Serena Sutcliffe

1989

P9-AFO-550

CHAMPAGNE

THE HISTORY AND CHARACTER OF THE WORLD'S MOST CELEBRATED WINE

SERENA SUTCLIFFE

SIMON AND SCHUSTER
NEW YORK LONDON TORONTO SYDNEY TOKYO

Champagne

Copyright © 1988 Mitchell Beazley Publishers
Text copyright © 1988 Serena Sutcliffe
Illustrations and maps copyright
© 1988 Mitchell Beazley Publishers
All rights reserved
including the right of reproduction
in whole or in part in any form.

Published by Simon and Schuster
A Division of Simon & Schuster Inc.
Simon & Schuster Building
Rockefeller Center
1230 Avenue of the Americas
New York, New York 10020

SIMON AND SCHUSTER and colophon are registered
trademarks of Simon & Schuster Inc.

Edited and designed by Mitchell Beazley International Ltd.,
Artists House, 14–15 Manette Street, London W1V 5LB.
Simultaneously published in Great Britain
by Mitchell Beazley Publishers
under the title *A Celebration of Champagne*.

1 3 5 7 9 8 6 4 2

Library of Congress Cataloging in Publcation Data

Sutcliffe, Serena.
    Champagne: the history and character of the
world's most celebrated wine.

    Includes index.
    1. Champagne (Wine) I. Title.
TP555.S97   1988   641.2′224   88-3142
ISBN 0-671-66672-X

The author and publishers will be grateful for any
information which will assist them in keeping
future editions up to date. Although all reasonable
care has been taken in the preparation of this book,
neither the publishers nor the author can accept any
liability for any consequences arising from the use
thereof or from the information contained herein.

Editor Dian Taylor
Designer Suzie Hooper
Editorial Assistant Nicola East
Map Research Alison Melvin
Proofreader Ray Granger
Index Annette Musker
Picture Research Brigitte Arora
Production Ted Timberlake

Senior Executive Editor Chris Foulkes
Senior Executive Art Editor Roger Walton

Illustrations Paul Leith
Commissioned Photographs Nic Barlow
Maps Lovell Johns Ltd.

Typeset by Servis Filmsetting Ltd., Manchester, England
Reproduction by Colourscan, Singapore
Printed and bound in The Netherlands by
Royal Smeets Offset

CONTENTS

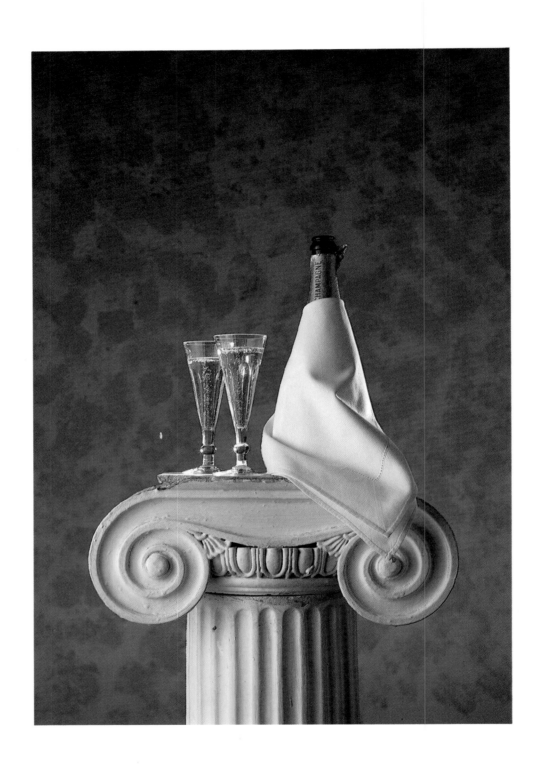

*To all those with whom I have
shared a bottle of champagne.*

INTRODUCTION

It often happens when one writes a book that, suddenly, the subject matter is all around, even in the most unexpected places. You simply cannot get away from it – not that, with champagne, anyone would wish to. These subject-related references have usually always been there; it is just that, without a book in mind, you miss many of them. But with all the senses keyed up, you are aware of any aspect of the current obsession, for this is what a book becomes. In my case, where the reflective period is always far longer than the writing, the mind is almost crowded with facts, gleaned from all corners of the world and the most unlikely sources.

In the summer of 1987, I went to the Peloponnese and more especially to its Byzantine capital, Mistra, in the Vale of Sparta. As I stumbled between the exquisite churches perched on their steep slope, I read again Sir Steven Runciman's brilliant study of the ruined city. Lo and behold, the Champenois had been here, in the form of two crusading lords, Marshall William of Villehardouin and his nephew Geoffrey, who became more interested in the rich pickings of Byzantium than in regaining the Holy Places. By 1213 they had carved up the Peloponnese between them, and considered the Vale of Sparta to be their personal patrimony – it must have seemed a near paradise after the cold north of Champagne.

Then, when I started actually writing this book over Christmas 1987, the music in my ears, helping the words to flow, might have come from heaven. In reality, it was the Procession and Third Mass of Christmas as it might have been celebrated in Reims Cathedral in 1361. The spellbinding plainchant was an exact reconstruction of the Reims rite, but performed in Lincoln Cathedral; Reims, sadly, no longer has the choir screen and cloisters necessary for the Mass to be sung as it would have been centuries ago. The sound lingers with me now, as I finish the book.

Champagne itself has never been far from me throughout my life. It has been a constant companion and permanent delight, and I did not need the excuse of writing about it to adopt it as a faithful ally and an inspiration. When I was very young, it was always a part of celebrations and special anniversaries in the family. New Year's Eve at home involved my father appearing on the stroke of midnight with a laden tray of sparkling flûtes. To my grandfather, returned to England after almost a lifetime in China, ordering a "bottle of wine" in a restaurant automatically meant a bottle of champagne, which we drank throughout the meal. Actually, with the brand fidelity of his generation, it meant a bottle of "The Widow", which appeared summarily on the table. If, by some misfortune, Veuve Clicquot was not available, the occasion was slightly marred, and it was always with a sigh of relief that the family saw the arrival of that reassuring yellow label.

Brand loyalty was less marked with my parents' generation, and I certainly inherited their love of variety and desire to compare and enjoy the differences between the champagne houses. I was brought up with the great names, and this book is written in homage and appreciation of them. These are the houses that have stood the test of time, that have honed their art and skill over the years, and will live on into the future. With the one exception of a new house that looks destined to become a fixture in the gallery of great champagnes, I have wished to honour those dynasties that have created the greatest tastes and held aloft the unassailed reputation of this most regal of wines.

I have not included the far-flung fields of the "joint venture"; the champagne houses have exported their skills to many countries, often with considerable success, but this book is about the source of the inspiration: champagne itself. Nor has this been the place for dissertations on grafting, pruning and diseases of the vine, or on the purely technical side of champagne making – although I have aimed to find out and explain what makes a champagne great. Above all, I have wanted to describe the *tastes* of champagne and how they are achieved.

Champagne should be a companion for life, with us to celebrate the great moments and to console us in the bad. If we are lucky, it can become part of the fabric of our days, on hand to mark a birthday or a piece of good news, and equally accessible when we need cheering up. I do not know if I would go as far as Henry Vizetelly, the wine historian who, when speaking about the place of champagne in England at the end of the 19th century, remarked that its eclipse would almost signify a collapse of our social system. One cannot help feeling that threat lies perhaps in other directions, but champagne is most certainly with us to stay.

Now, as in the heyday of the Belle Epoque, we have a multitude of uses for champagne. We launch ships with it, we inaugurate buildings and open galleries and exhibitions with it. Even books, when publishers are feeling generous, are launched with it. We can drink it anywhere in the world: its language and appeal are international. Enjoying champagne in exotic locations is an extra bonus, even if it means buying it duty free on departure and taking it there yourself. It was very soothing on Grenada, the beautiful Spice Island, at the height of the revolutionary regime – in fact, the champagne passed Customs better than the biography of Mussolini brought in for holiday reading. A bottle of Lanson Demi-Sec was offered to us as a palliative on the Thai island of Phuket when our guestroom and luggage were ransacked within hours of arriving; champagne is a very successful comforter. Drinking champagne in flight is a part of travel, now that the myth of it not tasting good in the air has finally been laid to rest (the wine had probably just been badly stored). The large airlines wield champagne as a weapon, shrewdly assessing that every passenger likes to boast of having drunk this or that brand while winging between continents. And the Orient Express seems to run on champagne.

While researching this book, I even had cause to wonder if I had Champagne antecedents. The Deputy President of the Administrative Committee of the Syndicat des Négociants en Vins de Champagne in 1870 was a certain G. de Barry, the name of my maternal grandfather. At the time, the Honorary President was Comte Edouard Werlé, of the house of Clicquot, and the Vice President Eugène Roederer, so Monsieur de Barry was in good company.

It is probably evident from the pages that follow that I am a champagne addict but, I hope, sufficiently detached to criticize where necessary, to defend where justified, and to praise where deserved. The very best ambassador for champagne, of course, is the wine itself, and I would not profess to the same eloquence. Love of subject has made writing this book a genuine pleasure, frequently encouraged as I was by a glass at the elbow. If I had dedicated this celebration of champagne to only one person, I might have said, as Thomas George Shaw wrote when he dedicated his *Wine, The Vine, and the Cellar* to Gladstone (an amusing choice, given the statesman's abstemious tendencies!) in 1863: "Your sanction is the more gratifying, as I have informed you that I have expressed opinions, on some points, not in accordance with your own." This is my personal perspective of the wine, its history and place in our lives, which is no doubt as individual as the tastes of the great champagnes themselves.

My deep-felt and sincere thanks are due to all who have helped me to understand champagne (I think I knew how to *enjoy* it from birth!) and therefore to write this book. My especial thanks go to the CIVC, both in Epernay and London, and to those houses that did me the honour of talking so frankly to me. Their honesty is often in direct relation to the quality of their wines.

S. D. Churchill, a wine merchant in the heady champagne days of the end of the 19th century, tells of the maxim of a friend in his *All Sorts and Conditions of Drinks*: "There are only two occasions when I drink Champagne, and those are when I have game for dinner, and when I haven't."

I find I am in total agreement.

SERENA SUTCLIFFE,
LONDON 1988.

CHAPTER ONE

THE RISE OF CHAMPAGNE

It would be picturesque to say that the rise of champagne was as inexorable as the bubbles that float up the centre of a glass. But champagne's prominence was hard won and covered centuries of varying social conditions. The graph did not go steadily upwards; it wavered and turned, and occasionally dipped alarmingly. The popularity of wines can follow fads and fashions, and demand and sales can be dependent on wars and alliances and all sorts of political manoeuvres. Added to these imponderables is the fact that champagne, however glamorous, is agricultural in origin and therefore as vulnerable to blight, disease and bad weather as any other crop.

From the beginning, there were threats to the establishment of vineyards in Champagne. Originally game-filled forest, the Marne region under the Romans was not as widely planted with vines as the more amenable countryside to the south. Then in AD92, after a year when the grape harvest had been as abundant as the cereal crop was poor, the Emperor Domitian ordered that all the vineyards in Gaul should be uprooted. It was almost two centuries before the Gaulois were allowed to plant vines again, by the Emperor Probus – his own troops replanted vines around Reims and Châlons.

Champagne has always known this dichotomy between cereal crops and the vine. The fear was of not having enough corn and wheat, so periodically the vineyards had to be reduced. In 1566, for example, Charles IX decided that not more than a third of the land of each canton should be occupied by vines. Happily, this was modified in 1577 by Henri III, who only warned against excessive planting of vines.

The "mountaineous island", as the Montagne de Reims was known, seems to have been given over to viticulture towards the end of the 6th century. The Church played an important part, as it did in Burgundy (but not in Bordeaux). The monks of the abbey of St-Basles near Verzy were keen winemakers, and wine from Champagne was served at the feasts that followed religious processions and on festival days. St Rémi, who was bishop of Reims for 74 years until his death in

530, is said to have performed miracles that involved wine – but his most far-reaching achievement was the baptism of Clovis, the King of the Franks, in Reims in 496. Ten years earlier, Clovis had virtually ended Roman rule in Gaul; now he was fulfilling a vow made in battle to become a Christian if he won against encroaching rivals from the east. He also, apparently, enjoyed a special cuvée which came from one of St Rémi's own vineyards in Champagne.

Many great abbeys, including those of Epernay, Hautvillers and Avenay, were founded in the 7th century, with the consequent planting of vineyards in the ecclesiastical domains. The cultivation of the grape steadily progressed, so much so that in the 9th century the distinction was made between the wines of the Rivière de Marne and those of the Montagne de Reims. In this century, too, in 816, came the first of the coronations in Reims which did a great deal to spread the popularity of Champagne's wines throughout France. Charlemagne's son, Louis, was crowned with due pomp, and during the ensuing festivities the high-born participants became acquainted with the local wine.

Exquisite carvings adorn the stalls in the church of Rilly-la-Montagne.

The custom of crowning French kings in Reims was well established by the time of the coronation of Philip VI in 1328, when the Court and the local inhabitants drank some 300 casks of wine from the Coteaux Champenois. Foreign rulers also came to Champagne. In 1397 Wenceslas, King of Bohemia and Holy Roman Emperor, arrived in Reims to make peace with Charles VI on the schism which was splitting the Church. But it seems that the Church was not his main preoccupation; Wenceslas wanted to see if the wines of Champagne lived up to their reputation. Clearly, he was not disappointed, because he imbibed a serious amount throughout his stay and signed everything he was given in order to be left in peace to drink. Henry V of England, however, had another view. He judged the wine to be strong and foaming and injurious to the health and, after the battle of Agincourt, forbade its use by his army except when tempered with water. One would have thought that the bowmen deserved better than this.

Henri IV is surely the monarch most beloved by French vignerons. Nearly all claim he has some special links with their area, but André Simon informs us that champagne was his favourite wine and that, although not crowned at Reims, he was the first monarch to introduce champagne at Court. Henri's headquarters were at Damery in 1592 during the siege of Epernay, and some sources assert that he went by the name of Sire d'Aÿ. His chancellor and ambassador at large, Bruslart de Sillery, was also a close friend, which probably had an influence on what was drunk at the royal table.

The wine of Aÿ seems to be mentioned more than all others in the history of Champagne. The 16th-century Medici Pope, Leo X, reputedly had a vineyard at Aÿ, and three great European kings of that time, Charles V of Spain, François I of France and Henry VIII of England, kept agents there with the express purpose of furnishing them with its wine. However, Aÿ did not have it all its own way. As early as 1200, Henri d'Andelys, in his *Bataille des Vins*, praises the wines of Epernay, Reims and Hautvillers as among the best in Europe.

Vines had now been planted in Champagne on a wide scale since the 14th century, and by the end of the 17th century changes were taking place in the kind of wine made. There was more white, rosé and "honey-coloured" wine on the market, rather than the red still wines of the past. Most important of all, the interloper, sparkling white wine – vin blanc mousseux – made its appearance at this time.

Throughout much of the 17th century (and well into the 18th) there was close and bitter rivalry between Champagne and Burgundy over sales of their light red wines. The Champenois were particularly efficient in the export markets, as they are today. Poems, odes and prose were written by both sides to support their wines, and the case was taken up by the medical faculty in Paris. Eventually, after a century of tussling, the faculty arrived at the compromise that a man has to have both wines, just as he needs two legs – a judgment worthy of Solomon. There was also fraudulent nomenclature during this period, with "burgundy" being made in the Marne Valley.

Louis XIV, crowned at Reims in 1654, reputedly sent both champagne and burgundy to Charles II in England. The Sun King himself favoured champagne, but towards the end of his life his physician, Fagon, only allowed him to drink well-watered burgundy – apparently Nuits-St-Georges. However, Du Chesne, who became physician to the Dauphin when Fagon was promoted to attend the King, followed a different regime: he lived to 91, ascribing his longevity to the fact that he ate a salad every night and drank only champagne.

Luckily for champagne drinking in England, a young French nobleman, the Marquis de St-Evremond, fell out of favour at Louis' Court and in 1661 sought refuge across the Channel. By all accounts he was warmly welcomed for his great social qualities, which endeared him to both Charles II and William III – the latter was very fond of the still red wines of Champagne. St-Evremond had been one of the founders in France of the Ordre des Coteaux, formed to promote the wines of Champagne, and champagne soon became the fashion at the "petits soupers" given by society hostesses and Charles II's mistresses – the two were often indistinguishable.

It was at this timely point in the story of champagne that a young Benedictine monk arrived on the scene. Dom Pérignon became Cellarer at the Abbey of Hautvillers in 1668 and remained in charge until his death, in 1715, at the age of 77. He did not "invent" sparkling champagne, but he was the first to take full advantage of the natural effervescence of the local wine – he brought "champagne mousseux" to glory.

There were undoubtedly white wines before Dom Pérignon's time, probably more by accident than design, but he perfected the art of producing starbright white wines from black grapes by clever manipulation of the presses. He saw, too, the great advantage of blending the wines from different villages and crus, of balancing one element with another in order to make a better whole. (However, the idea of individual crus sold separately persisted for many years among certain négociant-owners – the snobbery of the single cru.)

The 19th-century Dom Pérignon window at Moët & Chandon in Epernay, by Gaudin of Paris. Donkeys have disappeared from the harvest scene, and so have the monks.

• • • • • • • • • • •

Dom Pérignon also enhanced the tendency of the white wines of Champagne to keep a large part of their natural sugar, so that in the Spring after the vintage there was a re-emergence of fermentation activity. He judged the right moment to bottle these wines to capture that delightful bubble. Next an effective seal was clearly needed to preserve the mousse, so Dom Pérignon substituted cork for the wood and oil-soaked hemp stoppers then in use. Now sparkling champagne was well and truly trapped.

Once into the 18th century, champagne's real history begins, and it stayed in favour. The somewhat reprehensible Duc de Vendôme gave it popularity in his racy world, and the Regent, Philippe Duc d'Orléans, declared himself a protector of champagne. Madame de Pompadour and the Duc de Richelieu were customers of Moët, Ruinart made a speciality of English Dukes, and the royal courts and aristocracy of all Europe found that champagne had become an essential part of their lives.

Frederick William I of Prussia (father of Frederick the Great), who reigned from 1713 until 1740, was a devotee. One day, while drinking champagne at a meal, he asked if anyone could explain why the wine sparkled. The reply was that only the Academy in Berlin could answer such a tricky question. The Academicians, however, said they would like to perform some experiments and asked the King for 40–60 bottles. The King was outraged. "I have no need of them to drink my wine, and I prefer not to know all my life why it sparkles, rather than to deprive myself of a drop!" Champagne was introduced into Russia in 1724, at the end of Peter the Great's reign, and under the Empress Elizabeth it

By 1700, the heavy "verre anglais" bottles, developed by the English around 1660, were being made in France. Thus it was that Dom Pérignon could procure suitable bottles for his sparkling wine. Indeed, he may well have been a catalyst in their production: the glassworks were very near his birthplace, Ste-Ménehould.

took over from Tokay as the official drink for toasts. Count Razumovsky, Catherine the Great's field marshal, ordered 100,000 bottles of French wine at one time, including 16,800 of the best champagne.

The Grand Tour, that 18th-century progress around Europe, caused many a sheltered Englishman to encounter champagne for the first time. A fellow traveller, Adam Walker, reports spending a sleepless night in Milan because of the high jinks of about a dozen English who drank, rather incongruously, "thirty-six bottles of burgundy, claret, and champaign (as our landlord showed us in his book) and made such a noise till six in the morning we could not sleep." Horace Walpole, on his Grand Tour, makes no mention of the local wine in his letters from Reims in 1739. But, writing to a friend in 1750, he does divulge how much champagne was enjoyed by the upper classes in England in the middle of the 18th century. He describes how Lord Granby joined his party at the glittering Vauxhall Gardens in London under the influence of the champagne he had consumed at "Jenny's Whim", a noted tavern.

Exports to America suffered during the War of Independence, but in 1790 Senator Johnson of South Carolina could write of a dinner where he enjoyed the company of the wife of George Washington and drank an excellent champagne.

It was during the 18th century that the courtiers-commissionnaires, who sold the champagne, became négociants (both making and selling the wine) and the oldest "maisons de champagne" date from this time. If Moët & Chandon are the biggest house now, it is perhaps because Claude Moët, the founder, dared to make more bottles of mousseux than other people. The year 1776 was notorious for breakages (the yeast activity must have been particularly explosive that year), causing financial disaster, so in the following years most producers made only small quantities. In 1780, a bottling of 6,000 bottles was exceptional, but Moët risked 50,000. Moët even survived their bank going bankrupt in 1794, a potential catastrophe for such a young business, but Jean-Rémy Moët paid all his creditors, although he himself lost more than half his capital. An early example of the integrity of a top champagne house!

So the 18th century slipped into the 19th, and new converts were won for champagne. Lord Nelson was dining with Sir William and Lady Hamilton as a guest of the British Resident at Dresden in 1800; Lady Hamilton drank enough champagne to lose her inhibitions, and favoured the company with her imitations of classical statuary (Goethe had marvelled at a similar performance in Rome in 1787).

Napoleon certainly drank champagne, and took it with him onto the battlefields. The Champagne region, as usual, fell in the path of the warring factions of Europe. On the evening of February 7, 1814, 222,000 men from the invading armies of Russia, Prussia and Austria camped in the town of Epernay – the city was bursting with Kalmucks, Cossacks, Tartars, Baskirs and Prussians. Jean-Rémy Moët was mayor of Epernay, and the beleaguered Napoleon stayed with him, making him a Chevalier of the Legion of Honour for his services. It was a traumatic time for the Champenois, as the battle raged back and forth – on

The Marquis de Sillery, who owned vineyards in Champagne, advanced champagne's cause in the early 18th century by offering it at one of the famous "soupers" given by the Duc de Vendôme in the magnificent Château d'Anet, former home of Diane de Poitiers. Sillery presented the bottles in baskets of flowers carried in by young girls clad as priestesses of Bacchus. There is no need to go as far as this nowadays to cause a stir – the sight of a good bottle is enough – but the tradition of champagne enlivening parties lives on.

Le Déjeuner d'Huîtres, by Jean-François de Troy (1679–1752). At this rollicking oyster party, the glasses are quite wide-brimmed and the bottles are still the old "dump" shape with narrow necks.

Le Petit Souper, by Ch. Thevenin, an engraving owned by Pol Roger and used by them since the 1920s to support their marque. At this rather racy supper party the bottle shape is closer to that most commonly used today and the flûtes are narrow.

February 16, 15,000 Russian soldiers were encamped outside Reims Cathedral. When Napoleon eventually entered the city, he stayed in the house of Monsieur Ponsardin, the brother of Madame Clicquot (even at this early stage, there was no brand loyalty!).

The reverse side of this catastrophe, for the troops weighed heavily on the towns' supplies, was that they took back a taste for champagne to their native countries. In the summer of 1814, Clicquot wines landed in Koenigsberg to much acclaim. Mr Bohne, Madame Clicquot's famous agent, reported that the wine was considered there as nectar – "the pink wine is perfect". Naturally. It *was* the famous 1811 Comet vintage.

The role of the champagne agents, or commercial travellers, of those days was considerable. They travelled constantly, following in the wake of victorious armies, prudently avoiding the battlefields and appearing as soon as the fighting was over to see that victory was toasted in their champagne and not that of a competitor. But their life was not a soft one. They were often trapped in bombardments, narrowly escaped shipwreck or were caught in other vicissitudes such as blockades, political intrigues and tussles wth exchange rates. Their clients, too, were choosy. They liked their wines to be clear, with a fine, persistent sparkle – not "cloudy wines and those whose thick froth resembled toad's eyes". This is eminently understandable, but it must have been a terrible strain for the salesmen in those oenologically hit-and-miss days.

The indefatigable Mr Bohne looked after Clicquot's sales in Eastern Germany, Austria and Russia. He spent about half of the eight years between 1806 and Napoleon's abdication at St. Petersburg and from there made frequent

A mural from 1868 shows the whole champagne process at Mumm. 1. Vendange, with natural wastage due to pickers with a liking for grapes. 2. Collage, to clarify the wines, and recoupage (blending). 3. Remuage, or riddling, in pupitres; dégorgement (disgorging the sediment); dosage, the addition of the liqueur d'expédition. 4. The bouchage, or corking, and ficellage, attaching the wire muzzle. 5. Habillage, "dressing" the bottle with label and foil, and emballage, the packing in wooden cases. A veritable do-it-yourself champagne-making manual!

visits to Memel, Riga, Hamburg and Vienna. He was nothing if not observant, vying with the popular press of today in his vigilance over the Royal houses. In 1806 he wrote to the Widow Clicquot: "The Tzarina is with child. If it is a Prince, gallons of Champagne will be drunk in this vast country. Do not mention it, all our rivals would be here at once."

Roederer also conquered the Russian market, and the Tsar became the firm's best customer. Monsieur Louis Roederer must have had a lively sense of humour, as shown by his reaction to what could have been the first champagne begging letter: "Sir, I have no money, but I adore Champagne. Be a Christian, and send me a basket of your worthy bottles. Thanks to them, I shall be able to forget my misery for a time. Yrs, etc." The reply was succinct: "Sir, Your idea of drowning your misery is bad; the perpetual presentation of my little account would only recal [sic] to you your sad position. Believe me, your sincere friend, etc." Business, however, did not suffer from this reluctance to open a new account, and when Louis Roederer II took over from his father in 1870, annual sales were averaging an impressive two and a half million bottles.

By the 1870s some 18,000 hectares were producing grapes for champagne, with an average yield of approximately 636,000 hectolitres. But not all this was converted into mousseux; "choice" red wine was made at Rilly and Bouzy, as well as large quantities of ordinary red. What is particularly noteworthy about this period is that whereas production almost trebled between 1844 and 1870, and exports abroad increased at an even faster rate, there was a rise of only some 37 percent in French domestic consumption.

It is interesting to look back at what champagne was actually like in the 19th century. Remuage and disgorging had been practised on a small scale since Dom Pérignon, but it took the Widow Clicquot and her employee, Antoine Müller, in the early 1800s to develop a system of remuage which resembles today's methods. Madame Clicquot, as befits a woman's practicality, did her first experiments on her kitchen table, and real remuage, or riddling, in angled holes soon followed. However, cloudy wines continued to be a salesman's nightmare. Thomas George Shaw in his *Wine, The Vine, and the Cellar*, 1863, writes: "Champagnes formerly became often 'scuddy', which means that they lost their

limpidity and brilliancy; but this is now rarely the case." The growers, it transpired, said that the improvement was due to blending, with the wine not coming solely from one vineyard or grape variety or locality. Thus, by the 1860s, one disgorging was generally found sufficient, whereas three had not at one time been unusual.

Writing in 1896, N. E. Legrand in *Le Vin de Champagne* says that you have to go back to 1746 to find the first attempts to bottle sparkling champagne on an industrial scale. Sugar can be added to wine to improve its flavour, which seems a highly likely practice in the early days of champagne, or to increase the wine's potential alcoholic content – Monsieur Chaptal's notable contribution to wine production. But in the early 1800s it seems clear that some champagne makers added sugar later, prior to bottling, to induce the secondary fermentation in bottle – the prise de mousse. The problem was to judge the quantity; too little and the wine was not bubbly enough, too much and there were costly, and dangerous, breakages (Shaw, in 1863, said he knew of one cellar in which three men had each lost an eye when bottles exploded during the secondary fermentation). But in 1836 a distinguished chemist of Châlons-sur-Marne, Monsieur François, invented the "gleuco-oenomètre", which determined exactly the quantity of sugar to be put in each bottle of champagne in order to produce "une belle mousse". The system was not immediately adopted by everyone in Champagne, and it was only in the 1880s that the liqueur de tirage as we know it became common practice.

According to Shaw, the champagnes of the mid-century were fortified by brandy, to add to their apparent body. However, by the 1860s the "natural colour and grape flavour are preferred by all who know what true good wine is", rather than the former brown and amber and "partridge-eye" (pinkish-tawny) brews that looked, and tasted, nearly as strong as "golden sherry". Charles Tovey, writing in 1870, describes the liqueur d'expédition – the liqueur added to champagne after dégorgement – as the "very finest sugar candy, the best Champagne, and the oldest and finest cognac". (By 1896, Legrand could write that the dosage was a liqueur of cane sugar dissolved in top champagne – he makes no mention of brandy.)

It is worth knowing, especially for those who might one day come across an historic bottle, that Sillery used to be famous for dry, still wines bottled at 16 months and then left in the cellar for 8–10 years. It was made only in fine vintages and its price was very high. This was the true Sillery, much prized by the British aristocracy from the late 18th to the mid-19th century. It is possible to find Sillery bin labels in salerooms; they might now be a better bet than the wine. Apart from this speciality, many people of the time considered Sillery's reputation to be overblown – due, no doubt, to the earlier promotional activities of Vendôme's friend, the Marquis.

Shaw compared the average degrees of liqueur in the mid-1800s among the principal export markets. For England it was 12–13 degrees; for France 14–15; for Belgium it was the same as for France but with more brandy; for Germany 16–18; for Russia 20–22 ("only good for savages or children", says Professor Saintsbury); for Sweden and Norway 24–28, and even 30; and for India about 9. Legrand, near the end of the century, says that cuvées destined for Russia had the most sugar, with a little less for Germany, France and Belgium. The dosage was reduced still further for the United States, and the cuvées for England were hardly sugared at all – they were très sec (extra dry), and sometimes brut.

Charles Tovey throws more light on the question of champagne's colour, particularly rosé. He points out that champagne varied occasionally in shade due to natural circumstances – apparently the wines of 1865 and 1868 took on considerable colour from the grape skins and acquired a tawny-pink hue. He avers that around 1845 pink champagne, made so "by a decoction of cochineal", was much in demand, "but like many other novelties of a specious type, had but a brief existence". This bears out Shaw saying in 1863 that amber or rosé champagnes used to be made by boiling elderberries. But, he then says, the Champenois were also "allowed" to add must from red grapes in order to achieve that pretty colour.

Tovey describes a mid-century dinner when the host, the banker-poet Mr Rogers, had received as a gift a case of pink champagne from Louis Philippe, and to do it special honour he had the first bottle produced after dinner instead of with "the roast". Tovey thought that the saucer-shaped champagne glasses, fashionable in 1870 but in the mid-1800s just coming into use, made that other novelty of the day, pink champagne, look singularly beautiful "when poured into them and crowned with its snow-white foam".

As for how champagnes were labelled throughout the 19th century, Shaw wrote: "Until not many years ago, Champagnes were made from the grapes of certain vineyards; from whence has, no doubt, arisen the names of Vin d'Aÿ, Vin de Silleri, Fleur de Silleri, etc" – with their beautiful labels. "But now, all the wine of the best houses is composed of various growths mixed together; for experience has proved that when this is done the quality may be made not only superior to any one kind, but the wine thus blended is also hardier, and not subject to the diseases that formerly prevailed."

Shaw also describes the composition of a cuvée at that time: "The black grapes form generally about two-thirds, giving strength and body; while the white impart richness, delicacy, and bouquet; and the cuvée, with these proportions, will turn out to be Champagne of the finest quality." It is fascinating to compare this recipe with the proportions given for the top champagnes today. Certainly, the prestige blends now, with some notable exceptions, have a higher percentage of Chardonnay, but this is because they are designed for apéritif drinking and a life style that favours lighter food and wine.

The early years of the 1860s were difficult for those champagne houses that were trying to make their mark in the United States – the Civil War was something of a preoccupation, and trade was catastrophic for such a relatively luxurious new product. Krug produced a special label with the head of George Washington and the American eagle. Krug's labels for the French market at the same time were Sillery, Verzenay Mousseux, Crème de Bouzy, Carte Blanche, Goût Français (with a three-coloured cockade) and Oeil de Perdrix, or Partridge Eye. The English market received Private Quality, First Quality, Second Quality, Extra, and an Extra Dry for Invalids.

This last label was only in recognition of what had been known for some time – that champagne is an excellent healer. In 1789 that great agricultural pioneer, Arthur Young, had gone to Reims, which he found both magnificent and spacious. "At dinner they gave me also a bottle of excellent wine. I suppose fixed air is good for the rheumatism; I had some writhes of it before I entered Champagne, but the vin mousseux has absolutely banished it." Two days later, however, he complains bitterly because he has discovered that at Châlons and Ste-Ménehould he has to pay three livres for his bottle of "execrably bad" vin de Champagne, whereas at Reims it cost 40 sous and was "excellent". "So there is an end of my physic for the rheumatism – 25 miles."

The Franco-Prussian War of 1870 was another time of trial for the Champenois. It is really brought home to anyone reading Charles Tovey's book of that date, to which he adds a sad postscript, saying that at publication many of his friends in Champagne were in the grip of a grim war, losing sons and watching their vineyards trodden brutally underfoot.

However, as the century drew to its close there was a series of fabulous vintages and a period of great prosperity. Ironically, there was also viticultural disaster, as phylloxera finally reached the northern vineyards. But every Golden Age has to have its tarnished corners.

Champagne has always had trouble from false "competition", from within France (the Loire) and abroad. In the 19th century, many of the judgments of the Appeal Courts in these cases of other wines being "passed off" as champagne were pronounced in Angers. Apparently there was even a so-called champagne house at Aÿ that turned out to be just a poste restante address, with letters forwarded to Tours!

A collection of invoices to some famous clients of Moët & Chandon. The Bonapartes were frequent customers – Napoleon is reputed to have said of champagne: "In victory you deserve it, in defeat you need it." Other customers included the Duc d'Orléans and the poet Alphonse de Lamartine.

CHAPTER TWO

THE GOLDEN AGES

The Belle Epoque started the century. It came after the Naughty Nineties, and social life was as coruscant as champagne itself – sparkling, witty and gloriously uninhibited. It was the era when people went out to be seen, to be entertained and to enjoy themselves. If you had it, you flaunted it. New money was being made, and old money still existed. And, somehow, they met over "un verre de champagne".

The Belle Epoque was all curves: vases, chair legs, tables, there wasn't a straight line in sight. Of course, it began earlier; the scene was set in the Second Empire, in the pleasure-loving society of Napoleon III's France. Then the rich, powerful, high-class cocottes held sway. The three great demi-mondaines of the 1890s were Liane de Pougy, la Belle Otéro and Cléo de Mérode – and heaven knows how much champagne drinking they inspired. The private rooms of Lapérouse were much in use.

Maxim's was the great meeting place. The 1900 Paris Exhibition fixed it firmly in the firmament of truly international haunts, and oysters and lobster were on the menu. The men lingered at the bar with their champagne, and the women (both respectable and less so) eyed each other with ill-concealed curiosity. The champagne, regrettably, tended to be sweet: it was its sole defence against its diabolical positioning in the meal, after the Sauternes and before the brandy. Only the British were well and truly launched on brut.

The French were consuming some seven million bottles of champagne and sparkling wines from the Marne a year at the turn of the century. But the pattern of drinking bore no comparison with that of today. No one bought a bottle on the way home and shared it in connubial bliss. One went out to the smart restaurants of the day, to the grand hotels, to the fashionable night spots, and was *seen* to be enjoying oneself. In Paris, this meant the Café de la Paix, Drouant of literary fame, the Ritz, the Grand Hotel, and Lucas at the Madeleine, with Majorelle's magnificent Ceylon lemonwood panelling. Somehow, this finds an echo in contemporary Champagne, where so many homes have a panelled room or two,

Two views of dining
out in Paris in 1904.
The provinces saw
such goings-on as
orgies of illicit
pleasures. The reality
could be far more
sedate – but
champagne had a
place in both.
• • • • • • • • • •

well padded and substantial, the perfect setting for contemplating bubbles.

And what did all those mirrors of the era reflect? Colours, and flowers, and flamboyance. The Belle Epoque was not quiet: it was flashy. Everything was "worked", nothing was left alone. It was art nouveau and Tiffany, encrustation and marquetry. It was colours that clashed and, it has to be admitted, ornate vulgarity. But it was fun. Against a social fabric that was far from stable, and not a little malicious, everybody went out – "on sortait". The most unlikely people mixed: the louche and the ladylike sat on the same banquette. It was the last fling of an age that was to end in the trenches. It was dying embers in Europe, but pioneering new money in America.

Mumm have some fascinating records of the booming champagne market in the United States. They sent 420,000 bottles across the Atlantic in 1877, and 1.5 million in 1902, their best year for that market. Veuve Clicquot's sales only caught up with the 1905–6 figures in 1973. In 1882, 36 million bottles of champagne were produced, a quarter for France and three-quarters for export. In 1900, Perrier-Jouët needed 200 people to ship one million bottles; now about 70 people handle three times as much. In Britain, in that first decade of the 1900s, André Simon was selling quantities of Pommery. In America, sales of champagne nearly quadrupled between 1900 and 1909.

North America, at that time as now, was the second-largest champagne market after Britain. Champagne was everywhere, but especially on the West Coast, where gold had made the hostelries of San Francisco magnets for both the hopeful and the hopeless. Genuine finds were celebrated with the best that money could buy, and that meant French champagne, just as one celebrates a stroke of good luck today. By 1900, it was the land barons who dominated the West and ordered the bubbly. Champagne was drunk with the same abandon in the steamy districts of New Orleans as in the altogether more tight-lipped ambience of New England. By 1909, it was well established in bars, certainly from the pictorial evidence of the time – although there is a degree of confusion as to what actually constituted "champagne", especially when scrawled on a bar blackboard.

The two Paris World Fairs of 1889 and 1900 had done much to enhance the reputation of champagne. Here the houses did not exhibit as individuals but as members of the Association of Champagne Merchants. They had a Champagne Palace, designed by the Reims architect Kalas, where remuage and dégorgement were demonstrated and the public could buy glasses of champagne. This group presentation won the highest award at both Fairs.

Escoffier was the great chef of the Belle Epoque. In his autobiography, he recalls a gala dinner given by the Comte de Lagrange after his horse won the Grand Prix de Paris: Veuve Clicquot was sandwiched between Lafite 1846 and Yquem. He transformed London's Savoy Hotel, cooking for Edward VII, Emile Zola and Sarah Bernhardt. A Savoy wine list of 1901 shows a variety of champagnes and an even greater variety of "dosages". Not only could one choose one's vintage, but also the exact degree of dryness desired, with accompanying descriptions such as "extra quality extra dry" (Bollinger), "dry England" (Clicquot), "extra sec" (Deutz), "extra superior brut cuvée exceptionelle [sic]" (Dagonet). The vintages ranged from 1884 to 1893.

In fact, the heyday for menus was the period between 1880 and 1914: they were often decorated by noted artists and have great value today. But not much can be gleaned from them with regard to how and when the champagnes were served. The very disparate list of wines could appear at the side of the food or grouped after it, but it was all very haphazard. What appeared to be a frightful mismatch (Louis Roederer Doux with roast duck) may not actually have been so: the printer may not always have lined up the food with any particular wine.

Gradually other markets followed the British predilection for brut: in 1905 Mumm launched a drier version of Cordon Rouge in New York, although in France dry champagne only started to have any impact after 1910. Brand promotion began to be important: Mumm's accounts for 1907 show lists of gifts to the diplomatic corps, associations, and restaurant personnel, as well as all sorts of objects which would have borne the name Mumm.

The artists of the era twirled and swirled with enthusiasm. The painters were Bonnard and Mucha, the designers and decorative architects Gaud, Guimard, de Feure, Majorelle, Vallin and André, the artists in glass Gallé, Daum and Tiffany, while sculpture was represented by Maillol. Some furniture, posters, jewellery and glass remain, but the wrought-iron fantasies are fast disappearing, none more so than the nostalgic entrances to the Paris métro.

In London, at the height of Edwardian splendour, the great houses of the aristocracy on Park Lane (most of them now replaced by hotels) were the centre of the capital's social life. Parties were lavish, hospitality grand, and the champagne flowed. It is interesting to note that champagne never fell into either

A fascinating detail from the 18th-century décor of the Paris restaurant Le Grand Véfour, set in the Palais Royal Gardens and owned by the Taittinger family. For more than 200 years, personalities from the worlds of politics, art and literature have made it their haunt. Colette, Victor Hugo, Cocteau and Callas, Balzac and Flaubert – all have sat on the red velvet banquettes and sipped champagne from flûtes.

• • • • • • • • • •

• • • • • • • • • • •

*Madame de
Pompadour, a
customer of Moët, is
reputed to have said:
"Champagne is the
only wine that leaves
a woman beautiful
after drinking it".
Advice such as this,
from one of the
great "horizontales",
should be taken
seriously.*

the exclusively male or female domain: men could order it without feeling effeminate, women could enjoy it without appearing brazen. There have been periods when red wine was thought to be a "man's drink", while women sipped a little Hock, but champagne carefully treads between all the social pitfalls and has always been "correct".

The Edwardian gastronomic chronicler, Colonel Newnham-Davis, gives us a very clear picture of how champagne was served throughout a meal: this was the time, of course, when champagne was vintage and certainly weightier (more black grapes in many cases) than the cuvées we have now. It accompanied caviar, consommé, sole, tongue, salad, asparagus and ice cream (a tall order, even for this most noble of wines!), while a rosé was called to service for a meal consisting of caviar, clear soup, sole, lamb, foie gras, quails and ice cream. (Caviar, clear soup, sole and ice cream seem to have been consistent favourites to begin and end a meal.)

Little did the urban partygoers realize that in Champagne itself a battle was raging. Phylloxera, the dreaded predator of the vine, had taken its time in reaching the north of France, but its progress was inexorable. L'Abbé Dervin, in 1896, wrote the most illuminating book on the subject I know: *Six Semaines en Pays Phylloxérés*. It is the account of a marathon journey through all the viticultural regions of France in 1894 with the aim of giving advice to the vignerons of Champagne. Phylloxera had existed in France since the 1860s, when it was discovered in the Bouches-du-Rhône and in the Gironde: by the time this book was written, it was in the Marne. L'Abbé Dervin brought the Champenois encouragement that their vineyards could be rebuilt using phylloxera-resistant American rootstock, but there were many who did not share this draconian view, and the process of grafting all the vines in the Champagne region was not completed until after World War I.

In 1908, the first law was passed which restricted the use of the name Champagne to the wines of the Marne and the Aisne, but excluded those of the Aube. The situation was exacerbated by a string of poor vintages from 1907 to 1910, and in 1911 the government restricted still further the use of Aube grapes. The Aube growers promptly protested, causing the government to talk of abandoning geographical delimitations. This in turn angered the Marne growers, who rioted, destroying many cellars in Dizy, Damery and Aÿ; Epernay was protected by a large contingent of soldiers. In the end a compromise was worked out, whereby the Marne was termed Champagne and the Aube and other outlying districts were classified as Champagne Deuxième Zone. This lasted until 1927, when a single designation was made and the communes eligible for the appellation Champagne were defined.

As if all this were not enough, World War I had a dramatic impact on the people of Champagne, although they continued to cultivate their vineyards during the hostilities. The trench warfare of the Marne took a terrible toll. Then, in 1917, came the Russian Revolution and ten percent of champagne's sales disappeared. Following the war, Germany and what had been the Austro-

Lapérouse, on Paris' Left Bank, was already a tavern in 1660; the panelling and mirrors installed in 1850 have recently been beautifully renovated. All the traces of time remain, including the scratches on the mirrors in the private rooms, where the demi-mondaines tested the diamonds they were given to see if they were genuine by drawing them across the hard surface. Champagne was brought in by waiters who always knocked before unlocking the doors of the intimate little salons.

A glimpse of low life in New Orleans at the turn of the century, captured by the renowned photographer Eugène Bellocq. His subjects were often the prostitutes of the Storyville section of New Orleans – here playing cards and whiling away the wait with a bottle of Veuve Clicquot. The city was an early centre of champagne drinking in the United States – perhaps the steamy climate made it all the more tempting. In these "hot and plush" bordellos, champagne was said to have assisted the birth of jazz – Jelly Roll Morton was a fan of Clicquot.

Champagne has always featured prominently in poster art, with its heyday in the Belle Epoque and the 1920s. There is something about the fizz and the pop, the naughtiness of champagne, that lends itself to the skills of the poster artist – dancing girls, flirtatious scenes, risqué vignettes.

Hungarian Empire were in no financial state to buy champagne, and Prohibition in America prevented legal imports. Britain remained a good customer, although economic depression in the 1930s did not encourage the spread of champagne drinking. The champagne houses at last turned their attention to the domestic market, and between 1927 and 1935 sales in France more than trebled.

It is often thought that in the 1920s (the Roaring Twenties) the cocktail usurped the position of almost every other drink. But from the number of times champagne appears in diaries of the day, it is clear that its popularity continued. Nancy Cunard, that peripatetic lover of liberty and alcohol, describes her life in Paris: "And then we would go and dance somewhere else in Montmartre. It was always champagne, and our heads were often swimming." (*Nancy Cunard*, by Anne Chisholm, 1979, Sidgwick & Jackson.) Evelyn Waugh's *Diaries* (Weidenfeld & Nicolson, 1976) are chock-full of champagne; in June 1924, he took a train from Oxford to London: "We found nothing to eat that seemed tolerable except bread and cheese but we drank some brown sherries, some champagne, many liqueurs and, smoking great cigars, got out at Paddington with the conviction that we had lunched well." Champagne often confers this illusion upon the most meagre repast. A few months later, he gave "a tiny dinner party with prodigious quantities of champagne at the Carlton Club. . . ."

We know that copious amounts of champagne were drunk on the steamers that crossed the Atlantic. Joseph Wechsberg, who played the violin in a French ship's orchestra, describes how six bottles of Veuve Clicquot were kept in the cello of one of his colleagues. The Captain's Dinner, that obligatory social

From the archives of
Charles Heidsieck:
definitely *not* the way
to pop a cork, but the
diner would soon be
soothed by the bubbly
about to be served in
the coupe which was
so fashionable at the
time.

occasion, included an amazing array of dishes, but "the stewards did not bother to show the wine card, simply asking the passengers if they preferred Mumm Cordon Rouge or the more expensive vintages of Charles Heidsieck, Reims, without mentioning the lesser brands" (*Looking for a Bluebird*, Penguin, 1944). In New York, when Ludwig Bemelmans was a waiter at the Hotel Splendide, the cases of champagne for big parties had to be broken open and iced "under the watchful eyes of Pommer, the old German bar-tender" (*Life Class*, Penguin, 1948). And a famous cartoonist at the hotel gave wonderful parties, ate grouse out of season and drank vintage champagne at ten in the morning.

During World War II, Champagne was occupied by enemy troops, and the only good thing that came out of this sad period was the formation of the Comité Interprofessionnel du Vin de Champagne, the CIVC. Robert-Jean de Vogüé was the driving force, representing the champagne makers – he was eventually arrested, sentenced to death and·despatched to a concentration camp, but miraculously survived. The CIVC acted as a buffer between the champagne houses and growers, and the demands of the Germans, and its fine organization has held to this day. Now the governing body of the champagne trade, it oversees production, distribution and stocks, decides the price of grapes, effects quality control, instigates research, and budgets and plans for the future based on estimated demand and world trends. Naturally, it treads a delicate path between the various vested interests in Champagne, but without it this complicated trade would be much the poorer, and considerably more anarchic.

Since World War II total sales of champagne have crept inexorably upwards, almost quadrupling between 1945 and 1966. But progress in the last 20 years has been even more meteoric, culminating in champagne's new Golden Age today.

French humour on
Prohibition in the
United States, by Léo
Fontan. The caption is
"How will America
regain her smile?" but
in fact France regained
her smile when
America started to buy
champagne again;
Prohibition had hit
sales hard, in spite of
the ingenious ways
found to smuggle it in.

CHAPTER THREE

CHAMPAGNE TODAY

More champagne is being drunk today by more people than ever before – it is the solid Golden Age. Champagne has been democratized and taken out of the gilded cage of the very rich or the very privileged (they are not always the same, although one can lead to the other). The previous Golden Age saw comparatively few people drinking a great deal of champagne. Now a far wider public has more than a passing acquaintance with it. Some have made champagne their usual tipple; others drink it occasionally and aspire to drink it frequently. Once we alight on champagne as our favourite celebratory liquid, the celebrations tend to present themselves more often – acquiring a champagne taste is a very easy thing to do.

Champagne has permeated every aspect of life, from the serious to the flippant. It makes its presence felt in politics and sport, in business and the arts. It is always welcome and rarely refused. When has anyone, of whatever nationality or culture, ever felt insulted by the offer of a glass of champagne? Even a non-drinker would appreciate the gesture. The invitation to join someone over this most convivial of wines always strikes the right note. It has style, but could never be seen as "de trop". And, somehow, having accepted, the world always feels a better place.

Monarchies and republics alike seem to run on champagne. There is never a state occasion worth its name that does not have champagne featuring somewhere on the programme. Buckingham Palace inform me that champagne was most definitely present at Queen Victoria's Diamond Jubilee in 1887, but their records do not show the names of champagnes served during this period, only that both sweet and dry were consumed. At Queen Elizabeth II's coronation in 1953, there was a plethora of Clicquot 1934, served at a state banquet and two royal dinners, while Pol Roger 1934 took over at the other state banquet. There was a similar sharing-out of the honours at the Queen's Silver Jubilee in 1977. Bollinger 1964 was served at one royal dinner, Lanson 1969 at the other, and Moët & Chandon was poured at the evening reception.

*In 1982, at the first
banquet ever given for
an American
President at Windsor
Castle, the Queen
served President
Ronald Reagan and
guests Pol Roger 1969
with the fresh
raspberries – a wise
choice as a young
champagne would
have been too brut
and fresh at this stage
of the meal. (The
glasses were 19th
century.)*

To the victors, the laurels – and the champagne. Tony Jacklin leads the celebrations for a European "first" in the 1986 Ryder Cup golf tournament.

Krug 1969 was served at the wedding breakfast (the lunch for relations and close friends of the family) of the Prince and Princess of Wales. When the Duke and Duchess of York married, Krug 1973 was served at the reception before the wedding breakfast. But do not think for a moment that these wines are reserved solely for crowned heads and their intimates. A magnum of each was sold at the auction held in Bordeaux on the occasion of Vinexpo 1987. The buyer was an Australian wine merchant who intended drinking them "at a very special function" to coincide with Australia's great racing event of the year, the Melbourne Cup.

Naturally, champagne is firmly ensconced at the Elysée Palace, where the President entertains in great style. But here the champagne is almost invariably served at the end of the meal, with "le dessert", in time-honoured French tradition. One cannot help feeling that these superb brut champagnes would be even more glorious at the other end of the repast, but it would be almost lèse majesté to say so. Mrs Margaret Thatcher had the honour of being served Comtes de Champagne Taittinger 1979 at a lunch given by Monsieur François Mitterrand in 1986, but it arrived with the profiteroles. How I would have preferred to drink it over the poached salmon, but I expect they had other things to talk about than the harmonious marriage of food and wine. For the Prime Minister of India, Rajiv Gandhi, it had been Taittinger Comtes de Champagne 1976 with glace montmorency (cherry ice cream), and the Prime Minister of Japan, Yasuhiro Nakasone, did not escape either (Comtes de Champagne 1975 with coupe Grand Marnier). Krug 1975 entered the lists with that meringue and chocolate confection, a marjolaine, at a lunch in honour of Chancellor Helmut Kohl of the Federal Republic of Germany.

The presence of
champagne in Grand
Prix motor racing is
far from discreet. If
you are anywhere near
the winners you are
sure to be sprayed
with bubbly, in this
case by Derek
Warwick, Nikki Lauda
and Ayrton Senna.

• • • • • • • • • • •

Is all this worth noting? Does it tell us anything more about the image and the real position of champagne today? It most certainly does, because it is loudly proclaiming that, to do honour to our guests, we have to give them the best, and that means champagne. After all, France has a good many other wines in her garden.

Since politicians, and not monarchs, are now our masters, it would be sad indeed if they neglected this most royal of drinks. They have taken a keen interest in the subject throughout history. George Canning, Britain's early 19th-century foreign secretary and (briefly) prime minister, reportedly avowed that any man who said he really liked dry champagne simply lied! Much more recently, when the English politician and ex-ambassador to Paris, Christopher Soames (later Lord Soames), was sent on the delicate mission to Rhodesia, as it then was, to secure its peaceful transition to independence, he took with him a quantity of Pol Roger (he was also Churchill's son-in-law from whom, no doubt, he acquired this particular taste). In the midst of proceedings, he surprised an interested party by affirming: "Rhodesia will be at peace in exactly 30 days". "Why?", asked his slightly puzzled questioner. "I only have 30 bottles of Pol Roger left", was the calm reply.

Who drinks champagne today, where, and why? Geographical trends are often linked to events. A serious amount of champagne is consumed in Florida, for example, from January to March, but that is where wealthy Americans and tourists from overseas spend their winter breaks. The more agile of the winter holidaymakers go to ski, often to smart Aspen or Vail, so up goes the champagne consumption there. An impressive two-thirds of the State of Colorado's champagne drinking is in the mountain resorts – après-ski in earnest. Or take

Champagne al fresco
always has a special
ambience, although
the attire need not be
as formal as when
picnicking during an
early-evening interval
at Glyndebourne,
England's summer
opera festival. The
cows, however, seem
unimpressed.

• • • • • • • • • •

Long Island and the Hamptons in the summer, where New Yorkers escape from the stifling city for a holiday or just for a weekend, and seem to party without a break. Enter champagne again.

And the timing is all important: champagne always goes where the fun is. The biggest peak, of course, in most countries is Christmas and New Year. In The Netherlands, a staggering 62 percent has been recorded for champagne sales during the fourth quarter of the year. The Dutch, apparently, have an absolute mania for popping corks on New Year's Eve, when the volume peaks in quite alarming fashion.

Then there is the summer, which draws champagne like a magnet. It seems that June weddings are part of our mores, whatever the sociologists might say about changing customs and attitudes. People like to get married with at least a chance of the sun shining, and lots of bubbly engenders the right sparkling atmosphere for the couple's departure into a new life. The champagne may only be produced when it is time to cut the cake, but it is still the "only" toasting wine. I personally prefer a champagne with more body with the weighty fruitcake that is the traditional British recipe, something like Roederer Rich or Clicquot Demi-Sec (which the Queen Mother has specially labelled as Rich). The French, of course, go in for a full meal, with champagne as the finale. But then they often indulge in some energetic dancing to work it all off.

All weddings do not follow the orthodox pattern, however. Captain Edouard Chemel, who flies Concorde from Paris to New York (and presumably back again), has married a couple from Las Vegas on board, taking over where the captains of ocean liners left off. He has also taken groups of Japanese tourists for "joy rides", for the heady delights of flying fast, taking photographs – and drinking champagne. There must be something about Concorde. Queen Elizabeth, the Queen Mother, requested a flight for her 85th birthday. When they could persuade her away from the cockpit there was a light lunch awaiting: some Scottish lobster, Angus beef (after all, she *is* Scottish), suprêmes de volailles, followed by raspberries and redcurrants surmounted by a dome of cream, all washed down with Krug.

In Britain, summer means "The Season", and this means champagne. Being Britain, most of the frenetic activities revolve around sport, although the season is, naturally, accompanied by an enormous number of parties, and the odd cultural event is allowed to creep in. Metaphorical kick-off is the Derby, followed fairly briskly by Royal Ascot (after all, racing is the sport of kings), then Henley Royal Regatta and Wimbledon usually managing to clash, more racing at Goodwood – a scenically lovely, somewhat bucolic gathering – and yachting at Cowes. Throughout there is a sprinkling of rather royal polo, and cricket at Lords. To the uninitiated, this all probably sounds like tribal rites – and so they are. But they are also an inextricable part of champagne drinking. With the exception of the Members' Pavilion at Lords, where beer is more the order of the day (well, what do you expect of all-male enclaves), a huge amount of champagne is consumed on these occasions. The obvious reason is that people are

"Nor should the existence of Champagne Stakes be forgotten. There are now several races of this name at different meetings; but the oldest is that established at Doncaster in 1828, and taking its title from the fact of the owner of the winner having to present six dozen of Champagne to the Doncaster Club." (Henry Vizetelly in A History of Champagne, 1882.) Now, a champagne house will sponsor a race and make a presentation to the owner and sometimes the jockey.

out to enjoy themselves and champagne has a marked tendency to enhance this. But the more subtle explanation is that all these activities are out-of-doors, and fresh air simply cries out for shimmering champagne. After all, eating outside, picnics and hampers are just the modern extension of the glorious fêtes champêtres of our ancestors.

Champagne has always been present in the partying society, but how has the champagne of today permeated almost every event of note, be it ceremonial, sporting, cultural or just sheer fun? The short answer is sponsorship. Subtly and with infinite taste, the great champagne houses have appeared on the scene with offers of help and bubbly, and they have been warmly received. Often the sums involved are not large, but champagne provides the magic ingredient that lifts a function into a memorable event.

Champagne X will have a box at a race meeting and entertain a few people in great style, while Champagne Y will perhaps splash out on a whole tent to which a large number of friends, customers and a social diarist or two will be invited. Often this largesse is accompanied by sponsorship of a race, the Champagne Z Stakes. And at all the race meetings, from the grandest, couture occasions to the small, country, mud-bespattered events, champagne is available at the bar, and the houses will make great efforts to see that they are represented. Then, when the marque is "listed", you have to see that the bar employees "push" it. I never realized the influence those slightly nannyish bar ladies can have – a very English feature of racing life: they can simply lead the punter by the nose to the brand they currently hold in favour. Strong men are like putty in their hands. I know one house that used annually to fly some of these jolly ladies out to Champagne for a day's intensive indoctrination into the mysteries of their particular brand. Apparently it worked like magic – but they were all, I think, slightly in love with the very gallant chairman of the English importers.

Most champagne houses have dabbled with racing at one time or another – placing bets and drinking bubbly seem to be intimately linked. In England, Bollinger each year present the award to the leading amateur and professional National Hunt jockey – the tough, macho part of racing that sorts out the men from the boys. Other houses have backed the new sport for the super-rich, ocean racing. Mumm was the quaffing champagne for the 1983 America's Cup in Newport, Rhode Island, but the tiller passed to Moët-Vuitton for the return match in Perth, Australia.

Moët, of course, are the champions of sponsorship. A whole study in itself could be made of the development of promotion "behind the scenes", as opposed to advertising – a trail that Moët has so brilliantly blazed. They traditionally provide the celebratory champagne held aloft by Grand Prix racing-car winners around the world. Moët & Chandon (magnums, if you please) even went on two recent voyages to the North and South Poles. And in America, Moët was poured (and poured) at the Statue of Liberty Restoration Fund party on Staten Island, while just about every champagne house produced a special label for the cleaning up of that rather daunting female.

Big business runs on champagne. It would seem that the so-called Crash of 1987 was a mere lacuna between two popping corks. One City of London hostelry charted "progress" in the numbers of bottles ordered, and claimed that the event merited no more than the proverbial hiccup in overall sales. The man was a seasoned seer, because the end-of-year figures for champagne consumption were astounding. Britain retained its position as the foremost export market for champagne with a record 19.2 million bottles imported in 1987. This shows a staggering increase of 19.5 percent over the figures for booming 1986. It has to be admitted that everyone, from the CIVC in Epernay to individual shippers, is somewhat mystified by this soaring rise, but figures have a habit of being figures. America took second place with 15.8 million bottles, followed by West Germany (10.5 million), Switzerland (7.2 million) and Italy (7.1 million).

If you ask the head of any top champagne house where he is looking for the future, he will say Germany. As for new, as yet relatively uncharted markets, we must include Spain, with her burgeoning "Champagnerías". Perhaps this indicates that countries where sparkling wines are already appreciated (Sekt and Cava) are the most fertile ground for the invasion of champagne – one will just have to hope that eventually they will renovate their nomenclature. Clearly, Japan also has great potential, particularly for the Moët-Vuitton group – the classy Vuitton luggage is already a best-seller there.

So what is champagne today? It is a fact of life, and yet still frivolous. It is an accessory of seduction, sales patter and social manoeuvring. It is part of our joys and our travails. It goes a-wooing with a will, but is just as amenable when the whole edifice comes to grief. Champagne is simultaneously a fair-weather friend and an ally for life. It is often with us at birth, and more of us should make sure it is with us when we go. Above all, we need it for that period in between.

There is a nostalgia about water and rushes and ripples that is not explained by logic. This couple have wisely opted for an ice bucket for their champagne. Tying the bottle to a string and trailing it alongside the boat can result in tepid champagne or, at worst, no champagne at all.

• • • • • • • • • • •

CHAPTER FOUR

THE WINE
OF THE MUSES

For every occasion when champagne appears in a painting, an opera, a novel or a poem, there must be ten times as many artists and writers and composers (perhaps not singers, anyway not just before a performance) who have been inspired by the bubble. Hemingway, who was a Krug man, describes Scott Fitzgerald drinking (and drinking) champagne at the Dingo bar (now the Rosebud) in Paris' rue Delambre. Could it have been this bout that produced the cruel description of "Mrs. Abrams' face, cooked to a turn in Veuve Cliquot [sic]" in *Tender Is The Night*? William Carlos Williams, one of America's greatest 20th-century poets, made a pilgrimage to Reims to see the cellars of Veuve Clicquot; it replaced a visit to the cathedral.

Oscar Wilde considered that only those who lacked imagination could not find a good reason for drinking champagne. In his case, much of it was consumed at the Savoy Hotel, London, where the champagne that was reputedly his favourite, Dagonet, was listed. "There was no harm in your seriously considering that the most perfect way of passing an evening was to have a champagne dinner at the Savoy, a box at a music hall to follow and a champagne supper at Willie's as a bonne-bouche for the end. . . . The heavy amber-coloured indeed almost amber-scented champagne – Dagonet 1880, I think was your favourite?" (Letter to Lord Alfred Douglas, *Oscar Wilde – Letters*, published by Hart Davis). At the sad end in Paris, when virtually all had abandoned him, Monsieur Dupoirier at the Hôtel d'Alsace fed him without payment and even bought him champagne.

Sir Walter Scott had a great love of champagne: it circulated briskly at his Scottish home, Abbotsford, at Sunday dinner, before the claret. His publisher also arranged an exchange with a Frenchman: Scott's books against champagne. Scott certainly increased the popularity of champagne in Scotland during the 19th century: he ordered "white champagne and red, both sparkling". No wonder French guests felt so at home at Abbotsford.

In Somerset Maugham's *The Summing Up*, his commentary on his life and art (we are not allowed to call it an autobiography), he talks of another writer's love

Where there's music, there's champagne, from the "Moet and Chandon" song – George Leybourne's celebrated music-hall hit of 1869 – to the Teatro alla Scala in Milan, the heart of Italian opera, where Veuve Clicquot sponsored a production of Rossini's *Il Viaggio a Reims* in 1985. Naturally, the stage was aglow with bright yellow, to match the famous label. The story turns on a disparate group of people on their way to Reims for the coronation of Charles X in 1825.

of champagne: "There is in Victor Hugo's *Choses Vues* a passage, touching in its unconscious humour, in which with awe, astonishment and a spark of envy for such wildness, the sensible little man describes a supper party with an actress. For once in his life he felt a devil of a fellow. Good gracious, how the champagne flowed and what luxury, what silver, what tiger-skins, were to be seen in her apartment!" (William Heinemann, 1938).

George Bernard Shaw was more succinct: "I'm only a beer teetotaller, not a champagne teetotaller" (*Candida*). So was Noël Coward, who is reported to have said: "Why do I drink champagne for breakfast? Doesn't everyone?" And then there was Rudyard Kipling, who observed: "If the aunt of the vicar has never touched liquor, look out when she finds the champagne".

In a lovely vignette, *Proust as a Soldier*, Anthony Powell describes the stresses of life in the army for someone so obviously illfitted for the role. Lighter moments were provided by champagne parties given by the volunteers, of which Proust was one, in rooms hired in the town of Orléans – a practice expressly forbidden, but watched rather enviously by less affluent officers, who were sometimes invited in to take a glass.

Emile Zola's love of good food and drink was such that they inevitably took their place in his novels. His Nana was always drinking champagne – sometimes with fruit, which is not the ideal accompaniment. She also drank it at the races, notably the Grand Prix de Paris in the Bois de Boulogne, where there were hampers of champagne. Corks came out with "feeble pops", and when the champagne ran dry the servants ran to the refreshment bars for more.

The Café Anglais in Paris was a well-known haunt of Nana's. It reappears evocatively in the Oscar-winning Danish film *Babette's Feast*, Isak Dinesen's story of how a French woman came to cook a Lucullan feast for an austere community in Jutland. The one hedonist at the table, General Lowenhielm, is reminded of earlier days at the Café Anglais: the chef, of course, had been Babette. At the feast, they drank Veuve Clicquot 1860, which Babette had ordered specially from France.

Among poets, Byron was certainly acquainted with the delights of champagne: "Champagne with its foaming whirls/As white as Cleopatra's pearls" (*Don Juan*). But by far the most lyrical poem to champagne is *Le Vin de Champagne* by J-L Gonzalle (1860). Could any other wine have inspired such a work? In his preface, the poet says that in "la coupe de cristal où sa mousse pétille" – the crystal coupe where its mousse sparkles – one finds both hope and oblivion, "ces deux enfants de la même heure" – these two children of the same hour, which alone help us to live. The style is, necessarily for the time, florid, but it captures the dream of champagne, its purpose in our lives, its capacity to make, and to cause us to relive, memories.

Longfellow had a penchant for Verzenay and Sillery, while Pushkin compared "the blessed wine of the Veuve Clicquot to the fountain of Hippocrene from which poets drew their inspiration". Here champagne as muse is given a very strong endorsement.

Clicquot seems to have had more than its fair share of literary praise, for Mérimée, in one of his letters, says that "Madame Clicquot quenches the thirst of

Screen sophistication, stage extravaganza, the sheer fun of a waltz – champagne has been used to evoke every mood.
• • • • • • • • • • • •

It is altogether appropriate that the name of Colbert, Louis XIV's powerful and cultured adviser, who was born in Reims in 1619, has been given to the Comité Colbert, an association formed to promote all that is best and most luxurious in French design and creativity, from jewellery to luggage and couture clothes, glass and porcelain. The champagne houses that are members of the Comité are Bollinger, Krug, Moët & Chandon, Roederer, Ruinart and Veuve Clicquot.

all Russia. They call her wine 'Klikofskoe' and drink no other". This seems a slight exaggeration. Where was Roederer? In 1852 the famous Porte Mars, one of the finest monuments of Reims, was on the point of crumbling; Mérimée wrote to a certain Monsieur Vitet: "We have sent le Marquis de Pastoret to Madame Clicquot, who is queen of Reims. It seems that if she deigns to say the word, the arch is saved." The arch is still standing.

Not only the wine, but the buildings of Champagne can inspire art. I have enjoyed some wonderful champagnes in the Lalique glasses modelled on the "angel of the smile" over the northern doorway of Reims cathedral. In return, champagne houses are often patrons of the arts, none more so than Mumm. Maurice Utrillo painted *Champagne in Montmartre* for Mumm, with Sacré Coeur and the famous "moulin" in the background, and an outsize bottle of Cordon Rouge dominating the foreground. Utrillo refused payment but accepted 100 bottles of champagne. Foujita, the Japanese artist, revelled in the bounty of René Lalou, head of Mumm. There is a slightly mischievous story that he said he wanted to give a present to the "patron": a church. In the event, René Lalou bought the land and had the chapel built, next to Mumm's premises in Reims, and Foujita decorated it with frescoes. The great designer of tapestries, Lurçat, was a friend of René Lalou – his *Champagne* in the series *The Song of the World* must be one of the most joyous explosions of life ever depicted. The "mousse" rises from a wooden cask in a flight of butterflies, deep blue, red and yellow. No one could stand in front of this and feel sad.

Moët has embarked on a remarkable artistic venture, the Australian Art Foundation. The Moët Art Fellowship gives an Australian artist the chance to work and study in France for a year, and a touring exhibition ensures that the work of some 20 young Australian artists is seen by a wide variety of people across the continent. The Art Acquisition Fund enables the State Galleries or the Australian National Gallery to purchase contemporary Australian art, giving artists the seal of recognition.

Where films are concerned, the lucrative (and totally unartistic) practice of "merchandise placing" has become big business. I prefer the age of delightfully gratuitous remarks such as: "Champagne tastes much better after midnight, don't you agree?" that graced the Max Ophüls melodrama *Letter from an Unknown Woman*, with an ingenuous Joan Fontaine and a rakish Louis Jourdan. It is irresistible to associate Louis Jourdan with champagne, never more memorably than in the film of Colette's *Gigi*, with the enchanting Leslie Caron and that heady song, *The Night They Invented Champagne*.

The theatre frequently uses champagne as a legitimate prop. In Christopher Hampton's adaptation of Laclos's *Les Liaisons Dangeureuses*, played by the Royal Shakespeare Company, champagne is prominently displayed in the courtesan scene. For Russian plays, it seems to be almost mandatory: in Alexander Ostrovsky's *Artists and Admirers*, the characters are constantly asking for "more champagne". A London champagne shipper ensures a steady flow of publicity for his wine by supplying stage managers with dummy bottles:

the contents pop like champagne but are, alas, only soda water. And still in theatrical vein, every year London's Garrick Club marks the birth of that great actor, Sir Henry Irving. In February 1988, his 150th anniversary was celebrated with a menu based on the supper that was given to Irving at the Garrick in 1883 on his departure for his first North American tour. With the port and lemon jelly and iced pudding we had Pommery Brut Royal – and very splendid it was too.

And what of music and champagne? It surely could not be the banal trillings to be heard on every champagne house's telephone while you are waiting for your call to be put through, a particularly popular fashion in the champagne capitals of Reims and Epernay at the moment (at least Roederer has Vivaldi's *Four Seasons*). Champagne produces musicians of the highest order: Eric Heidsieck, who was Alfred Cortot's last pupil, is a pianist of immense sensivity. Jean-Philippe Collard, of the Philipponnat family, is another pianist of the greatest ability, regularly collecting Record of the Year awards in the United States.

Opera embraces champagne – although I have always wondered about the famous "Champagne Aria" in *Don Giovanni*: as it was set in Seville, what was really in the glass? Perhaps another case of fraudulent nomenclature? Rossini's *Il Viaggio a Reims*, so gloriously revived in 1984 at Pesaro under Abbado, would seem a natural for champagne sponsorship throughout the world. In fact, it is difficult to amass such a fine array of singers as the opera requires in one spot at any given time, although Clicquot managed a sparkling production at La Scala, Milan, in 1985.

However, the ultimate operatic accolade must come in Johann Strauss' *Die Fledermaus*, which ends on a high note of praise to King Champagne. There is something bewitching about a New Year's Day performance of this glorious romp – followed by a champagne supper for artists and audience alike!

"There are people constitutionally unable to find pleasure in anything but variety. But a man who sings the praises of Champagne at the expense of the wine of Bordeaux is only saying with a certain amount of eloquence: 'I prefer Champagne'. Each of these wines has its partisans, and both sides are right." Stendhal.

Wife, Wine and Song, by the American artist John Haberle (1856–1933). The violin and its bow rest against a sheet from the music of *The Merry Widow.* The champagne is Veuve Clicquot; the painting was sold by Sotheby's, New York, to the champagne house in 1988.

CHAPTER FIVE

WHAT MAKES CHAMPAGNE

I may shock a good many people by saying that the fundamental reason why champagne is so special is not primarily the champagne method, the méthode champenoise. So many people, for so long, have tried to initiate us into its mysteries that we have missed those points that are really important to the making of champagne. But N. E. Legrand in *Le Vin de Champagne*, 1896, drives straight to the heart of the matter: "Champagne, this delicious wine that sparkles on our tables, to the greatest satisfaction of the eye and the pleasure of the stomach, is above all a French product, unique and inimitable, drawing its qualities, not from any artifice, but from the special nature of its soil, from its noble grape varieties and from its geographical position in the ancient province of Champagne."

These are the pivotal ingredients of champagne. The champagne method, or the secondary fermentation in bottle, is a mechanical manoeuvre that certainly aids quality but, on its own, is by no means enough to ensure it. It can be, and is, carried out in many places in the world, on many different types of wine. However, Monsieur Legrand, although identifying absolutely correctly what gives champagne the potential to be great, fails to pinpoint the most vital element of all: the art of blending. The assemblage, marrying cru with cru, grape with grape, is what distinguishes great champagne from the merely good. Blending is that extra manoeuvre that gives complexity to a wine. If the blender is experienced, if he has innate talent, and if he has access to a fine palette of villages and growths and, in the case of non-vintage wine, reserve wines, there is no limit to the spells he can weave.

So all the energy of a champagne house should be concentrated upon producing the best possible raw material: the still wines from which the blend is made in the spring after the vintage. Every detail of growing, pressing and first fermentation is geared towards this end. Skilled blending is what gives champagne its balance, that high-wire act between freshness and depth of flavour, fruit and body, delicacy and length on the palate.

Stainless-steel fermenting vats at Laurent-Perrier, Tours-sur-Marne. Nearly every house now uses similar equipment, except for a very few that are still devoted to casks. Temperature control is easy in vats of this type and they are no problem to maintain and keep clean, especially when huge quantities of wine are being handled.

First, the grapes must be picked. This is always done by hand; mechanical harvesters are not permitted in the Champagne region. There is a special reason why this rule is upheld: because so much champagne is made from black grapes, the slightest damage to the skins would result in variously tinted wines. Fortunately there has never been a labour shortage in Champagne (it was largely the labour factor that decided the southwest of France to turn so decisively to the machine). Since the 1987 vintage, the timing of the start of the harvest has been more flexible, with an overall opening date for the region being fixed centrally and then each village choosing the precise starting date for their vineyards. Given the three grape varieties of the region, the diversity of sites and the distance between the areas, this is an eminently sensible move, enabling the grapes to be picked at the optimum moment. In some cases, this improved and more locally exact timing will allow grapes to be harvested at higher natural alcohol levels, thereby necessitating less chaptalization.

This is one of the innovations introduced by the new Charte de Qualité, which is aimed at extending quality, not just maintaining it. The Charter's first concern is the soil, where it all begins. Now, before planting a new vineyard or replanting an old one, the soil and subsoil must be analysed to see if any additions or corrections are required and to select the right grape variety and graft for the soil type. The Charter covers the selection of clones, so that the right balance is struck between a grape's ability to produce quantity and to deliver a true and characteristic taste.

Yield is a touchy subject, affecting as it does the growers' pockets, but exaggerated production results in neutral wines, in Champagne as anywhere else. In 1983, the decision was taken to increase from 150 kilos to 160 kilos the amount of grapes required from which a hectolitre of must is pressed, and this could be adopted as general policy. It is, however, more difficult to advocate in small vintages such as 1984. Yields are fixed every year with regard to the harvest forecasts and the prevailing economic situation. In 1987, yield was limited to

The other approach is that of Krug, where the wine goes through its first fermentation in old oak barrels. Clearly this is more small scale but there is great individuality in the crus, which can be kept apart, enabling a house such as this to make very complex blends.

11,250 kgs/hectare plus 20 percent, the equivalent of 75 hectolitres/hectare plus 20 percent. In practice, much should depend on the type of vintage: a very good, sunny year should be allowed to produce more than a poor one, but the 160 kilos formula should be employed, thus creaming off the very top-quality wine.

The Charter of Quality also covers pruning and the control of foliage. The most dramatic proposal concerns quality control at the press (the press houses are nearly all in the vineyards and wine villages and not in the town cellars of the champagne houses), when payment to the growers would vary according to the health and maturity of the grapes. This is controversial but, in my view, must gradually be implemented – after all, this is what happens at the best cooperatives elsewhere in France. There are also plans to replace old presses with new ones over a period of five years: a challenge to the authorities, as there are nearly 2,000 presses in the region to inspect.

By far the most common press is the traditional, vertical "coquard". Its great virtue is that it is simple to operate – "like Deux Chevaux cars, everyone can drive them", as a Champenois put it picturesquely. These round or square presses take 4,000 kilos of grapes which yield 2,666 litres of juice. Of this, the first 2,050 litres, the "cuvée", is by far the best quality, producing wines of finesse and breed. The second part of the juice as it comes off the press is called the "première taille" (410 litres); the quality of the Chardonnay première taille can often be good, much better than the equivalent from black grapes, which gives a coarser wine. The last part of the juice is the "deuxième taille" (205 litres), which has a distinctive smell and taste and is used for less expensive champagnes, such as the second marques of some houses and certain buyer's own brand (BOB) champagnes. As with everything else in this world, you get what you pay for. Any juice pressed out beyond the 2,666 litres is called the rebêche, which should never be used in the production of champagne.

Modern versions of the coquard are being produced that work horizontally; they are easier to manoeuvre, quicker and less costly to run than the vertical press and give the same good results. There are also both hydraulic and pneumatic horizontal presses. Sizes can vary from a 2,000 to a 12,000 kilo content, with Moët very happy with their 12,000 kilo pneumatic Willmes model, after adapting the shape to be shorter and wider, with two entries for loading and a modified "pressurage". This gives them juice with the same analysis as from their traditional presses, but there is more colour in the deuxième taille from the Willmes.

If I have dwelt on the quality of grapes it is because research has now largely switched from the cellar to the vineyard. So much has been perfected and refined in the winemaking process that future concentration will be on the balance between quantity and quality (that age-old battle) and true viticultural research. The Moët & Chandon group is working along three lines of in-vitro culture: development of facilities for the production of grafted vine plants; formation of a collection of in-vitro genotypes under ideal hygienic conditions; and improving the health of the grape varieties and rootstocks.

Most rosé champagne is produced by blending red wine of the region with white (interestingly, this is the only area in France where this is allowed). A few houses obtain the pink colour by skin contact through pressing, maceration or "bleeding" (saignée). The difference between blending and skin contact does not affect quality – that, as always, rests on the basic class of the wine. With both methods, the exact shade is difficult to judge because the wine loses colour during the prise de mousse.

• • • • • • • • • • •

*Charles Tovey had
his own view of the
tasting characteristics
of different villages.
In 1870 he wrote:
"Aÿ – very delicate
Verzenay – full,
vinous and spirituous
Bouzy – full flavour
and spirituous
Cramant – delicate in
the mouth, but as it
goes off the palate,
somewhat coarse [I
think he must have
been unlucky here]
Avize – very fine and
delicate."*

The juice, or must, then goes through the process of débourbage, which is a natural clarification, or decanting of solid matter, effected at about 5°C (40°F). The clean juice is now ready for its first, alcoholic fermentation, nearly always in stainless-steel vats, although a very few houses – Krug, Bollinger (partially), and Alfred Gratien – still ferment in cask. The Champenois use their own cultured yeasts, so they can control the fermentation to a very great degree. It also means that they have fermentations that do not "stick", or stop before all the sugar is converted into alcohol, which has been a problem in many areas of France where anti-rot treatments have to be used in the vineyards.

Fermentations are usually carried out at between 18° and 20°C (65–68°F) and last for about ten days. In Champagne, a good must contains a minimum of about 9–9.5 percent alcohol. It is then necessary to chaptalize the must (to add sugar as it is fermenting) to bring it up to about 10.5 percent alcohol as a vin clair after the first fermentation. The liqueur de tirage, which induces the second fermentation in bottle, will add about 1–1.5 percent alcohol after the prise de mousse, and champagne is sold at around 12 percent alcohol, less than both red and white burgundy.

With regard to acidity, in good vintages the must measures between 7.5 and 9 grams before fermentation. The final acidity in a vin clair depends on whether a house causes its wines to go through malolactic fermentation (the majority do), which is the process by which the greener malic acid is transformed into the milder lactic acid. Thus, a vin clair after bottling can have an acidity reading of from 4–4.5 grams up to 6 or 6.5 grams. A house like Krug, where the champagnes can be laid down, will be at the top end of the acidity scale. In all cases, good balance between sugar and acidity is essential to the quality of a champagne and its potential for ageing.

The still wines are kept separately, according to the logistical possibilities of the house. Vats, and sometimes barrels, will be marked with grape variety and village name: the more elements available, the greater the palette for making up the assemblage.

Assemblage is not for amateurs. At first, distinguishing between an array of rather thin, acid, still white wines seems daunting, but after practice, enormous differences emerge. In the process you learn much about the Champagne vineyards and the characteristics of the villages and crus. Knowing how to put them together comes with experience and a clear vision of what you actually want your champagne to taste like. This image has to be projected beyond the prise de mousse, or second fermentation, to the mature wine, and therein lies the ultimate skill. The virtue of the assemblage is that one cru can act as the catalyst to another. You play with contrasts, the yin and the yang of champagne.

As an indication of how tasting characteristics of the villages and grape varieties emerge during the assemblage, I have picked out some notes of the many vins clairs tastings I did with the 1987 still wines (actual assemblages are much more complicated than this, involving anything from 20–40 crus). **Bollinger** (tasting from casks): ***Chardonnay – Oger:*** good bouquet. *Villers-*

Depart le   LUN. 16 NOU. 1987 10h05
Caisses de Droite remuees le
LUN. 16 NOU. 1987 18h35
Tenue N.01   2/16 Dr. 1 Degr.
LUN. 16 NOU. 1987 19h05
Caisses de Gauche remuees le
LUN. 16 NOU. 1987 19h05
Tenue N.02   2/16 Dr. 1 Degr.
MAR. 17 NOU. 1987 03h06
Caisses de Gauche remuees le
MAR. 17 NOU. 1987 03h06
Tenue N.02   2/16 Dr. 1 Degr.
MAR. 17 NOU. 1987 03h06
Caisses de Droite remuees le
MAR. 17 NOU. 1987 07h06
Tenue N.03   2/16 Dr. 1 Degr.
aisses de Gauche remuees le
Tenue N.03   2/16 Dr. 1 Degr.
MAR. 17 NOU. 1987 11h07
Caisses de Droite remuees le
Tenue N.04   * 4/16 Ga. 3 Degr.
MAR. 17 NOU. 1987 15h07
Caisses de Gauche remuees le
Tenue N.04   * 4/16 Ga. 3 Degr.
MAR. 17 NOU. 1987 19h08
Caisses de Droite remuees le
Tenue N.05   2/16 Ga. 3 Degr.
MER. 18 NOU. 1987 03h08
Tenue N.05   2/16 Ga. 3 Degr.
aisses de Gauche remuees le
Tenue N.06   2/16 Ga. 3 Degr.
IER. 18 NOU. 1987 03h08
Caisses de Droite remuees le
Tenue N.06   2/16 Ga. 3 Degr.
MER. 18 NOU. 1987 07h09
Caisses de Gauche remuees
enue N.06   2/16 Ga.
MER. 18 NOU. 1987

The highly skilled art of poignetage – giving the bottles a swift shake to stop the sediment from settling during the second fermentation, or prise de mousse – at Pol Roger, in the days when electricity was a somewhat mysterious new phenomenon.

• • • • • • • • • •

Marmery: more earthiness. *Avize:* finesse on bouquet; often drier and more "metallic" than other crus on the Côte. **Pinot Noir** – *Verzenay:* good length on palate. *Bouzy:* scented, but Verzenay fuller. *Aÿ:* shorter on palate.

Lanson: *Chardonnay* – *Oger:* very scented, marked acidity. **Pinot Noir** – *Verzenay:* scented, good and clean, much less acidity than the Chardonnay. (It was always said that in those hot years of 1959 and 1976 at Verzenay, "one made wines like elephants"!)

Laurent Perrier: *Chardonnay* – *Avize:* a little sharper on the nose than the others. *Cramant:* elements of grapefruit, more marked taste than many Chardonnays this year. *Oger:* a little broader than the Avize and the Cramant. *Chouilly:* acidity main characteristic. *Sézanne:* broad acidity. **Pinot Noir** – *Ambonnay:* nice nose, toasty taste (normally, Ambonnay is riper than Bouzy). *Tauxières:* some exotic fruit. *Tours-sur-Marne:* straightforward, direct. *Verzenay:* rounder, some grapefruit. *Verzy:* Neutral middle palate, more marked on finish.

Moët & Chandon: *Chardonnay* – *Cramant:* slightly musky, supple, strong taste of liquorice (in this year, when the Chardonnay overproduced, the yield at Cramant was not quite as exaggerated: hence the wines are less hollow than other villages on the Côte des Blancs, such as Chouilly). *Villers-Marmery:* delicate, floral, finishes a little shorter than the Cramant (yield not excessive here nonetheless). **Pinot Noir** – *Verzenay:* finesse, austerity, class and delicacy. Very clean, with breed. *Mailly:* deeper colour, goût de terroir, as always here. Fruity, soft and full. **Pinot Meunier** – *St-Martin d'Ablois:* smell of warm bread, a "millstone" quality, good acidity balance. *Châtillon-sur-Marne:* more typically Meunier, some astringency and tannin. (The Pinot Meunier is the grape that "fills up" between the high points of the Pinot Noir and the Chardonnay – the wadding, if you like.)

Perrier-Jouët: *Chardonnay* – *Cramant:* good bouquet and character. Can often be round and "fat". *Le Mesnil-sur-Oger:* good fruit, less finesse than the Cramant. **Pinot Noir** – *Aÿ:* finesse (as 1987 a lighter year), elegant for an Aÿ. *Mailly:* open

Gyropalette at Veuve Clicquot: these "cages" hold the bottles at an angle, gradually manipulating them so that the sediment from the second fermentation can fall onto the crown cap and be easy to remove. In many houses, gyropalettes have replaced manual remuage to bring the sediment down the bottle more quickly. The computer printout from the totally automatic gyropalettes at Bruno Paillard records the date and time of every manoeuvre – even at 3 o'clock in the morning. A brief look at the printout tells the chef de caves the position of every gyropalette.

• • • • • • • • • •

nose, body, steely, earthiness (typical of cru), lacking finesse but contributing power. *Verzy:* sprightly acidity, good. *Verzenay:* less acidity and more floral on nose. More powerful on palate. *Bouzy:* between Aÿ and Verzenay in character, softer than Verzenay, more bouncy than Aÿ. **Pinot Meunier** – *Vinay:* more neutral nose, soft and easy. *Venteuil:* cru known as La Reine de la Petite Marne – very good bouquet.

Louis Roederer: *Chardonnay* – *Avize:* three samples, one with greengagey fruit, one combining acidity with fullness, and one with appley acidity. *Vertus:* finesse and keen character. **Pinot Noir** – *Verzenay:* rounded. *Ambonnay:* most complete of all.

Veuve Clicquot: *Chardonnay* – *Cramant:* almost animal muskiness, aromatic. **Pinot Noir** – *Verzenay:* good fruit – in hotter years, often has a nose of red burgundy!

Overall impression of vintage: clean wines, without great keeping potential and often short on palate, due to high yield, especially with Chardonnay. The Ambonnay wines impressed me most, as well as some very good Verzenay, with Cramant on the Côte des Blancs consistently more scented than its neighbours.

When juggling with the vins clairs, the house has to decide how much wine, if any, to put aside for vintage, and the proportion that must be kept for reserves. The vintage wines, of course, go through the village and grape variety blending, while remaining with the same year. Vintage champagne is thus an intriguing blend in the bottle between the climatic characteristics of one year and the house style.

After a cold stabilization treatment to eliminate crystals, the wine is ready for the second fermentation, or prise de mousse. This is obtained by adding the liqueur de tirage, a mixture of wine, sugar and selected yeast culture, the latter carefully calculated to give the right amount of bubble in the final result. Future

• • • • • • • • • •

A team of workers at the house of Madame and Monsieur P. Barthélemy at Aÿ, with the solemn faces more associated with anxiety about the unfamiliar camera than the sparkle usually induced by the product.

At Laurent-Perrier, remuage is still entirely by hand, even though the house sells more than 7 million bottles a year. Moët & Chandon, the region's giant, also uses this system for all its wines. Some houses retain manual remuage for their cuvées de prestige, but have gone over to gyropalettes for their other champagnes.

• • • • • • • • • • •

The modern dosage machine at Louis Roederer. These machines have become much more accurate and consistent in recent times, and the disparities measured in the dosage between bottles of what should have been the same wine have largely disappeared. The wines themselves are becoming drier, especially among the top cuvées.

• • • • • • • • • • •

research might well concentrate on the mousse in champagne, an element that is little understood and frighteningly idiosyncratic. Highly refined beet sugar is mostly used nowadays and the yeast chosen will take account of whether remuage later will be manual or in gyropalettes, as it affects the type of deposit to be removed. The liqueur de tirage cannot add more than 1.5 percent alcohol or produce more than six atmospheres of pressure, or mousse. The wines are bottled and closed with either the more common crown cap with plastic insert or in some cases (usually cuvées de prestige) a cork and metal clasp.

The bottles are then stacked horizontally, either sur lattes in huge piles or in pallets. The important thing is that the second fermentation in bottle should take place at a cold, constant temperature of between 10° and 12°C (50–55°F) and the process can take up to three months, leading to great complexity in the champagne. The prise de mousse marries the reserve wines and the base wine, but above all it underlines the qualities in a wine and exaggerates any faults. It also, of course, adds the bubble. The bottles are moved several times during the process, either manually, when the shaking is called the poignetage, or by forklift truck (incidentally, beware these lethal vehicles when they appear around corners at breakneck speed in Champagne cellars). Shifting the sediment in this way helps make remuage easier.

Remuage, or riddling, is done either manually in pupitres (boards with holes in which the bottle necks are inserted) or mechanically in gyropalettes, which may be computer controlled. The aim, in both cases, is for the sediment to fall down onto the plastic lining of the crown cap. In pupitres the bottles are gradually inverted; in gyropalettes they start neck downwards, the pallet movements causing the sediment to fall. In gyropalettes this can take a mere week, whereas manual remuage can take two to three months. Pupitres also, of course, take up a great deal of space, so some houses use this method only for their cuvées de prestige.

The residual sugar in champagne is measured in grams per litre. It is interesting to see the results of tests on a number of non-vintage champagnes by the French Consumers Association, published in January 1988:

Ayala 9.6

Billecart-Salmon 13.9

Bollinger 9.0

Deutz 13.2

Gosset 8.9

Charles Heidsieck 12.4

Heidsieck Monopole 13.8

Krug (Grande Cuvée) 8.5

Lanson 15.0

Laurent-Perrier 13.2

Mercier 12.4

Moët & Chandon 12.4

Mumm 10.4

Perrier-Jouët 13.7

Philipponnat 12.4

Piper-Heidsieck 9.9

Pol Roger 12.4

Pommery & Greno 14.0

Louis Roederer 12.8

Ruinart 14.1

Taittinger 14.4

Veuve Clicquot 12.4

Dosage figures do not, however, remain constant: a house judges what is best for each cuvée.

Moët & Chandon, where remuage is still entirely manual, have done a great deal of research into encapsulated yeasts, les billes, together with the CIVC and the Institut National de la Recherche Agronomique. The second-fermentation yeasts are trapped in double-walled beads made of alginate, which allows the sugar, alcohol and carbonic gas to pass through while remaining impervious to the sediment caused by the second fermentation. The encapsulated yeasts can thus descend almost immediately to the neck of a bottle. One of the problems that will have to be faced before commercial use can be made of the billes is the cost of the machine or system that injects them into the bottles. The actual billes will also, no doubt, be expensive – they will be Moët's patent, which is only fair, as Moët have done the work. As to quality, there seems to be no measurable difference between champagnes made in this way or "normally". In comparative tastings I have wondered if, when you leave the two wines in the glass, a small difference appears with the effects of oxidation, resulting in a slightly "fresher" bouquet on the traditionally made champagne. If so, that could lead to ageing problems for champagnes made with billes, but many more trials on small quantities will be carried out before final decisions are taken. Experiments with "levures agglomérantes", or flocculent aggregating yeasts, have not been as successful organoleptically, with some noticeable reductive tastes. But improved yeasts of this type could be found.

After remuage, the bottles are aged sur pointes, or vertically, with the neck of each bottle in the punt of the bottle below. The longer this maturing period "on the yeasts", the better the champagne – it can vary from months to years and will be reflected in the ultimate price you pay. A champagne that has been sur pointes for two to three years, or even better for four to six years, such as some cuvées de prestige, will have a more complex bouquet and a deeper flavour.

Dégorgement, or disgorging, is now nearly always done à la glace. The necks of the bottles pass through a tank of freezing brine, and when they emerge upright the sediment has gathered in sorbet-like consistency in the plastic top. This is easy to remove on the automatic line and the wine is now perfectly bright. Even bottles disgorged by hand, à la volée, have often been through the brine bath: this is the method used for some top cuvées and always when the closure for the second fermentation was the cork and metal clasp – the liège et agrafe.

The bottles now have a small space into which goes the liqueur d'expédition containing wine (similar to that being dosed) and, usually, cane sugar. Some old wines need no dosage, and of course there is no dosage in champagnes sold as Ultra Brut, Brut Sauvage, or other names indicating total dryness. Non-vintage champagnes, being younger, have more dosage than vintage champagnes, which are themselves often launched onto the market with a slightly higher dosage at the beginning, when the vintage is "new": later dégorgements have the dosage reduced. When there is no dosage, the bottles are topped up with the same wine from other bottles.

Much has been written about dosage: certainly, cheap champagnes, to disguise their somewhat common character, usually receive a liberal "dose". But there were also anomalies among good champagnes, largely because the dosage machines were not very exact and there were wide disparities between bottles of supposedly the same wine. Now, improved machines ensure absolute accuracy and the tendency of the top marques is towards even greater dryness, the fullness coming from the quality and maturity of the wine itself.

The champagne is then ready to be corked. All good champagnes will have a cork where the upper part is agglomerated cork, followed by several discs of natural cork, the part that is in contact with the wine. The bottles are now automatically given a shake to disperse the liqueur d'expédition and the label and foil are put on. Some houses prefer to keep their champagne after disgorging for further ageing in the cellars, especially for the British market. Most champagnes are now similarly dosed for all markets so that much-travelled customers can always find the same taste wherever they are, although there are markets, such as Germany and Africa, which have a penchant for sweeter styles.

There are those who ask if the champagnes made now will last as well as their ancestors. The answer is probably not, if you are thinking in terms of 40 years or more. The wines now are likely to have less vinosity, due to higher yields (often because of better husbandry in the vineyard, as well as different clones), and more Chardonnay in the blends as opposed to the very black-grape champagnes of yore. The old corks were also made in one piece, so they would have lasted better — essential if you wish to lay down a champagne for half a century.

But the attention to detail in champagne making has never been greater. With huge worldwide sales, consistency of quality has certainly never been better, backed by competent technical knowledge: 30 years ago, there were no oenologists working in Champagne, now there are about 150. Above all, the fascinating individuality of the champagne houses has been preserved, which I consider the most vital element of all.

Terms used on labels to indicate the sweetness (or dryness) of champagne are very subjective — one person's sweet may be another's dry. However, the following, with the limits of the residual sugar in grams per litre when the dosage has been added, is a guide.

Ultra brut: very dry indeed (no dosage at all).

Brut: very dry, 0–15g.

Extra sec: dry, 12–20g.

Sec: slightly sweet, 17–35g.

Demi-sec: sweet, 33–50g.

Doux: very sweet, more than 50g.

"Champagne PLOIX-JOLY"   ÉPERNAY — Scènes de vendanges

Collection des Nouvelles Galeries

Pickers enjoying a well-earned rest and sustenance. The Champagne vineyards have remained traditional at vintage time, with mechanical harvesters banned and a grand feast when picking is over.

CHAPTER SIX

AN ATLAS OF CHAMPAGNE

Driving up to the Côte des Blancs, across the plain from Fère-Champenoise, is like being a pilgrim coming upon Chartres; but instead of the cathedral rising up in front of you from the flat fields of the Beauce, you see Mont Aimé jutting out, a great bluff of vineyard. At the end of January 1988, in especially mild weather for the season, little puffs of smoke appeared all over the Mont, as everyone burnt their first prunings in preparation for the real "taille". It looked tranquil, but the growers were worried because there had been no cold snap to cleanse the vineyards. What if the frost came later, when they had already pruned? The saying is that where there are no crows, there is no cold weather – and we looked in vain for these harbingers of snow and frost.

The open views, the broad-brush landscape, the hard weather in (most) winters, these are the physical facts of Champagne. This is no close-knit land of hidden vineyards amid woods and valleys. It is a landscape wrought from chalk, with the open plains, the steep-edged hills, the long prospects of chalk country. The Marne River Valley which runs east-west through the heart of Champagne is wide and flat-floored, reminiscent on a grander scale of one of the rivers cutting through England's South Downs chalk. And indeed the parallel is close: the chalk is part of the same geological series, the southern rim of the great basin which dips beneath the Channel and reappears in southern England.

Champagne covers a wide area, very wide if you take the old frontiers of this historic province. To trace these frontiers is to discover links which still underlie life in Champagne. The northern edge of the old province touches Belgium, and it includes the département of the Ardennes, the cool, forested hill country which abuts the frontier. The southern neighbour is Burgundy, where not many kilometres separate the Champagne vineyards and those of Chablis. To the west lies Paris, to the east, Alsace and Germany. Champagne is thus at the crossroads of two of the oldest and busiest highways in Europe, routes which have brought trade, prosperity and war: five times in four generations (1814, 1815, 1870, 1914, 1940) invaders captured Reims. A happier result of geography was the great

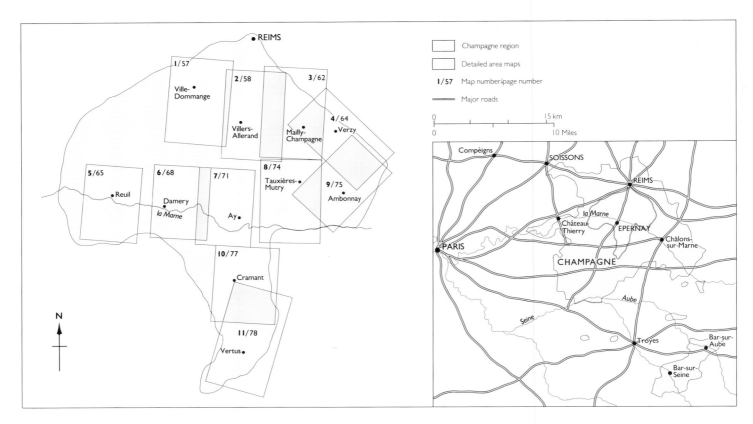

medieval Champagne Fairs, where traders from Flanders and farther north bartered cloth and leather with merchants from Italy, who brought the produce of the Mediterranean and the East. It is perhaps from these fairs that the cosmopolitan attitude of the Champenois stems.

Vineyards make up only scattered patches of the land within the appellation boundary. The bold patch portrayed on many a wine map, running from north of Reims south to the Seine and with outliers beyond, gives the impression that here is a broad swathe of continuous vineyard such as is found in the Midi. But most of this tract of country is corn or sugar-beet fields, woods or pasture. The vineyards run in narrow strips along slopes and edge the forests.

The greatest vineyards in Champagne lie in three sweeps along the edges of the Montagne de Reims, the Marne Valley and the Côte des Blancs. These three vineyards are on the slopes of chalk hills, carefully poised at an altitude high enough to be clear of frost and flood, low enough to be sheltered. Great debate centres around the geology of Champagne, and the contributions made by the various kinds of chalk. Drainage, exposure and slope are at least as important as the type of chalk beneath the subsoil.

It is possible to trace the quality levels of the Champagne vineyards by their échelle rating, shown in broad terms on the maps in this chapter. Every wine commune has a rating, agreed by the experts of the CIVC, with 100 percent for 17 Grand Crus and 90 percent plus conferring the honorary rank of Premier Cru on

The heartland of Champagne is conventionally split into three: the Montagne de Reims (from Villedommange through Verzy and around to Champillon); the Vallée de la Marne from here westward, and the Côte des Blancs from Epernay down to Bergères-lès-Vertus.

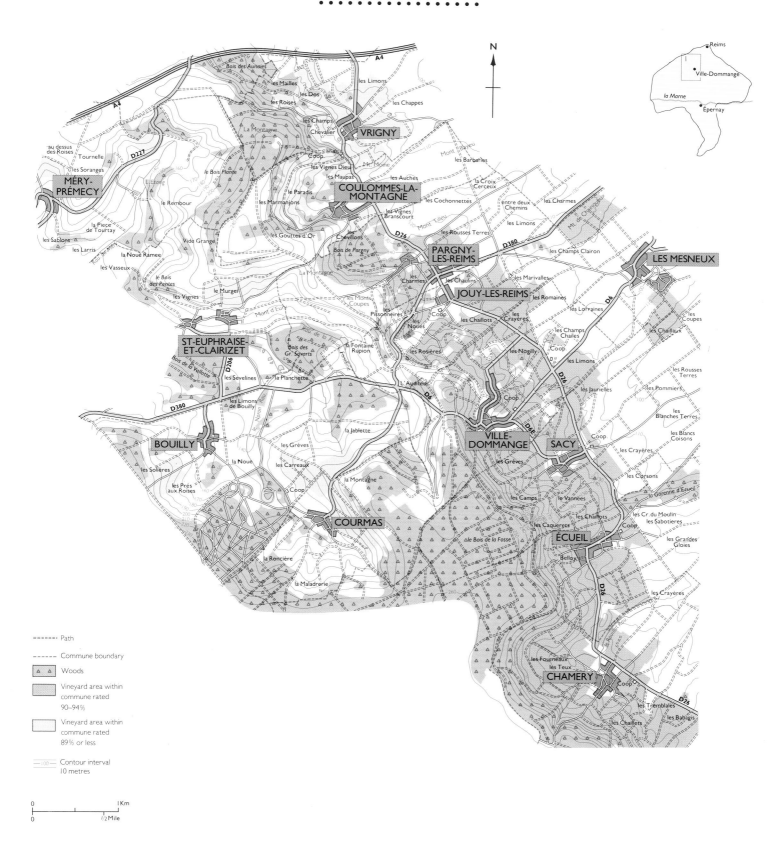

Reims

Ville-Dommange

la Marne

Épernay

N

Bois des Aunaies
les Mailles
les Roises
les Dos
les Limons
les Chappes
les Champs
Chevalier
VRIGNY
La Montagne
A4
au dessus des Roises
Tournelle
les Soranges
D227
L'Etang
le Bois Planté
le Paradis
le Rembour
Coop
Les Vignes Dieu
les Maupas
les Auches
Mt Moine
Mont Baveu
les Barbaries
la Croix Cerceux
MÉRY-PRÉMECY
COULOMMES-LA-MONTAGNE
les Cochonnettes
entre deux Chemins
les Charmes
les Marmanjons
les Vignes Branscourt
Mont Tilleu
les Limons
la Piece de Tourtay
Vide Grange
les Gouttes d'Or
Chevillons
Bois de Pargny
les Rousses Terres
D380
Mt de Chanqueu
les Champs Clairon
les Sablons
la Noue Ramée
La Montagne
D26
PARGNY-LES-REIMS
les Larris
le Bois des Pentes
les Charmes
les Chaulins
les Marivalles
LES MESNEUX
les Vasseux
le Murger
les Vignes
les Monts Coupes
JOUY-LES-REIMS
les Romaines
les Lorraines
D6
les Coupes
Mont d'Eur
les Pissonneires
Coop
les Noues
les Chaillots
les Crayères
les Chaillaux
Rau de la Fro
la Fontaine Rupion
les Rosières
les Nogilly
les Champs Chailes
Coop
les Rousses Terres
ST-EUPHRAISE-ET-CLAIRIZET
Bois des Gr. Sqvarts
les Limons
D26
les Pommiers
D206
Bois de la Vallotte
les Sevelines
la Planchette
L'Auditeur
Coop
les Jaurielles
les Blanches Terres
D380
les Limons de Bouilly
D6
les Blancs Coisons
la Jablette
Coop
D6E
Coop.
les Crayères
BOUILLY
les Grèves
VILLE-DOMMANGE
SACY
les Corsons
la Noue
les Carreaux
la Montagne
les Grèves
la Garenne d'Ecueil
les Solières
les Prés aux Roises
Coop
les Camps
le Vannees
les Chaillots
Cr. du Moulin
les Sabotieres
COURMAS
les Caquerets
ÉCUEIL
les Grandes Gloies
la Roncière
le Bois de la Fosse
Belloy
les Crayères
la Maladrerie
D26
les Fourneaux
les Teux
les Crayères
CHAMERY
Coop
D26
les Tremblales
les Babagis
les Chaillets

====== : Path

– – – – : Commune boundary

△ △ : Woods

Vineyard area within commune rated 90–94%

Vineyard area within commune rated 89% or less

—100— : Contour interval 10 metres

0   1 Km
0   1/2 Mile

N

VILLE-DOMMANGE

LES MESNEUX

MONTBRÉ

SACY

ÉCUEIL

CHAMERY

SERMIERS

VILLERS-
ALLERAND

RILLY-LA-
MONTAGNE

Path
Railway
Commune boundary
Woods
Vineyard area within
commune rated
90–94%
Vineyard area within
commune rated
89% or less
Contour interval
10 metres

0   1 Km
0   1/2 Mile

Reims
Villers-
Allerand
la Marne
Épernay

les Lorraines
les Coupes
les Champs
Chailes
les Chaillaux
Coop
les Limons
les Jaurielles
les Rousses
Terres
les Pommiers
les Recevresses
les Pas
les Blanches Terres
les Blancs
Coisons
les Terres
aux Buissons
Coop.
les Crayères
la Pierre Pouilleuse
les Créneaux
les Corsons
la Garenne d'Écueil
le Champ du Puits
le Vannées
les Cr. du Moulin
les Sabotieres
Coop
Belloy
les Chaillots
les Grandes Gloies
les Epinettes
les Crayères
les Crayères
les Limons
les Longues Raies
les Longues Raies
les Teux
Coop
CHAMERY
les Bruyères
la Grande Terre
les Tremblaies
les Babagis
la Garenne
du Cosson
la Mottelle
les Chaillets
les Bourges
les Quartiers
le Procureur
Coop.
les Hulots
les Presies
les Gros
Grés
le Château
la Noëlle
les Fiers
Monts
D22
les Verillats
les Plantes
Jeannin
le Bury
les Gouttes
d'Or
les Sablons
Mont
Trouilly
les Crêtes
les Blanches Bornes
les Jugelles
les Blancs Monts
les Chênes
Brûlés
les limons
la Garenne
les Paimelles
la Croix Ferlin
la Bastille
les Chênets
les Locambins
les Bichottes
les Faux
les Charmes
les Cumines
les Teux
les Vaukillons
D26
Mont
Tisset
le Ch. de Chigny
les Longues Raies
les Preux
les Gr. Bornes
les Vicomtes
la Côte
Henrion
Montreval
les Moulins
à Vent
le Trèso
les Maladries
le Mont
des Grues
les Ternigots
les Serbies
Bois la Dàux
N51
D409
Forêt Domaniale
Sermiers
les Chaufours
les Terres St. Denis
Bois de l'Hôpital
de Reims

The 17 grands crus of
Champagne, with a
100% échelle
(vineyard rating),
are:
Ambonnay
Avize
Aÿ
Beaumont-sur-Vesle
Bouzy
Chouilly (for
Chardonnay)
Cramant
Louvois
Mailly
Le Mesnil-sur-Oger
Oger
Oiry
Puisieulx
Sillery
Tours-sur-Marne
(for Pinot)
Verzenay
Verzy
In 1960, 1 hectare of
Grand Cru was worth
10,000 Fr. Now
(1988), 1 hectare is
worth 1 million Fr.

another 140. The lowest figure is 80 percent, but you need to leave the Marne département and venture to the Aisne or the Aube to track down an 80 percent commune. Naturally, a rating is not absolute: there are good and less good sites in each commune. Another indication of the quality of a commune's vineyards is the list of landowners. Where the information is available, names of the major houses owning vineyards have been added to the descriptions of the villages. This information has been drawn from questionnaires filled in by the houses themselves. It is not infallible: land is bought, sold and swapped; there are various grades of "ownership" including leases to growers who actually farm the land, and long-term grape-buying contracts made with small growers are sometimes discussed as if they confer proprietorial rights. Nor are all the great houses totally forthcoming: the information available varies from the meticulous to the vague. Interestingly, some houses own no vines at all, relying on their buying power in the open market to keep them supplied with grapes.

Reims lies on a broad plain, which slopes gently south and southwest up to the edge of the forested Montagne. Along the slope between the two is a string of vineyard communes, beginning with Vrigny, beside the Paris autoroute, and sweeping down, first south and then east, to Verzy, where the slope makes an abrupt turn to the south. Consequently the vineyards of this northern part of the Montagne face east and north, a most unusual circumstance in viticultural France, especially considering how far north they are. Pinot Meunier predominates in many of these villages, as it is less prone to frost damage than Pinot Noir. The Champenois have been known to call this district "Siberia".

The northernmost villages of the string, down to Chamery, are called the Petite Montagne. The first, Vrigny, rates 89 percent, and its produce appears nowhere in the vineyard registers of the Grandes Marques. Coulommes-la-Montagne is rated the same, but Pargny and Jouy rise to Premier Cru level. The cooperatives, shown on the map as "coop vinicole", are important in this area. Most land in Champagne belongs to individuals, not to the great houses. Many of these 18,500 small farmers sell their grapes to the big concerns, often on long-term contracts. Others take their grapes to the local cooperative, and a minority make their own champagne from their own grapes. Very few of the great houses own enough land to supply even half their needs. They rely upon carefully

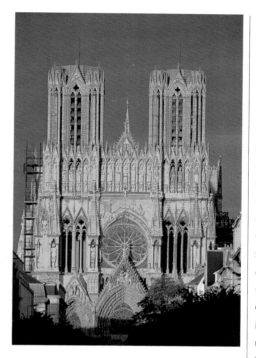

Reims cathedral, built between the 13th and 15th centuries, is a monument to tenacity: it was virtually destroyed in the fighting of World War I. Its magnificent stained glass is now an assemblage of old and new, including three contributions by Chagall, and a Jacques Simon window which depicts the stages of winemaking in Champagne. Reims itself is the capital of the province and headquarters of many of the great houses. Its few vineyards are rated at 88%; Pommery & Greno have some Chardonnay here.

The River Marne
traverses the heart of
Champagne, flowing
from east to west and
forming a major route
for travellers
throughout the
centuries.
• • • • • • • • • • •

les Basses Hayes
les Molles Fosses
les Hayes
Mont Ferré
les Trésors
la Garenne
les Champs St. Rémy
la Sobinette
Terres des Moussets
les Couraux
la Glacière
D8
les Carres
D8E
les Montouzons
le Mont
de Gelus
la Garenne des Cesses
les Chauds Champs
D8
la Vesle R.
D8E
le Champ
Brûle
les Paradis
la Crayère
A4
la Souris Blanche
le Chemin de Coureaux
SILLERY
D9
D409E
D409
les Crochets
les Termes
les Vigneuls
les Trésorières
les Petites Vignes
les Grands Jardins
PUISIEULX
MONTBRÉ
Fort de
Montbré
le Mont
de Montbré
Mont
Thibe
le Mont
Fournois
Pilon à Four
Gros Ventre
Mont
de la Cuche
Champ Baillard
Franc Alleu
Croix la Voizelle
le Bauchet
D33
le Chemin
de Chigny
les Trois Saules
D208
les Rouages
A4
le Ch. de
Chigny
Champ Elin
Sersuits
la Cuche
le Buisson St. Jean
les Gloies
le Chemin
de Mailly
Fosse Blanc
la Reculée
les H. Blanches Vóies
Champs Thomas
les Blanches Vóies
Sainfoins
les Champs Perchaux
les Champs St. Jean
les Haies de Mailly
Ch. des Robéaux
les Voyéttes
les Grèves
les Pelles à Four
les Egrimoussets
le Grosse Pierre
les Corigniers
Champs aux Fromges
les Crayats
Champ de la Guerre
les Potences
les Rochelles
D7
Longues Raies
de Livry
les Epinettes
Champ Tortus
Vauréages
les Hermisseaux
le Parc
Champs la Hache
Montaigu
les Bruyères
Blancs Fosses
la Barbarie
les Maladries
D409
Bas Moutions
les Beaunes
Coop. C!
les Mauvais
Champ
la Maie
None de Mailly
les Villiers
les Voies de Reims
Champ St. Martin
les Dernis Fosses
les Perthois
**RILLY-LA-
MONTAGNE**
les Hauts Moutions
le Moulin à Vent
Nid d'Agace
D808
les Coutures
les Godats
les Corrêtes
les Cumines
la Maladrie
les Carisets
le Champ Richard
les Bassignons
Chemin d'Armis
Terres
des Garennes
Champs
aux Buissons
Haut
de Villiers
les Bórneaux
VERZENAY
D26
les Crêres
les Coutures
les Pécherines
le Noyer L'Herbier
les Mignottes
les Sentiers
D26
les Clos
Bois le Dou
les Bruches
les Champs Bayard
les Carelles
les Grimpants
les Croix
**MAILLY-
CHAMPAGNE**
Bois de Verzenay
le Châtelet
les Carrières
Coop
la Perte
Mocquebeaux
**CHIGNY-
LES-ROSES**
les Beaux Regards
les Verbonnettes
LUDES
les Vigneulles
le Cran
D9
Baudets
Seigneurs
les Greffières
la Vauselle
le Bauchet
la Plaine
les Fays
le Chêne Martin
Plaine de
Verzenay
le Roset
le Bas Bois

Path
Railway
Commune boundary
Woods
Vineyard area within
commune rated
100%
Vineyard area within
commune rated
90–94%
Contour interval
10 metres

Reims
3
Mailly-
Champagne
la Marne
Épernay

1 Km
0
0   ½ Mile

nurtured relationships with the thousands of individual growers: partnerships which become vital in years of shortage, when the best-quality grapes are hard to buy in the free market. Some of the land along the Petite Montagne is, however, owned by the houses: Veuve Clicquot have Pinot Noir at Pargny.

The vineyards become more densely spread from Villedommange onwards through Sacy, Ecueil and Chamery, all rated at 90 percent. Only Villedommange figures in the holdings of the Grandes Marques houses, providing Pinot Noir for Veuve Clicquot. The slope here faces east, with one or two corners having a southeast exposure.

Behind this line of vineyards and its sheltering forest is a valley, that of the Ardre, which has a string of champagne-growing villages. Bouilly and Courmas, both in a side valley, rate 86 and 87 percent respectively. Chaumuzy and Sarcy, off the map to the west, manage only 83 percent. Mercier have some 12 hectares of Pinot Meunier at Sarcy, a small percentage of the firm's total holdings. Some new planting is being allowed here, which seems sad when there is better land left fallow elsewhere in Champagne.

Back on the north slope of the Montagne, Villers-Allerand has 90 percent status but a fairly small area of vines. The commune straddles the main Reims-Epernay road, which here climbs up through the vines and the woods to start its ruler-straight progress across the forested plateau of the Montagne. Rilly-la-Montagne, to the east, is more considerable both in size and quality, the first commune of the true Montagne vineyard. All three grapes are grown: Billecart-Salmon buy Chardonnay here on contract, while Gosset own land producing Pinot Noir. The échelle is 94 percent. The villages which come next – Chigny-les-Roses and Ludes (both 94 percent) – face due north and are over 60 percent Pinot Meunier, this grape being chosen here for its relative hardiness. Mailly-Champagne is the first Grand Cru of the Montagne, with a name for Pinot Noir: Moët & Chandon, Heidsieck Monopole and Perrier-Jouët own land here; Pommery & Greno have 21 hectares, Mumm 25 hectares.

Verzenay, the next village, is also a Grand Cru. It is often described as Pinot Noir country, but some Chardonnay is also grown. Bollinger have 17.1 hectares in six plots, including la Barbarie (see map), all Pinot Noir, and Lanson own Pinot Noir vines here. Pommery & Greno have 30 hectares, and Veuve Clicquot own land. Billecart-Salmon buy Pinot Noir on contract, and Moët have a 25.75 hectare holding, 70 percent Pinot Noir and 30 percent Chardonnay. Heidsieck Monopole have 21 hectares, Mumm 39, and Roederer own vines. Verzenay has one of the highest reputations of the Montagne communes, making up for its northerly exposure by gently sloping vineyards well protected by the forests. A spur gives some easterly and northwesterly exposures.

North of here, on the plain rather than the Montagne slopes, is Sillery, another Grand Cru and once, up to Edwardian times, a name redolent of luxury and excellence in champagne. Being low and flat, the Sillery vineyards face the threat of frost, and the soil is far from ideal, but Sillery has history on its side. Great fame adhered to the village through its links with the eminent Brulart family,

Within the Marne département, there are outlying vineyards around Sézanne, southwest of Epernay, and in the valley of the Vesle northwest of Reims. Beyond the Marne "heartland", there are vineyards in the Aisne, around Château-Thierry to the west, and the Aube to the south. Few of the Grandes Marques own land or buy grapes from these regions, but many BOBs and bottlings from lesser-known houses contain these wines. The Aube vineyards are on the same Kimmeridgian clay as Chablis, while the Aisne shares the same chalk geology as the Marne.

Path

Commune boundary

△ △ Woods

Vineyard area within
commune rated
100%

Vineyard area within
commune rated
95–99%

Contour interval
10 metres

0   1 Km
0   1/2 Mile

les Logettes

D8E

L'Espérance

N44

D7

Grevière

A4

les Voyettes

les Cheneyieres
Joudion

la Voie de Sillery

Champs du Gré

la Voyette

BEAUMONT-
SUR-VESLE

les Madeleines

Champs
Cordier

les Précheux
en Thulin

les Chaillots

Longues Raies
de Livry

les Sainfoins

la Passe Renard

Champ St. Martin

Blancs Fossés

les Voies de Reims

la Barbarie

Vignes Goisses

la Croix Guignon

les Courzines

D34

les Perthois

les Champs Brulés

Champ des Lapins

la Pistole

D326

Canal de l'Aisne

VERZENAY

Dimettes des
Lampages

A4

la Malonge

N44

les Mal Fosses

D26

Bois de Verzenay

les Bussets

Côte des Gt Champs

la Voie Creuse

les Maladries

D34

les Epinettes

la Conge

Champ Guillard

les Montants

Mont
des Loges

Haute Naise

D26

les Murs

les Cumaines

les Champs Chauvry

Blanche Voie

Côte des
Bergères

Côte des
Noyers

D34

VERZY

Bois la Souris

Teisseignères

les Saint-Bets

les Vivandes

D26

Bois de Charrière

le Moulin a Vent

Bois Royal

les Epinettes

D326

les Faux de
Verzy

Perthelle

sur Perthelle

VILLERS-
MARMERY

les Beguines

le Marmery

les Cugnets

D26E

les Vardulettes

Broco

les Pechins

les Oies

D37

A4

les Vardelles

D26

les Terres des Oies

les Maillys

les Culettes

les H. Leury

les Essares

Reims

4

Verzy

la Marne

Épernay

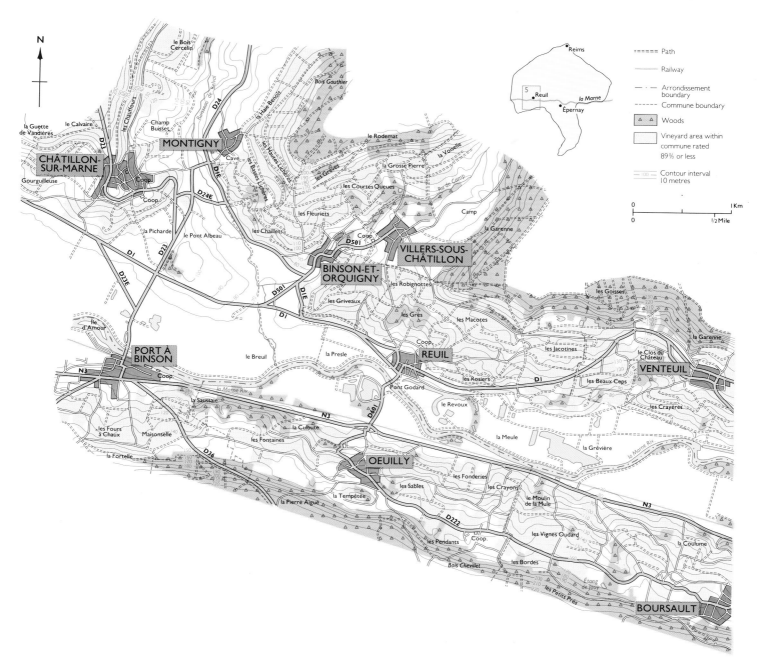

lords of Sillery. They owned vineyards here and in Verzenay, Mailly and Verzy, but all their wine was sold under the name of Sillery. Today this link is broken, and Sillery is not thought truly to earn its Grand Cru status. It does, however, have a certain name for Chardonnay, with Ruinart and Moët each owning 15 hectares planted with white grapes, and Pommery and Greno having a large (44 hectares) holding planted with Chardonnay (in 1986 they also listed some Pinot Noir). As map 3 shows, the Sillery vineyards are a continuation northwards of those of Mailly and Verzenay. Puisieulx, to the east of Sillery, is also a Grand Cru,

Below are the official
figures for the number
of hectares in
production, followed
by the CIVC's
forecast for the next
few harvests.

1919	12,010ha
1920	11,043ha
1925	11,551ha
1930	12,300ha
1935	11,930ha
1940	7,814ha
1945	10,728ha
1950	10,958ha
1955	11,471ha
1960	12,375ha
1965	15,069ha
1970	17,888ha
1975	21,707ha
1980	24,057ha
1985	25,249ha
1987	25,566ha

Forecast:

1988	26,000ha
1989	26,300ha
1990	26,700ha

(of about 27,500ha
total vineyard area)

but it has only a few vineyards (most in the west, on a low hill near Montbré) and even less of a reason for being in the top rank. Moët & Chandon grow Chardonnay on 3.25 hectares.

Back on the Montagne, Verzy ranks with its neighbour Verzenay. Lanson and Moët have Pinot Noir land here (two hectares), as do Veuve Clicquot and Roederer. The village to the east, Beaumont-sur-Vesle, is also rated at 100 percent, although failing by modern criteria really to justify its eminence. The few vineyards are on flat ground. Roederer and Lanson have holdings. Villers-Marmery is better situated, but only rates 95 percent. This commune concentrates on Chardonnay, and although no great houses own land here it is well known as a source of solid, strong-tasting white grapes.

From here, the Montagne swings around to face south, bringing a warmer exposure to the communes of Trépail, Ambonnay, Bouzy and on into the Vallée de la Marne. This southern stretch of the Montagne is mapped on Maps 8 and 9. Trépail has earned a 95 percent rating and is considered good for Chardonnay. Its neighbour Vaudemanges shares its rating.

Ambonnay, the next village, has Grand Cru status and is a source of Pinot Noir for Lanson, Mumm, Moët, who own 5.6 hectares here, and Heidsieck Monopole, major landowners with 21 hectares. Pinot Noir is the dominant variety, and the source of some good still red wines from here and the next few villages to the west. Bouzy's vineyards also have Grand Cru status, and a more southerly exposure. Pinot Noir again predominates, and the list of houses owning land begins with Bollinger, with 3.2 hectares, followed by Gosset, Heidsieck Monopole (three hectares), Lanson, Moët (9.4 hectares), Mumm (22 hectares), Pommery & Greno with 30 hectares and Veuve Cliquot. The ten percent or so of Bouzy's land planted with Chardonnay is considered by some experts an aberration: they far prefer the white wine of Trépail.

The Louvois vineyards continue from Bouzy's around into a little valley which pierces the slope of the Montagne. This is not a large commune, with around 40 hectares. Bollinger own more than a third of the vineyard land (14.35 hectares) on which Pinot Noir is grown. Roederer are also present. The village has Grand Cru status. Tauxières Mutry (99 percent) lies farther down the same valley. Its vineyards merge with those of Bouzy and Louvois to the east. As the map shows, only the quirks of the commune boundaries deprive the eastern vineyards around Mont Ecouvé of Grand Cru status. These fields are part of the same sweep of vines that start in Bouzy, cross a tongue of Tauxières (thereby losing status) and regain Grand Cru level with the crossing of the boundary into Louvois. The rest of Tauxières' vines are in two patches in the south and northwest. Bollinger have three parcels of Pinot Noir, totalling 17.3 hectares, with vines in Les Jolies and Les Vigneules, both in the northwest corner of the commune. Moët have 7.8 hectares with both Pinots (mainly Noir) and Mercier have a large holding of 28 hectares, mainly Pinot Meunier with some Pinot Noir.

Now there is a gap in the vineyards, separating those of the Montagne de Reims proper, from Rilly around to Bouzy and Louvois, from the stretch that

faces due south across the Marne Valley from Avenay along to Cumières. Fontaine-sur-Aÿ, the little village in the gap, is not classified, despite its auspicious suffix, and has more forest than vines. Tours-sur-Marne, away to the southeast, is beyond the low hill that bounds the Livre Valley to the south. It is a Grand Cru by virtue of its vineyards on the northern edge of the commune, which march with those of Bouzy. Tours is a Grand Cru for black grapes only; Chardonnay earns only 90 percent status – a reversal of the more common state of affairs where Chardonnay has been upgraded to put a premium on this popular grape. Mercier is the only Grande Marque to list land in Tours, with seven hectares of Chardonnay, although Laurent-Perrier have their home here.

To the west, Bisseuil (95 percent) is another Marne-side village, but its vineyards, too, are away up the slope to the north, on the south-facing slopes of the hill which bounds the Livre Valley. Bollinger have 5.4 hectares of Pinot Noir in the Les Tuilières vineyard, and Deutz grow both Pinots. Mareuil-sur-Aÿ is also on the Marne, with vineyards on the Goisses spur which projects south from the hills to just above the village (see the map and photographs on pages 70 and 72–3), and on the Montagne slopes to the west of the little river Livre, which here has its confluence with the Marne. This 99 percent-rated commune should not be confused with Mareuil-le-Port in the Marne Valley. Ayala (5.9 hectares), Deutz, Gosset, Lanson and Roederer have Pinot Noir holdings in Mareuil-sur-Aÿ, Moët have 30 hectares of Pinot Meunier, and Philipponnat have 12 hectares here (of which 5.5 hectares are the Clos des Goisses) and in neighbouring villages, 80 percent Pinot Noir and 20 percent Chardonnay. The village is the headquarters of Billecart-Salmon.

Hautvillers seen from its vineyards, with the Forêt de la Montagne de Reims in the background.
• • • • • • • • • • •

HAUTVILLERS

N

VENTEUIL

les Pommiers
les Heurtemonts
les Geais
les Pruniers
les Grivas
le Bauchet
Bois des Loges
les Richelettes

le Pâquis St Médard

Hauts Murgers
les Fosses
les Brustins
les Chéneaux Rouges

Bois de St-Marc
Terres des Moines
les Noels
les Fosses Suffies
les Sellettes

les Courts Barons
la Folie
les Russelets
le Moulin de Brunet
le Genevrois
les Rouges Monts
les Pêchers
les Chênes
les Côtes à Bras
les Barilliers

Luteri
les Pommerats
les Lotonnières
les Vervannes

CUMIÈRES

D1

les Sussières
le Moulin à Vent
les Chèvres
Coop

DAMERY

les Pierres Martin
les Chalmonts
les Momignons
les Treilles Monet
les Haies de Bras

les Cerisiers
île de la Vanne
la Marne Riv

Barrage
les Crayères
l'Île

les Vieilles Eaux
les Glageres
le Fer à Cheval
les Longues Raies
l'Écu

la Haute Borne
les Maresses
le Champ Râpé
les Avinières
les Grande Corvées

N3
Fosse Tournisse
les Arches
le Grand Pré
le Cas
le Trésorier

BOURSAULT
D222
les Saints Rys
les Culots
la Mamelle
la Rue du Pont

le Moulin Jean Gueux
le Juberlu
les Beaunes
N3
Pré Cigny
MARDEUIL

les Aulnes
le Trou du Renard
les Dérozettes
la Rivette
D401

la Cohette
la Fabière
les Morlantins
les Clos

VAUCIENNES
les Louves
les Rocherets
N3

Bois Guillaume
Bois Écouart
les Heurte-Loups
Champs Fleuris
Mont de Bon

la Meleine

la Maloterie

• • • Path

—— Railway

—·— Arrondissement boundary

--- Commune boundary

△ △ Woods

Vineyard area within commune rated 90–94%

Vineyard area within commune rated 89% or less

Contour interval 10 metres

Reims
6
Damery
la Marne
Épernay

0 — 1 Km
0 — ½ Mile

North of Mareuil, up the Montagne slope, stands the beautifully named Avenay-Val-d'Or, with its 93 percent-rated vineyards tucked into a bend of the Livre Valley. Bollinger have 14.35 hectares in Champ Bernard and Monthurlet (in the extreme south and north of the commune respectively). Mercier have a small (1.9 hectres) holding of Pinot Meunier here, and Mumm own 41 hectares. To the west is Mutigny, also rated 93 percent, with its vines running along the steady south-facing slope of the Montagne towards Aÿ. The village itself is unusually placed, up in the woods above the vineyards.

Aÿ (see Map 7) is a small town rather than a village, a place of narrow streets and high walls hiding the buildings of the champagne houses which have their premises here: Bollinger, Ayala, Deutz, Gosset, plus several others of lesser renown. Its wide band of vineyards, rated as Grand Cru, clothe the hillside from above the town across to the west as far as Dizy. The slope is by no means even, as a glance at the contour lines on the accompanying map shows. Besserat de Bellefon have nine hectares of vines. Bollinger have 21 hectares of Pinot Noir, including their famed Vieilles Vignes plot of pre-phylloxera vines, and the Côte aux Enfants vineyard which sometimes, in hot years, makes a still red wine. Other named Bollinger vineyards include Cheuzelle, Valnon and Beauregard. Deutz (11.5 hectares) and Krug also grow Pinot Noir, Jacquesson have one hectare, Mercier 1.9 hectares, Perrier-Jouët some Pinot Noir vines, and Pommery & Greno a large 85 hectare vineyard which has a very small proportion of Chardonnay amid the Pinot Noir. Moët's 35 hectares consist of 80 percent Pinot Noir, five percent Pinor Meunier and 15 percent Chardonnay. Veuve Clicquot and Henriot have land for Pinot Noir, and Mumm have 16.4 hectares in Aÿ and Dizy.

Many other houses also own land here: Aÿ champagnes are thought of as a vital ingredient in a blend. The need for selection is, however, clear from the map: the Aÿ vineyards stretch from close to the Marne canal, on low-lying and frost-prone land, right up to an elevated enclave in the woods where, despite the southern exposure, the microclimate is cool. Taken as a whole, however, Aÿ is known to be "forward" in ripening compared to other parts of the Montagne.

The vineyards of Dizy are perfectly placed from one point of view: they stand on either side of the main north-south road through Reims and Epernay, and are thus for many a traveller their only glimpse of viticultural Champagne. Motorists using this road also realise how long and steep the slope of the Montagne is. The village of Dizy lies on the flat land where the road crosses the Marne Valley, and the vineyards climb up to the northeast and north, towards Champillon at the top of the hill. Dizy is rated at 95 percent and grows all three grape varieties. Jacquesson have four hectares, 80 percent Pinot Noir and 20 percent Chardonnay; Lanson a vineyard of Pinot Noir; Moët 5.8 hectares, 60 percent Chardonnay and 40 percent Pinot Noir; Mercier a small plot of Pinot Meunier, Roederer Pinot Noir and Perrier-Jouët some Meunier.

Champillon, being higher and cooler than Dizy, rates only 93 percent, but the well sheltered south-facing slopes produce well reputed wines. Lanson, Mercier

The Route du Champagne is a signposted drive around the vineyards. The CIVC produce a map which shows three variants on the route and gives detailed directions. Even the signposts are colour-coded to help visitors find their way around.

• • • • • • • • • • •

The Clos des Goisses at Mareuil-sur-Aÿ, a beautifully sited vineyard set on a low hill above the River Marne and its accompanying canal. It belongs exclusively to Philipponnat.

• • • • • • • • • • •

and Roederer have black-grape vineyards. The Champillon vineyards sweep around the top of the slope and merge with those of Hautvillers, another 93 percent cru with a village perched on the hill overlooking the Marne. The views from here, as from Champillon, are well worth the climb. Jacquesson grow Chardonnay here, Lanson have vineyards, and Mercier three hectares of Pinot Meunier. Moët are the largest single proprietors with 40.6 hectares split equally between the two Pinots. Hautvillers is the site of the abbey where Dom Pérignon made his great contribution to the development of champagne; Moët own the old abbey, which is now a museum to the winemaker-monk. The connection between Moët and Hautvillers is venerable: the firm, run by Jean-Rémy Moët in the 18th century, bought wine from the abbey vineyards.

From Hautvillers, the band of vines runs on above the village of Cumières (see Map 6). These vineyards, rated 93 percent, include 5.2 hectares of Pinot Noir owned by Moët. The exposure here is full south, and this, allied to the nature of the soil and the local rootstock used, causes the grapes to ripen quickly. The harvest at Cumières often starts early with a special derogation from the authorities. West of Cumières the slope steepens and the woods crowd close to the river, with only a narrow strip of vines between the flat alluvial land and the forest edge. To the west, where the slope broadens again, is Damery, which achieves only 89 percent status. The villages just described, from Aÿ through Dizy to Hautvillers and Cumières, are collectively known as la Grande Marne. West of here, Damery is the first commune of la Petite Marne. Ventuil, the next village, is called the queen of the Petite Marne. Between the two, the valley of the Brunet stream breaks the line of the Montagne. Several little villages farther up the valley grow grapes, but their rating is only 85 percent.

The Marne Valley vineyards stretch west from here for a good distance. The train from Epernay to Paris passes continuous vineyard for nearly half an hour

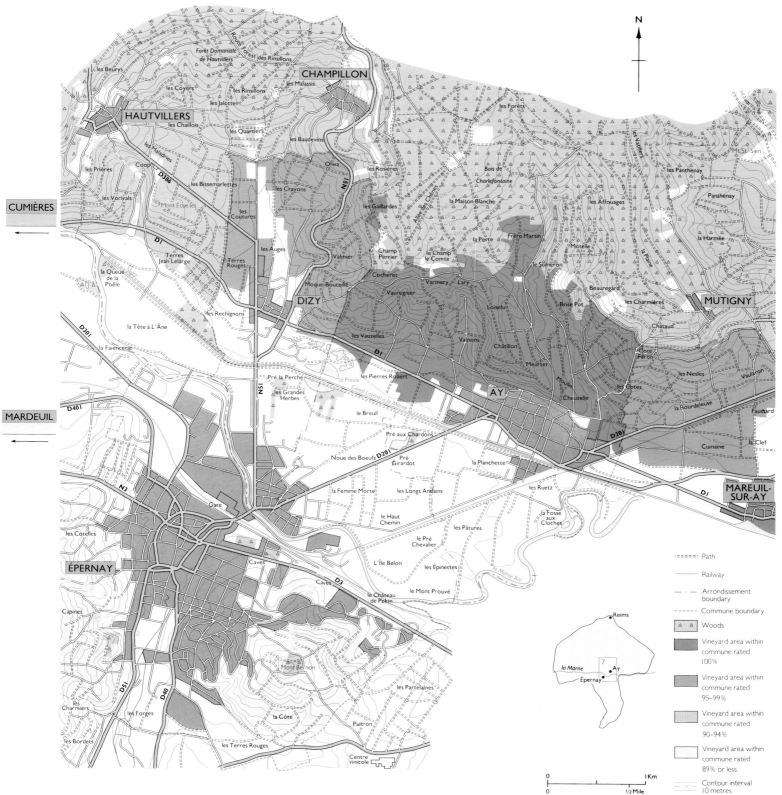

CUMIÈRES

AVENAY-VAL-D'OR

MARDEUIL

Path

Railway

Arrondissement boundary

Commune boundary

Woods

Vineyard area within commune rated 100%

Vineyard area within commune rated 95–99%

Vineyard area within commune rated 90–94%

Vineyard area within commune rated 89% or less

Contour interval 10 metres

Reims

la Marne

7   Ay

Épernay

0   1 Km

0   ½ Mile

Vines in the Clos des
Goisses above Mareuil-
sur-Aÿ.

• • • • • • • • • •

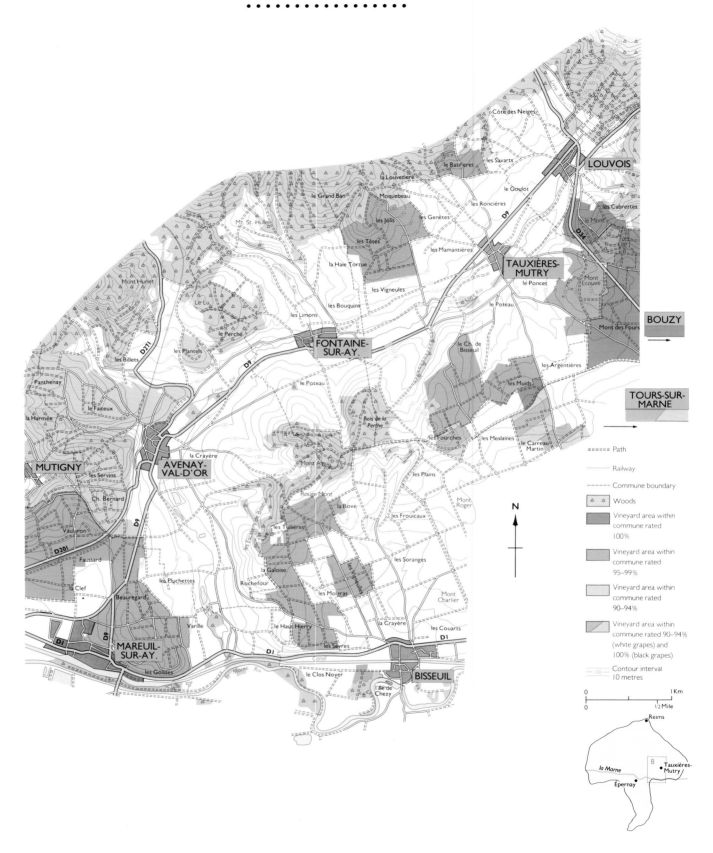

LOUVOIS

Côte des Neiges

le Batilleret   les Savarts

la Louvetière   le Goulot   les Cabrettes

le Grand Ban   Moquebeau   les Roncières   le Mont

Mt. St-Hulin   les Jolis   les Genêtes   D9   TAUXIÈRES-
                                                                          MUTRY

les Têtes   les Mamantières   le Poncet   Mont
                                                                          Écouve
la Haie Tortue

Mont Hurlet   les Vigneules   le Poteau   Mont des Fours

Le Lu   les Bouquins   BOUZY

les Limons   le Ch. de
                   Bisseuil

le Perché   les Argentières

les Plantels   FONTAINE-
D271   SUR-AY.   TOURS-SUR-
les Billets   MARNE

Panthenay   le Poteau   les Muids

le Faiteux

la Harmée   Bois de la   les Fourches   les Meslaines   le Carreau
                   Perthe   Martin

MUTIGNY   la Crayère   Mont Aigu   les Plains   N

AVENAY-
les Servins   VAL-D'OR   Path
                                    Rouge Mont   les Frouicaux   Mont
Ch. Bernard   la Bove   Roger   Railway

Vaularon   les Tuilières   Commune boundary
D201
Faussard   Woods
                                                  les Soranges
la Clef   les Pluchettes   Vineyard area within
                                    la Galoise   commune rated
Beauregard   les Molgras   Mont 100%
                 Rochefour   les Vigneules   Charlier
                                                                                   Vineyard area within
        Varille   commune rated
D8   la Crayère   95–99%
                 le Haut Hierry   les Couarts
MAREUIL-   les Sèvres   D1   Vineyard area within
SUR-AY.   D1   commune rated
                                                                                   90–94%
        les Goisses   le Clos Noyer   BISSEUIL
                                                                                   Vineyard area within
                             l'île de   commune rated 90–94%
                             Chezy   (white grapes) and
                                                                                   100% (black grapes)

                                                                                   Contour interval
                                                                                   10 metres

                                                                          Reims

                                                                          la Marne   Tauxières-
                                                                                            Mutry
                                                                          Épernay

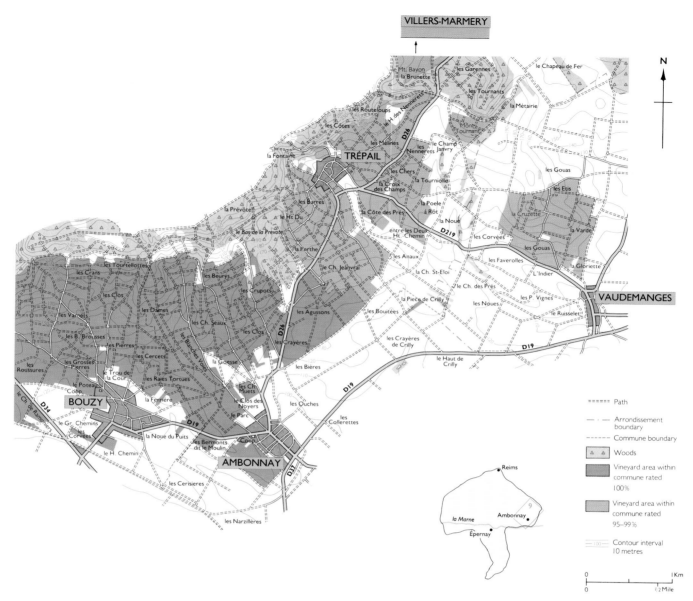

(and it is a fast train). In general, the villages along the north bank are much better than those on the south, because they face south and thus have better exposure to the sun. But there are exceptions south of the river, as at Leuvrigny (beloved of Krug and Roederer) and Festigny.

Venteuil, on the north bank, has an 89 percent rating and is the source of Pinot Noir grapes bought on contract by Billecart-Salmon. (See Map 5.) The next three villages – Reuil, Binson-et-Orguigny, Villers-sous-Châtillon – all have ratings of 86 percent. None of the three appears in the vineyard rolls of the great houses: increasingly, from here west, we are in the land of grower champagnes. Montigny and its neighbour Châtillon (both 86 percent) continue the vineyard sweep, with a break where the Belval stream flows down from the Montagne. Vandières and Verneuil also rate 86 percent. Vines also dot the side valleys to the

Between 1.15kg and 1.20kg of grapes are needed to produce one bottle of champagne. The difference is due to the fact that grapes give varying quantities of juice according to the climatic conditions of the year (hot year, thick skins, less juice, whereas rain before the vintage will increase the size of the grapes, and give a thinner skin and more juice) – the ratio of skin/juice is not fixed irrevocably to any one measurement. For the 1987 harvest, the price of grapes from 100%-rated vineyards was fixed at 21.77 francs a kilo.

north, where Bollinger, for example, have a six hectare plot of Pinot Meunier at Champvoisy (84 percent).

Of the south-bank villages, only one, Mareuil-le-Port (84 percent), figures in the Grandes Marques vineyard lists: Moët have a large vineyard (48 hectares) of Pinot Meunier here. Mardeuil (84 percent), opposite Cumières and just west of Epernay, boasts a fraction of a hectare of Moët Chardonnay.

Epernay, which rates 88 percent, is not really a Côte des Blancs commune. Indeed, its vineyards are far less important than its cellars, and it could be called the capital of vinous Champagne by virtue of the sheer density of chais, bottling halls, offices and other buildings which line its streets, and by the labyrinth of cellars beneath them. Moët and Mercier, two of the many firms with their headquarters in the town, own vineyards within the commune. Moët have 12.4 hectares growing all three grapes, with the emphasis on Chardonnay. Mercier have ten hectares, half Pinot Meunier, a third Chardonnay, the rest Pinot Noir.

The Côte des Blancs proper begins southeast of Epernay with the vineyards of Chouilly. To the southwest of Epernay, behind the Côte, are two small valleys (see Map 10). The first vineyard commune is Pierry, rated 90 percent, where Deutz have 5.75 hectares. Deutz also have a 1.5 hectare holding in neighbouring Moussy, growing the two black grapes, but the dominant landowners in this 88 percent-rated commune are Moët, with 81 hectares of Pinot Meunier. Moët have a small (1.6 hectare) patch of the same grape in Vinay (86 percent), as does Perrier-Jouët.

Mancy (88 percent) lies in the other valley, south of Epernay and directly west of the Côte. Moët have 5.3 hectares here growing Chardonnay (60 percent) and Pinot Meunier. Other villages in the same area are Monthelon and Chavot-Courcourt, both rated 88 percent. At the head of the valley is the Premier Cru commune of Grauves, whose black grapes earn a 90 percent rating, while its Chardonnay gets 95 percent. Bollinger have three parcels totalling 6.1 hectares, all growing Chardonnay. Moët have a similar-sized holding, three-quarters Chardonnay and the balance Pinot Meunier.

Chouilly, the first village of the Côte des Blancs, is just outside Epernay to the east. Its vines are close to Cramant in the south, and on the Mont Bermont slopes in the west (see Maps 10 and 7 respectively). The southern portion is on the north and northeast slopes of the Butte de Saran, which as Map 10 shows shelters Cramant to the north. The Butte is a forest-topped hill, split from the main slope of the Côte by the village of Cramant. Chouilly has the status of a Grand Cru for black grapes, but only Premier Cru (95 percent) for white, which make up the vast majority of the vines. Four Grandes Marques list Chardonnay vineyards in Chouilly: Lanson, Moët (48.7 hectares), Mercier (3.4 hectares) and Roederer.

Cuis is set on the northern corner of the Côte des Blancs, with a 90 percent rating for black grapes and 95 percent for white. Bollinger have one of their largest holdings here, with 18.75 hectares of Chardonnay in five parcels, including Les Fetes (or Les Faites) and Les Roualles. Moët are also sizable landowners, with 64 hectares of Chardonnay.

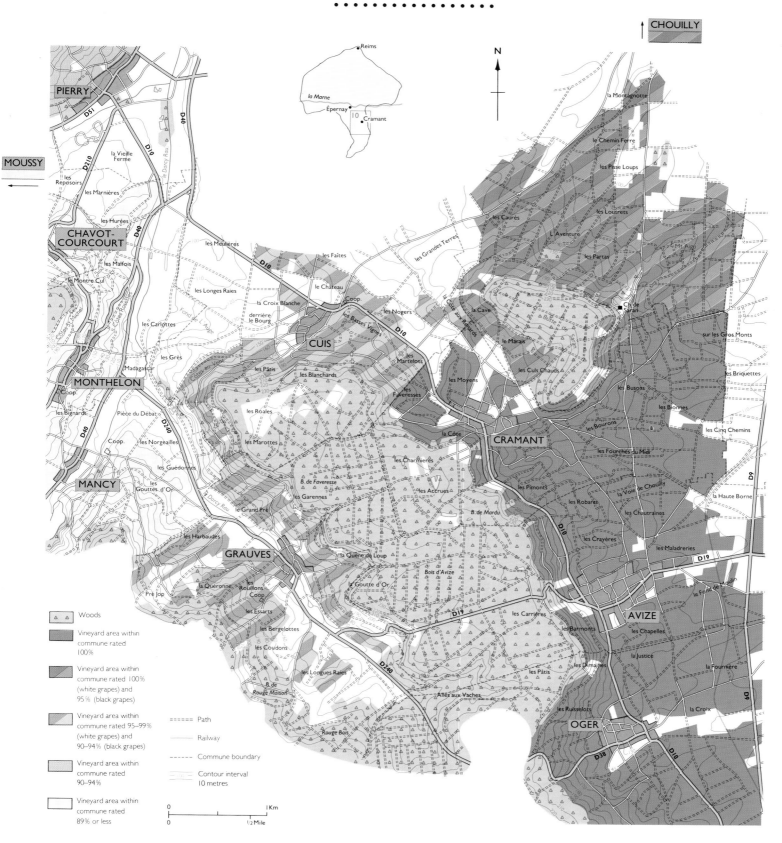

la Marne

Reims

Épernay

Cramant

MOUSSY

CHOUILLY

N

PIERRY

D51

D40

D10

D210

la Vieille Ferme

les Reposoirs

les Marnières

les Hurées

CHAVOT-COURCOURT

D40

les Meulières

les Faîtes

D10

les Grandes Terres

la Montagnotte

le Chemin Ferré

les Pisse Loups

les Malfois

le Montre Cul

les Longes Raies

le Château

la Croix Blanche

derrière le Bourg

les Carlottes

Côte Rosaltier

Fond de l'Auge

les Nogers

Coop.

CUIS

les Basses Vignes

D10

les Caurés

L'Aventure

Mt Aigu

les Loutrets

les Partas

les Grès

les Pâtis

les Blanchards

les Martelots

la Cave

le Marais

Butte St.

Côte aux Regards

Ch. de Saran

sur les Gros Monts

MONTHELON

Madagascar

les Roales

les Faveresses

les Moyens

les Culs Chauds

les Briquettes

Coop.

les Bignards

Pièce du Débat

les Marottes

la Côte

les Busons

les Bionnes

les Cinq Chemins

D40

D240

Coop.

les Norgeailles

les Charmières

les Bourons

B. de Faveresse

les Accrues

B. de Mardu

les Fourches du Midi

les Guédonnes

MANCY

les Gouttes d'Or

le Grand Pré

les Garennes

les Pimonts

la Voie de Chouilly

les Robarts

les Choutraines

CRAMANT

D10

Darcy Rau

les Harbaudes

la Quene du Loup

les Crayères

la Haute Borne

D9

GRAUVES

Bois d'Avize

les Maladreries

D19

la Quéronne

les Rouillons

Coop.

Pré Jop

la Goutte d'Or

le Fond de Moulin

les Essarts

les Carrières

AVIZE

les Barmonts

les Chapelles

les Bergelottes

les Dimaines

la Justice

la Fournière

les Coudons

les Pâtis

D240

B. de Rouge Maison

Allès aux Vaches

les Russelots

la Croix

les Longues Raies

OGER

Rouge Bois

D38

D10

Woods

Vineyard area within commune rated 100%

Vineyard area within commune rated 100% (white grapes) and 95% (black grapes)

Vineyard area within commune rated 95–99% (white grapes) and 90–94% (black grapes)

Vineyard area within commune rated 90–94%

Vineyard area within commune rated 89% or less

Path

Railway

Commune boundary

Contour interval 10 metres

0   1 Km

0   ½ Mile

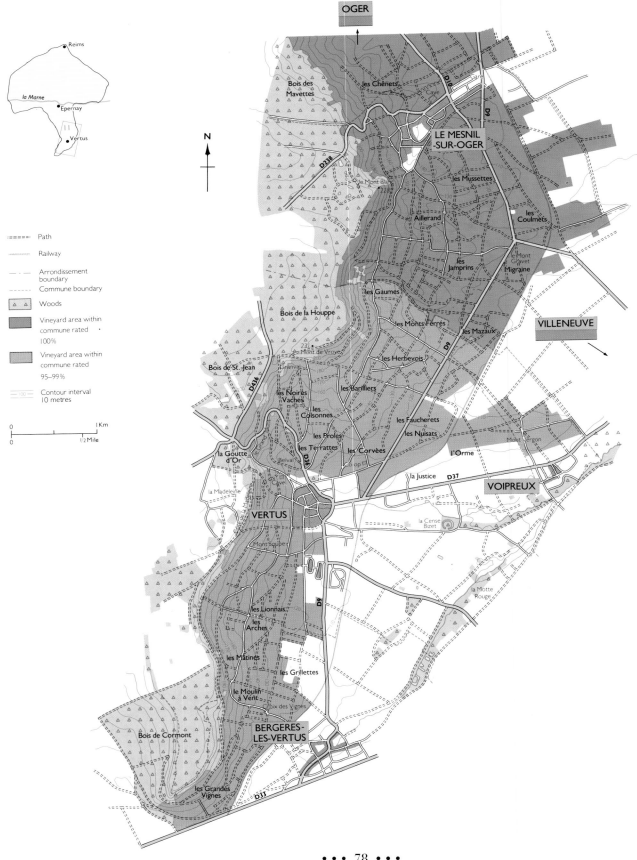

OGER

Bois des
Mavettes

les Chênets

Cave

Gare

D10

D9

N

LE MESNIL
-SUR-OGER

le Mont Blanc

les Mussettes

228

Aillerand

les Coulmets

D238

le Mont
Gravet

Migraine

les
Jamprins

VILLENEUVE

les Gaumes

Bois de la Houppe

les Monts Ferrés

les Mazaux

231

Mont de Vroye

les Herbevois

D9

Bois de St.-Jean

Oraval

180

Bois de St.-Jean

les Barilliers

170

les Noires
Vaches

160

les Colsonnes

les Faucherets

D436

les Proies

les Nuisats

Mont Vergon

les Terrattes

les Corvèes

l'Orme

la Goutte
d'Or

D36

la Justice

D37

VOIPREUX

la Madeleine

Cave

Coop

la Cense
Bizet

VERTUS

Mont Aimé

la Motte
Rouge

les Lionnais
les
Arches

D9

les Mâtines

les Grillettes

le Moulin
à Vent

Croix des Vignes

Bois de Cormont

BERGERES-
LES-VERTUS

les Grandes
Vignes

D33

Reims

la Marne

Epernay

Vertus

Path

Railway

Arrondissement
boundary

Commune boundary

Woods

Vineyard area within
commune rated
100%

Vineyard area within
commune rated
95–99%

Contour interval
10 metres

0   1 Km

0   1/2 Mile

Cramant is a Grand Cru, entirely Chardonnay, with landowners including Lanson, Moët (38.3 hectares), Mercier (less than one hectare), Perrier-Jouët and Pommery & Greno (36 hectares). Mumm's five hectare holding is the source of their Crémant de Cramant (now called Cramant de Mumm). Moët's Château de Saran is here. Cramant has vineyards on the slopes of both the Butte and the main Côte, thus enjoying good exposures to the east and south.

Avize, next, to the south, is another Chardonnay Grand Cru with land owned by Jacquesson (11 hectares), Lanson, Moët (1.75 hectares), Mumm (26 hectares), Pommery & Greno (38 hectares), Roederer and Veuve Clicquot. The vines slope down from the Côte, whose flat summit is crowned by the Bois d'Avize. Oger continues the line of Côte des Blancs Grands Crus. Lanson, Roederer and Veuve Clicquot own vineyards. Le Mesnil-sur-Oger is next to the south, again a Grand Cru, famous for Krug's walled Clos du Mesnil (less than two hectares) and with Deutz (11.5 hectares), Moët (29 hectares) and Veuve Clicquot also present. Salon, whose wine comes entirely from le Mesnil, own one hectare. Vertus is a "mere" Premier Cru, with a 95 percent rating and Moët, Roederer and Veuve Clicquot are among its landowners. Seventeen percent of the vines are Pinot Noir. Bergères-lès-Vertus (95 percent) marks the southern end of the Côte, with some vines around the isolated Mont Aimé which, like the Butte de Saran, stands sentinel over the approaches to the Côte proper.

The canal at Tours-sur-Marne, which links the Marne and the Saône near Dijon, forming one of the main north-south water routes in France. The easy communications provided by the rivers, and later the canals, helped champagne attain its status as a widely traded wine.
• • • • • • • • • • • •

CHAPTER SEVEN

THE GREAT CHAMPAGNE HOUSES

These are the houses that have made the glorious history of Champagne and that will continue to maintain its worldwide reputation. They range from multinational giants to small family firms where successive generations have maintained their house style. For this is what champagne is all about – the individual tastes of each marque and their fascinating diversity of bouquet and flavour.

In the pages that follow I have tried to get behind these tastes, to describe them and how they are achieved. Does the house own vines, from where does it make its grape purchases, what are the blends of the champagnes, is the equipment ultramodern or are there still casks in the cellars? How does the house itself see its champagne, and how does that correspond with my tasting impression of its wines? The vast majority of these tastings were done as this book was being written in winter 1987–spring 1988.

There is no correlation between size and quality: the huge concerns can make champagnes of as high a quality as the small firms, and vice versa. Integrity is not linked to size, and the most astute of those who run Champagne nowadays know that only constant vigilance will ensure a healthy future for the region. I am more encouraged now about the direction that champagne is taking than I was ten years ago. Stocks are high (a necessity if fine champagne is to be produced) and the Champenois are more aware of the socio-economic problems which could endanger quality in the long term.

Looking into the crystal ball, it is difficult to see where there is room for future mergers between the giants: the scene is dominated by the Moët-Hennessy-Vuitton group, with Seagram and BSN the other major influences. Perhaps the multinational Grand Metropolitan will wish to acquire a champagne marque?

Ultimately, whatever its size or ownership, each champagne house is judged by what is poured into the flûte.

The addresses of the houses that follow are given on page 218. Most of the champagne firms welcome visitors, although with a very few exceptions they ask

Jean-Rémy Moët (1758–1841), grandson of the founder of the house of Moët & Chandon and one of the great figures of Champagne history. He managed the firm during the difficult time of the Revolution and became a friend and admirer of Napoleon, who conferred the Légion d'Honneur on him for his loyal service.

that an appointment is made in advance. It is always worth checking beforehand in any case, because the hours when visitors will be received vary between the houses (but lunchtime is always sacrosanct) and are usually limited to Mondays to Fridays. These are, after all, working houses!

Ayala

If I have a special place in my heart for Ayala champagne, it may be because it has graced the hospitable table of *Decanter* magazine headquarters on so many occasions. A bottle of Ayala has often been on hand after gruelling tastings of tannic young Bordeaux – and nothing is more welcome as we sit and compare notes over the unveiling of the labels.

Somehow, the champagne is a reflection of the house: frank and "familial", honest and without pretension. It is a very personal operation, with Jean-Michel Ducellier the main shareholder and guiding light. A man of vision and intelligence, he supervises both his champagne house in Aÿ and the much-admired Bordeaux 3rd growth, Château La Lagune. In each case he has seen the importance of a close, loyal team, and Ayala's staff have decades of service behind them, which undoubtedly contributes to stability and consistency.

The Syndicat de Grandes Marques de Champagne was established in 1964, replacing the Syndicat du Commerce des Vins de Champagne. There have been additions to the list since then, but the membership is somewhat historic because a few of the names are only a second marque of a more famous house. While the great champagne houses are in this list, there are others outside the Syndicat that also make champagne to the highest standard. As always, it is not membership of any "club" that preordains quality, it is the integrity and commercial health of each house at any given time.

Ayala was founded in 1860, by the son of a Colombian diplomat who married a local, high-born girl with vineyards in her dowry. From 1937 until his death in 1969, René Chayoux owned Ayala, and it was he who added La Lagune to the stable in 1961.

The cellars of Ayala burrow under the slopes of Aÿ. The house owns 30 hectares of vines, Pinot Noir at Mareuil-sur-Aÿ and Pinot Meunier at St-Martin d'Ablois. These represent 20 percent of Ayala's needs. Thus 80 percent of their requirements are bought as grapes, divided between 50 percent Pinot Noir, 25 percent Chardonnay and 25 percent Pinot Meunier. Production runs at 800,000 bottles a year, and one forms the impression that Ayala are quite content with this. It is manageable and fits in with their aims and perception of their place on the market, which is to provide a good, satisfying champagne at an ungreedy price. Indeed, the value of a bottle of Ayala is usually remarkable.

Maintaining three years of stock, Ayala base their style on the Pinot Noir, confident that it will give them the balance they seek between body and finesse. Remuage is done entirely by hand.

Brut: This non-vintage always shows a solid, Pinot Noir influence; it is a champagne that is never neutral and fills the mouth. The cuvée based on the 1985 vintage is a clear example of the style.

Brut 1982: As so often with this vintage, there is an enticing, floral nose and an ethereal quality about the taste, firmly anchored by perfect balance.

Brut Rosé: Produced in clear bottles, the rosé colour is obtained by the addition of red wine from Mareuil. The blend is made in February, then fined, so there is time for the elements to "marry" before the tirage. The chef de caves does a trial bottling before the main tirage to see exactly how the colour turns out (there is always a considerable deposit of colour during the prise de mousse of a rosé champagne). The final result in the case of Ayala's Rosé is a bluey-pink colour, a bouquet of raspberries (typically Mareuil) and a delicious, round taste.

Blanc de Blancs 1982: The colour is a pale greeny gold and the bouquet is of flowers and hay, with a quite strong lemony influence. The taste is a little young and acid, and I do not find it a refined wine.

Grande Cuvée Ayala 1982: Launched at the end of 1987, this special cuvée comes from an excellent year and is, unusually for Ayala, made up of 80 percent Chardonnay grands crus and 20 percent Pinot Noir grands crus. The bouquet is both youthful and appley, yet ripe. The taste is very Chardonnay, like hazelnut biscuits. Very satisfying in March 1988, it needs another year in bottle to lengthen the finish.

Besserat de Bellefon

It took an outsider to create a real "maison pilote" in Champagne. From the technical point of view, the new cellars built in 1970 on the outskirts of Reims for Besserat de Bellefon, when they were owned by Cinzano, are some of the most practical in the region. Excavated from the surface and all on one level, the

Member houses of the Syndicat are:
Ayala & Montebello
Billecart-Salmon
Bollinger
Canard Duchene
Deutz & Geldermann
Charles Heidsieck
Heidsieck Monopole
Henriot
Krug
Lanson
Laurent-Perrier
Masse
Mercier
Moët & Chandon
Mumm
Joseph Perrier
Perrier-Jouët
Piper-Heidsieck
Pol Roger
Pommery & Greno
Ch. & A. Prieur
Louis Roederer
Ruinart
Salon
Taittinger & Irroy
Veuve Clicquot
Ponsardin

Champagne represents 20% of French wine and spirit production, 33% of exports of Appellation Contrôlée wines and 20% of exports of wines and spirits by region and category, just ahead of Cognac and well ahead of Bordeaux and Burgundy.

structure is in concrete, but an enormous amount of the local chalk soil was then put over the top to keep the cellar temperature naturally between 11 and 12°C (52–54°F), with no need to air condition. Stainless-steel vats are computer controlled, but the house is only just turning from manual remuage to 25 percent gyropalettes.

In 1976, Besserat de Bellefon was sold to Pernod-Ricard and, at first, the management was not of the happiest. But the group then had the good sense to appoint Jean-Jacques Bouffard as Président-directeur-général, with the result that in 1987 sales went up internationally by 67 percent. It is difficult to come into Champagne from the world of spirits, but Monsieur Bouffard's intelligence and grasp of matters Champenois are very evident. He is ably assisted by the technical director, Jean-Louis Dohr, whose arrival coincided with the construction of the new cellars.

Besserat own nine hectares of vines at Aÿ. There is also Salon's (owned by the group) one hectare of Chardonnay at Le Mesnil-sur-Oger, which is used by Besserat when there is no vintage Salon. Most cuvées contain 30 crus, and the malolactic fermentation is always carried out.

Besserat de Bellefon is much better known in France than on the export markets. Direct mail sales are very important on the home front and you are most likely to come across the marque when dining with French friends. However, annual production is now running at 2.3 million bottles, sales at 2.1 million bottles and exports at 305,000 bottles.

Crémant Blanc NV: As the word "crémant" is being phased out in Champagne, this will become the Cuvée des Moines. This has always been a big seller for Besserat, with justification. The cuvée in 1988, based on the 1985 vintage, is 60 percent Chardonnay with Pinot Meunier. In spring 1988 it was still young, with youthful acidity, but a perfect apéritif champagne, uplifting in all the senses.

Crémant des Moines Rosé NV (which will become Cuvée des Moines Rosé): Basically the same wine as its white counterpart but with the addition of red wine, including that of Aÿ. It is a popular champagne, which need not be drunk when it is very young.

Brut sans année: Not my favourite wine of the range, although there are some cuvées I like better than others. It seems to be variable – in 1987 it was deliciously fruity, in 1988 less so.

Vintage 1982: A splendid wine, made with 50 percent Chardonnay and 50 percent black grapes. It has a smell of hawthorn and is beautifully balanced and delicious.

Grande Cuvée B de B: This was first brought out in October 1984, when it was a blend of 1976 and 1979. The blend available in 1988 is 1979 and 1982 and has much more Chardonnay than the previous cuvée; it has a lovely creamy quality and is full of that hawthorn fruit and ripeness of the 1982 vintage, which seems to predominate in most wines of this year. It is always a treat when a ripe flavour is counterbalanced by freshness, and you see this well illustrated in the Grande Cuvée B de B.

Brut Intégral 1979: This non-dosage champagne was first brought out in 1976. The nose is slightly smoky and it is a wine that amplifies and becomes increasingly interesting in a large tulip glass. This is the wine that taught me that a champagne with no dosage is much less skeletal in a wider glass than in a very narrow flûte, and that the flavour is greatly enhanced if it is served at 11–12°C (52–54°F), rather than at 8°C (46°F), at which you might serve a crémant or a blanc de blancs.

It was also very good with fresh black truffles and asparagus, far more at home with these forceful tastes than when drunk on its own as an apéritif.

Billecart-Salmon

The Billecarts have been firmly entrenched in Mareuil-sur-Aÿ since the 16th century and today their houses, offices and gardens form an attractive enclave in the town. The picturesque "Salmon" part of the name dates from 1818, when the house was founded by Nicolas-François Billecart who had married Elisabeth Salmon. He became an intrepid traveller for the marque, with Russia his principal market. Now the fifth generation of Billecarts since the founder own and manage the firm, with Jean Roland-Billecart at the helm and his sons and the young oenologist François Domi backing him up.

Tradition is an intrinsic part of the Billecart philosophy, right down to the attractive "dump" bottles for the vintage, rosé and blanc de blancs vintage, used

The beautiful gardens in the Billecart-Salmon enclave in Mareuil-sur-Aÿ, where the houses and offices of this old family firm are clustered around mature trees and flowers ablaze with colour. Few working premises anywhere exude the same peace and calm – but the true business of the house is definitely not gardening.

The delicate tracery on some of Billecart-Salmon's labels today has been copied from their enviable collection of old champagne labels, featuring names such as Fleur de Sillery and Fleur de Bouzy.

• • • • • • • • • • •

since the foundation of the house, and the beguiling labels which date from 1838. But all does not stand still at Billecart. They have some very modern ideas on winemaking, particularly with regard to fermentation. After receiving the already "decanted" or "clarified" must, they effect another débourbage for 48 hours at an ambient temperature of 0°C (32°F), which is about 5°C (40°F) in the must. Because much of the natural yeasts are thus eliminated, dried local yeasts are then added and fermentation takes place in stainless-steel vats at 10°–15°C (50°–60°F) for three weeks. The temperature subsequently has to increase to 18°C (65°F) for the malolactic fermentation to take place; a malolactic bacteria base has to be added to start the process because the extra débourbage ensures that none is left in the wine.

Billecart have a battery of 50-hectolitre vats so they can keep separately a wide variety of crus, doing an immediate "préassemblage". They use cane sugar for the tirage, and the prise de mousse is carried out in all bottle sizes from halves to Jeroboams. Agrafes, or the cork and metal clasp, are still used, instead of crown caps, for Jeroboams and magnums of the vintage cuvée N.F. Billecart. Jeroboams are disgorged completely "à la volée", without going through the usual tank of freezing solution. I am under the impression that Cognac/eau de vie is sometimes used in the liqueur d'expédition of the non-vintage, and at Billecart there are definite differences between the non-vintage blends destined for France and England.

Billecart possess hardly any vineyards, with the exception of a few vines of 99 percent Pinot Noir at Mareuil-sur-Aÿ. But the house has contracts for supplies of grapes from very good areas, with particular emphasis on Chardonnay from Cramant, Avize, Le Mesnil-sur-Oger and Vertus on the Côte des Blancs, and Pinot Noir from Rilly-la-Montagne, Verzenay and Venteuil. These contracts represent about 40 percent of Billecart's requirements, with the remaining 60 percent of purchases being made in the three grape varieties.

In 1986 Billecart produced 420,000 bottles, rising to 450,000 in 1987. Just under half the production is exported, with the United States heading the list and Europe making up the rest.

Brut sans année: The French cuvée has more Pinot Meunier and is a younger blend than that destined for England, which appears rounder. The non-vintage is usually made from 25 crus and is composed of approximately 50 percent Pinot Meunier, 25 percent Chardonnay and 25 percent Pinot Noir. Billecart consider that they can "absorb" a poor year such as 1984 better than some houses because of their second cold treatment before fermentation, as well as adding up to 50 percent of reserve wines in difficult vintages. The brut non-vintage forms 70 percent of the house's annual production and can be relied on to show a floral, elegant character and very attractive taste.

Cuvée N.F. Billecart Brut 1982: The cuvée was created in 1968 on the occasion of the 150th anniversary of the foundation of the house. Rightly, it honours the founder, Nicolas-François Billecart, and often repays keeping – the 1976 was splendid in March 1988. The 1982 is a blend of Pinot Noir from Mareuil, Bouzy, Cumières, Chigny and Rilly, and Chardonnay from Cramant, Avize and Le Mesnil. The result is a wine of elegance and breed, with good, sustaining power behind it.

Blanc de Blancs 1983: Apart from the delectable label, a copy of those originating in 1846 proposing a Fleur de Sillery and a Fleur de Bouzy, the wine is somewhat tempting too. The composition of the cuvée is based on research into family archives of 1850. The Chardonnay comes from Cramant, Avize and Le Mesnil-sur-Oger, with the exact blend varying from vintage to vintage. The mousse is always particularly fine in the blanc de blancs, the bouquet is of hawthorn flowers and the taste is delicious on the palate.

Brut Rosé: Perhaps it is the intriguing combination of the house name with the colour of the wine, as well as the excellent quality of the champagne itself, that cause Billecart rosé sales to boom. Rosé represents ten percent of total production, which is unusually high. Nicolas-François Billecart made a rosé champagne under the label "Sillery Rosé" as early as the 1830s, the form, design and colour of which has been faithfully reproduced since 1950. Billecart call their wine the "blanc de blancs of the rosés"! It is certainly delicate, with its snowy mousse and dancing elegance and finesse. The base wine is 60 percent Pinot Noir and 40 percent Chardonnay, but the addition of red wine is less than that of most houses, seven to eight percent instead of 15 percent. All in all, the salmon-pink champagne is a treat.

Madame Lily Bollinger, a legendary figure in Champagne. She found the bicycle the best way of seeing at close hand how her vines were progressing, and it enabled her to keep in contact with those who worked for her. As a result, she was revered and loved in the region, and Bollinger prospered greatly under her constant vigilance.

Serious assessment by the Bollinger directorate, from left: Arnould d'Hautefeuille, Christian Bizot, Michel Villedey. Note that these connoisseurs are not using narrow flûtes but the standard tasting glasses designed by the ISO/INAO experts – wonderful for the big Bollinger taste, although not too encouraging for the bubbles.

Bollinger

Bollinger is not merely a champagne – it is an institution. It is a bastion of solid, reassuring proportions in what can sometimes appear as the shifting sands of champagne mergers. Founded in 1829, it remains a proud family firm, determined on its course and sure of its goals. It is equally uncompromising on its style, the Bollinger taste and how to maintain it. Bollinger does not set out to seduce people, to wean them to the marque by marketing gimmicks and "new" blends. People come to Bollinger, not the other way round. And once they have found it, the last thing in the world they want is for it to change. There is very little danger that it ever will.

Jacques Bollinger, German in origin as so many founding fathers of champagne houses, set up in business with a Monsieur Paul Renaudin. His sons and grandson extended and improved the vineyard holdings but, sadly, his grandson, Jacques, died young, in 1941. His widow, Madame Lily Bollinger, took over during the exceedingly difficult time of the German occupation, and proved as formidable as that other great widow, Madame Clicquot herself. Madame Bollinger was a woman of dynamic character, relentless in the pursuit of quality, unafraid of expansion (she doubled the house's production) and yet rooted to the traditions that are Bollinger. She presided over tastings of her wine both at home and abroad, implacable over standards and yet charming as a hostess. The most familiar image we have of her is bicycling through the Bollinger vineyards, keeping an eagle eye on activities and yet still managing to smile sweetly at the camera.

On her death in 1977, Madame Bollinger's nephew, Christian Bizot, took over. Aided by his two nephews, Arnould d'Hautefeuille and Michel Villedey, Christian Bizot is the perfect guardian of the Bollinger way of winemaking. And it *is* a wine, perhaps more than any other champagne. We tend to "think" Bollinger when planning a bottle of champagne to go with a meal. The great, uncompromising taste is almost a food in itself, but it also goes par excellence with a fascinating diversity of dishes. You do not create this kind of taste by accident, you construct it.

You start by having 140 hectares of vineyard, with an average rating of 97 percent. Your Pinot Noir vineyards are in Aÿ, Bisseuil, Bouzy, Louvois, Tauxières and Verzenay, your Chardonnay is at Cuis and Grauves, your Pinot Meunier is at Champvoisy. This meets 70 percent of your needs, with the rest made up of purchases of Pinot Noir and Chardonnay. With this you produce 1.5 million bottles a year, and you make wines that are predominantly Pinot Noir, often 70 percent to 30 percent Chardonnay. You make sure you have enough stock to cover five years of sales – there is no such thing as a "green" bottle of Bollinger. In between, you have your own way of making your wine, your house methods. And this is where Bollinger remains obstinately attached to its "habitudes" and, in this case, thank goodness for obduracy. A visit to Bollinger is like going back in time, but without the cobwebs. Everything is spruce and

When asked how she enjoyed her own product, Madame Lily Bollinger is reported to have replied: "I drink it when I'm happy and when I'm sad. Sometimes I drink it when I'm alone. When I have company I consider it obligatory. I trifle with it if I'm not hungry and drink it when I am. Otherwise I never touch it – unless I'm thirsty."

It is hardly surprising that Bollinger's adherence to quality and traditional standards of excellence has resulted in the establishment, in 1988, of the Madame Bollinger Foundation, to foster the highest levels of wine education and help safeguard wine-trade ethics and sound practices. The first beneficiary has been the Institute of Masters of Wine, which is using the grant to assist it to expand into an international body with members worldwide. The aims are as high as those that Bollinger set themselves.

businesslike, but there are not many sights like this left in the Champagne of the 1980s.

The first thing a visitor sees is a great many casks: in 1987, 1,000 barrels were used for the first fermentation. More acid wines are fermented in stainless-steel vats, where the malolactic fermentation can take place more easily – in the casks, the process is more haphazard – but you can be sure that most of the vintage wines and a part of the non-vintage special cuvée are barrel fermented. The casks are lined with tartrates and there is hardly any wood influence: the last barrels were made in 1964 and some even date from the 1930s. They vary in size, with the larger ones lined with more tartrates than the smaller ones. The wood originally came from the oak forests belonging to the Bollinger family at Cuis. Now a tonnelier (a cooper) is permanently employed (apart from during the vintage, when he is otherwise occupied) in maintaining the casks – he estimates that in 33 years more than 10,000 barrels have passed through his hands.

The second fermentation, or prise de mousse, takes place in all bottle sizes up to Jeroboams, and the vintage wines are still sealed with cork and clasp rather than crown caps. Remuge is entirely by hand. But Bollinger have another ace to play in the winemaking stakes. Uniquely, they keep their reserve wines in magnums, a work-intensive and expensive process which the house considers essential to the taste of their Special Cuvée. After each harvest they choose the best wines and bottle them in magnums for their second fermentation. These unblended, single-cru wines mature under carbon dioxide (CO_2) for several years before being decanted into casks and mixed with wines of a less exalted year, thus lifting the quality of the Special Cuvée. For devotees, this is the recipe that works and why they keep coming back for more.

Bollinger themselves sum up their taste as combining body and elegance – their wines have not been "sacrificed" to the fashion for a lighter style. The balance between Pinot Noir and Chardonnay is noteworthy, as well as the richness and complexity of the bouquet. It all comes back to the quality of their vineyard holdings and their fidelity to traditional methods of vinification. These are my tasting notes for an array of Bollinger wines.

NV Special Cuvée Brut: The current cuvée, in 1988, is made up of 1983 and 1984, with some 1975 reserve wine matured in magnums. The proportion of reserve wine can vary between six and nine percent of the whole. Tasting with Christian Bizot, I could not help exclaiming that the bouquet was that of a summer day in England – for me, the smell was inextricably bound up with that association, instant nostalgia for all those summer occasions when someone has cracked open a bottle of Bolly, on a lawn or beside a river, and that first whiff of scent has assailed the nostrils. The more technical assessment is that the wine has perfect balance between firmness and freshness, being both assertive and mature at the same time. It is an odd thing that Special Cuvée on its own always impresses, although it can be misjudged when it appears among a long line of wines in a blind tasting – rather like the way a Graves stands out in a tasting of Médocs.

Grande Année 1982: Quite a pale colour for Bollinger – but then, it is a young wine for this house. There is the true biscuity Bollinger nose (to be precise, it is the smell of crumbled digestive biscuits, probably only obtainable in Britain and in specialized shops elsewhere, but worth buying just to make the comparison), combined with the freshness of the vintage and a certain nuttiness. It fills the mouth and yet is quite light for Bollinger (the charming style of the year makes its mark here). However, the walnuts-hazelnuts taste on the palate brings you to order and reminds you of the label. The 1975, in magnums and bottles, is drinking superbly in 1988.

RD 1976 Extra Brut: The RD is, of course, a Bollinger trademark. It means récemment dégorgé, or recently disgorged, and it is the same wine as the Grande Année but kept for longer sur pointes. This extra contact with the yeasts gives it great vinosity – what Christian Bizot calls "une bonne colonne vertébrale", good backbone. It also provides a really toasty nose: ultra biscuitiness. The 1976 had no dosage and the assemblage was varied in this vintage to balance the heavy nature of the year, half Pinot Noir and half Chardonnay, thus giving more of the latter than usual. There could well have been a malolactic fermentation in bottle, but the extensive maturation causes all traces of it to disappear.

Aficionados of RD might be interested to know that in 1988, the 1976 is sublime. In January 1988 I tasted the 1966 and the 1964 within a few days of each other. The '66 was selected and disgorged in 1977 for the Silver Jubilee of Queen Elizabeth II. It was both younger tasting and paler than the '64, with little mousse but imposing steeliness and weight. The '64, disgorged in 1973, had slight sparkle but was rich, full and nutty. Christian Bizot is not too keen on

Christian Bizot of Bollinger among his barrels, in preparation for the arrival of the must from the presses. Most of the vintage wines and part of those destined for non-vintage Special Cuvée are fermented in cask – 1,000 barrels were needed for the 1987 harvest. Undoubtedly, this contributes to the majestic Bollinger taste, although the actual character of the blend is a more important factor in determining ultimate style.

Bollinger fans keeping their RDs as long as this, and most would agree that they are at their apogee when fresher, but it is nevertheless a wine-drinking adventure to sample the old beauties. The next RD to be released (during 1988) will be the 1979, followed by the 1981.

RD Année Rare 1973: This is not as complicated as it sounds. We are still with the same basic vintage wine but kept for even longer sur pointes, again making it perfect champagne for meals. It is quite golden in colour, and the malic acidity keeps it young and splendidly fresh. It is lovely, ample wine, with the customary biscuity finish. It is certainly the taste of Aÿ that marks the wines here, with about 25 percent from Bollinger's home base, together with the high-quality Pinots Noirs that make one sigh and say "Bollinger". It is interesting that Bollinger sample these wines in the tasting room in ISO/INAO glasses, which give a "big" champagne the space to show its paces, although they do discourage the bubbles that normally come up the centre of a glass with a more pointed base. Here, what you see is the "belle couronne", or the mousse around the rim of the wine, like a lacy crown.

1981 Vieilles Vignes Françaises Blanc de Noirs: This is always produced from the ungrafted Pinot Noir vines at Bouzy and Aÿ. Immediately, the hawthorn nose so typical of the 1981 vintage is evident, together with the familiar nuttiness. The wine is still tight and austere, packing a punch to come. I would love to wait three to five years for it. In 1987 we drank the 1970, which was total nourishment in itself. Immensely mouth-filling and ample, and awesome in its volume, it stops conversation in its tracks. It is not champagne as many people would know it – it is just Vieilles Vignes. Picking often poses a problem, as grapes from the vieilles vignes ripen earlier than those from the grafted grapes. Ideally, Bollinger would like special permission to start picking them before the official date, but that would still not resolve the need to have some "normal" grapes going through the press before the vieilles vignes.

Grande Année Rosé: Made with an addition of red wine, the sheer quality of Bollinger's rosé seems to defy Madame's distrust of any champagne that was not white! In 1988 the vintage is the 1982, but I am still on the 1981, with its classic champagne nose and full, fruity, satisfying taste. It is big and very Pinot, exemplary rosé, with the capacity to age.

Deutz

Deutz is the kind of champagne that wine producers in other regions of France tend to serve. Its reputation spreads by word of mouth rather than by massive publicity or exposure. While it is hardly an intimate secret, for 800,000 bottles of Deutz champagne are sold every year, it would often appear to be the favourite marque of people "in the know".

Deutz remains a family firm, now in its fifth generation. André Lallier heads this dynamic house – the name changed at the second generation, through the daughters. It is almost a "Dear Octopus" family, with tentacles in winemaking

The hugely ornate style of Napoleon III interior design, as displayed in all its splendour at the headquarters of Deutz in Aÿ.

enterprises in many parts of the world, but the heart beats in Aÿ. The house was founded in 1838 by William Deutz and Pierre Geldermann, who were born in Aix-La-Chapelle, as it was known then under the First Empire.

About 40 percent of the requirements of the house come from its own vineyards, a total of 42 hectares with an average rating of 97 percent. These are divided between Chardonnay at Le Mesnil-sur-Oger, Pinot Noir at Aÿ and Mareuil-sur-Aÿ, 70 percent Pinot Noir and 30 percent Pinot Meunier at Bisseuil, 75 percent Pinot Noir and 25 percent Pinot Meunier at Pierry and 70 percent Pinot Noir and 30 percent Pinot Meunier at Moussy. Deutz usually buy annually about 600,000 kilos of grapes for the rest of their needs, in the proportions of 55 percent Pinot Noir, 30 percent Chardonnay and 15 percent Pinot Meunier. Fermentation takes place in a battery of small, 100-hectolitre vats. The wines always go through a malolactic fermentation and remuage is entirely manual in the 18th-century cellars under the Aÿ vineyards. The prise de mousse takes place in all the large-sized bottles, including Methuselahs. Cork closures are still used at this stage for the Cuvée William Deutz, as well as for the Jeroboams and Methuselahs. There are some casks where the liqueur d'expédition is stored.

Deutz champagnes are characterized by the 100 percent-rated vineyard at Aÿ, which gives supple, elegant, fruity wines. They also include in their cuvées a significant amount of Pinot Meunier which gives roundness and length.

Brut NV: A blend of 30 crus from Aÿ, the Montagne de Reims, the Vallée de la Marne and the Côte des Blancs, this usually contains 45 percent Pinot Noir, 30 percent Pinot Meunier and 25 percent Chardonnay, and the liqueur d'expédition is a blend of crus from Aÿ, Pierry and the Montagne de Reims. It balances freshness and vinosity and is always reliable.

Blanc de Blancs 1982: This is presented in a clear bottle. The Chardonnays come from Avize and Le Mesnil-sur-Oger, both 100 percent-rated crus, and from Villers-Marmery, rated at 95 percent. Interestingly, the liqueur d'expédition is composed of Le Mesnil 1970, which went through second fermentation in magnum, and cane sugar. The nose has elements of blossom (a very 1982 quality) with lemony overtones. The taste is more hazelnuts and greengages, and the end result is a delicious, easy-to-drink champagne.

Vintage Brut: In 1988, the vintage is 1982 and is a blend of the three grape varieties. The liqueur d'expédition is cane sugar dissolved in Aÿ 1973, with prise de mousse in magnum. The taste is a good balance between power and finesse. When it is kept longer sur pointes, it is sold under a label designed by the painter Georges Mathieu – the flavour of the wine is more aesthetically pleasing than the art.

Rosé 1982: I like this, although it is not very "classic". A very roses and strawberries wine.

Cuvée William Deutz: In 1988, the vintage is 1982, although I have more experience of the 1979, which is on the pale side, light and elegant, a very apéritif style. It is seductive, and usually very good value, but there is no great impact on the finish. The blend is 30 percent Chardonnay, 62 percent Pinot Noir and eight percent Pinot Meunier. The liqueur d'expédition is cane sugar dissolved in Aÿ 1971 matured in magnum. In 1988 the house is bringing out, in very limited quantity, a Cuvée William Deutz Rosé 1982; it will be a totally Pinot Noir wine. **Cuvée 150ème Anniversaire:** Launched in 1988 for the 150th anniversary of Deutz, this was bottled in 1983 and is composed of the best cuvées from 1979, 1981 and 1982. The bottles are reproductions of the first bottle used by William Deutz when he founded the house, with somewhat startling engraved stars, a crown and "drapes". The blend is 70 percent Pinot Noir, 20 percent Chardonnay (vineyard rating 100 percent) and ten percent Pinot Meunier, because André Lallier likes the warmth and fruitiness this contributes to the whole. The colour is lemon-gold and there is a marvellous vigorous mousse. The bouquet is of comice pears and grapefruit and is very youthful, but the taste is impressively rich, full and bready. It is big, food champagne: just the sort to drink in the ornate Napoleon III reception rooms of Maison Deutz in Aÿ.

Gosset

There is little doubt that Gosset is the oldest established champagne house. In 1584, Pierre Gosset, mayor of Aÿ, started to sell his wines, and there is a document to prove it at the Bibliothèque Nationale. As to whether or not the family continuously traded as négociants, as well as producing vines, I hardly think it is my role to venture where many another researcher has foundered. Besides, such technicalities are of vastly less importance than the actual quality of Gosset champagnes as made today. And here it is easy to be unequivocal: they are very good indeed, and some are superb.

What is remarkable is that one family has wanted to make fine wine for more than 400 years. This puts the Gossets in the ranks of the Matuschka-Greiffenclaus and the Antinoris, who are, nevertheless, a few centuries ahead of them. Albert Gosset is now the head of the house, with Antoine and Laurent Gosset the sixteenth generation in the business. The year 1984 was, naturally, a big one for the family, with the 400th anniversary being celebrated in Aÿ and Paris with solemn Masses, balloon and vintage-car rallies, an art competition and concerts, galas and the creation of a rose christened Millésime. Naturally, there was also a very fine Cuvée Quatrième Centenaire to celebrate the occasion, but this, to no one's surprise, has disappeared from the scene – it was literally too good to last.

But it would take more than this to turn the head of the Gossets. They continue to make champagne with the same care as they always have. The family own 12 hectares of vines rated at 98 percent, all Pinot Noir, in the villages of Aÿ, Bouzy, Mareuil-sur-Aÿ and Rilly La Montagne. This accounts for a little more than 20 percent of their needs; the rest they obtain from more than 45 hectares in more than 30 villages and in all three grape varieties.

Clearly, there is a handmade quality about Gosset champagnes, from the oak casks among the vats to disgorging by hand and the intricate work of placing

987 a Noyon Millénaire du Couronnement de Hugues Capet proclamé Roy de France, le 3 juillet

Gosset produce some of the most beautiful and highly decorated labels in the region, especially when they commemorate historic events. As champagne so frequently marks great anniversary celebrations, the houses vie with one another to design eye-catching and glossy examples of the art.

● ● ● ● ● ● ● ● ● ●

Gosset's beautiful special labels on each bottle. The wines do not go through a malolactic fermentation and remuage is both manual and by gyropalettes. There are five years of stocks in the cellars – you can be sure that every bottle of vintage Gosset on the market is ready to drink. The millésimes and grands millésimes spend two to four months in old casks.

In 1987 Gosset produced 420,000 bottles; in 1988, 460,000.

Brut Reserve: In 1988 this was based on the 1983 vintage, with 25 percent reserve wines of 1982. It is made up of eight crus, 70 percent Chardonnay and 30 percent black grapes, of which 28 percent are Pinot Noir and the remaining two percent Meunier. The dosage is 1.25 percent by volume, made up of 1981 liqueur at 500 grams of sugar per litre (many houses use 750 grams per litre). The wine usually needs extra bottle-age for my taste, but is well made.

Brut Rosé: Undoubtedly, Gosset are masters of rosé, although they point out that pink champagne is really an "unstable marriage", with the red wine ageing more quickly than the white base. The current (in 1988) blend is made up of 1982 and 1983, 14 crus (70 percent Chardonnay, 30 percent Pinot Noir), with the addition of 11 percent Pinot Noir red wine from Aÿ and Mareuil. The shade is salmon and there is the usual very fine Gosset mousse, pink in this case. It is apéritif rosé, with its Chardonnay style, and combines fruit and austerity in a way that I find very pleasing indeed.

Grande Réserve: A blend of 1983 and 1982, with 1980 reserve wine, this contains 18 crus, 45 percent Chardonnay, 41 percent Pinot Noir and 14 percent Meunier. It is always good, combining delicacy with power, and has a lovely mousse.

Vintage: In 1987 I was lucky enough to taste a series of Gosset vintages, which gave me a real perspective on the style and ageing potential. These are my notes:

1982: Composed of 14 crus, 38 percent Chardonnay, 55 percent Pinot Noir and seven percent Meunier, the wine has a lovely ripe, hedgerows bouquet, redolent of sun on blossom, when the scent really emerges. Finesse and hazelnut flavour – will fill out even more.

1979: Very pale colour, a feature of all Gosset wines, even the old vintages (no malolactic). There is a family apple-blossom-and-petals bouquet and hazelnuts character. The wine is medium weight, with a lovely firm finish. A very pretty wine, superb as an apéritif or with oysters.

1976: Again, very pale. Delicate nose. Slightly almond finish. Obviously, very ripe wine. On this occasion, it was the wine that "said less" to me than the others, but it is a most serious champagne nonetheless.

1973: Golden straw colour, with a light toasty smell. Really elegant. Beautifully mature, while maintaining great freshness. Lovely floral finish. A marvellously successful 1973.

1971: Pale green-gold. Lovely floral, spring-hedgerows nose. Slightly nutmeg character? Lanolin elements. Full, rich finish. Roundest of them all – very ripe, with splendid balance. Really lives up to its fine reputation.

1969 (disgorged for the tasting): Very nutty smell. Still a pale colour. Vanilla-pod overtones, musky too, and almost jasmine. Nutty taste and a good deal more mature than the 1971. Yeasty/bready characteristics.

1964 (disgorged for the tasting): Pale, with that fresh, vanillin nose. More youthful than the 1969. Bready – or "briochy" to be more exact. Toasty finish. In fine form, like all great 1964s.

1961: A great deal of fruit on the nose, as well as a real smell of the boulangerie as one passes it early in the morning. Wonderfully youthful and bouncy. Quite a metallic taste, although not in a pejorative sense, with a walnuts finish.

1959 (disgorged for the tasting): Gosset hazelnuts bouquet. Really mature wine, with a soft cushiony finish. Powerful and strong, as befits the year (high natural alcohol and no chaptalization).

1952 (disgorged for the tasting): A splendid old wine with a very complex nose of hazelnuts, Spanish turron and even rosewater, as sprinkled on Tunisian sticky cakes! Vanillin elements and a somewhat rosy taste. Amazingly young wine, with an almost toffee-ish finish.

Grand Millésime 1979: This comes in an exact reproduction of the beautiful dark, heavy bottles that Gosset used in the 18th and 19th centuries. Composed of 18 crus and 61 percent Chardonnay, 34 percent Pinot Noir and five percent Meunier, and with a liqueur made up of the 1973, 1975 and 1976 wines. Charm and length and extraordinary finesse – this is remarkable champagne.

Grand Millésime Rosé 1982: In the same stunning presentation, this has to be one of the best rosé champagnes in the entire region. Composed of 15 crus and 100 percent Chardonnay, with 12 percent Pinot Noir red wine from Bouzy. The dosage is pink liqueur 1979 "dosée" at 1.25 percent. Gosset describe the colour as light pink, but in 1988 I found it more yellow topaz. It has a full, rich Pinot smell, with tiny seed-pearl bubbles. On the palate it is full with great vinosity, definite and oozing fruit, but with great breed and elegance underneath. Gosset recommend it as an apéritif; I found it perfection with smoked ham. However, I would jump at the chance to drink it with absolutely anything.

Alfred Gratien

A visit to Alfred Gratien in Epernay should be prescribed for all those who think there is nothing traditional left in Champagne. Not only have many of the winemaking methods remained unchanged for years, but there is an old-world charm in the welcome that could almost be from another age. This is not, however, to relegate the wine to something of the past – time-warp Champagne. The scale is small (between 120,000 and 180,000 bottles produced a year), but the taste is up to the minute, if it is quality you are seeking. The special excitement in the wines is their potential for ageing, as shown by some of the extraordinarily youthful, intriguing old champagnes.

Alfred Gratien is really the story of three families who have worked together through successive generations to safeguard quality and tradition. The firm was founded in 1864 by Alfred Gratien, who was joined later by Jean Meyer, born in Dr Albert Schweitzer's Alsace village of Gunsbach. Today the house is entirely owned by the direct descendants of the founders: Eric Seydoux and his two sons, Alain and Gérard Seydoux, and his cousin, Bernard de Bousquet. The commercial side is looked after by Christian Gallé and the cellars by Jean-Pierre Jaegger, rightly proud of their families' long association with Gratien.

The house owns no vines and buys in all three grape varieties, changing the composition of the cuvées according to the vintage characteristics. The first fermentation is carried out in 205-litre casks: some of the barrels are 30, 40 and 50 years old (the taste of oak is *not* required in a champagne). There is no malolactic fermentation and the non-vintage wines are aged for three to four years, the vintage for six to seven years. The vintage wines are matured under cork, not crown caps. Remuage is by hand and the prise de mousse takes place in all bottle sizes.

At Alfred Gratien they say their champagnes are often described as "old English style". They aim for, and achieve, a certain fullness and structure allied to suppleness, champagne both as an apéritif and for meals. This vinosity certainly allows the gastronome to experiment with different foods, as one might with a still white wine.

Cuvée de Réserve Brut NV: The cuvée in 1988 is based on the 1983 vintage and has a high (61 percent) proportion of Pinot Meunier, as well as Pinot Noir and Chardonnay. This explains the soft, supple character of the wine, while the bouquet has the Gratien hallmark of a certain biscuity quality together with some lemon and grapefruit overtones. At a blind tasting in 1987, I placed it very high because of its classy finish.

Rosé Brut NV: A favourite of Crown Prince Harald of Norway, this is a wine that repays keeping, especially if you do not mind the colour becoming more orange. The taste, however, will become rounder and softer.

In 1988 I was fortunate enough to taste a range of vintage wines from Gratien at their cellars in Epernay (sometimes these were marketed as crémant champagnes). These are my notes.

1979: Composed of 56 percent Chardonnay and 22 percent each Pinot Noir and Meunier, this had a lovely "nerveux" Chardonnay flavour, with the biscuity character just there (it develops with each year in bottle). The wine was already delicious and elegant, golden in colour and very scented. As there is no malolactic fermentation, acidities tend to be higher here, contributing to the propensity to age well.

1969: An assemblage of 39 percent Chardonnay, 22 percent Pinot Noir and 39 percent Meunier, the colour was more golden than the others. Both the bouquet and the flavour were reminiscent of fresh bread. The cork was slightly damaged, and I have had even better bottles of this remarkable 1969.

1966: Here the blend is 40 percent Chardonnay, 30 percent each Pinot Noir and Meunier. It was the oldest tasting wine of the line-up, but forceful and big.

1964: The Pinot Noir predominated with 38 percent, followed by 36 percent Chardonnay and 26 percent Meunier. The fresh-bread nose was in evidence as well as the austerity of this year. The toasty taste showed maturity, but also enormous class.

Following such a description of old wines, it is incumbent upon me to say that there are also innovations on the way at Alfred Gratien. In 1989 they will launch a "new" form of bottle – but I have a hunch it will be a replica of the old, heavy-based style which is now so à la mode. It is difficult to renounce tradition when it has served you so well.

Jean Saintot, the last barrel maker in Aÿ. The 205-litre casks, or "pièces", are rarely to be found now in the region, but houses such as Bollinger, Alfred Gratien and Krug remain faithful to the old methods. New barrels have to be aged before use, because the taste of oak is not desirable in champagne. Repairs and maintenance thus become very important, as casks can be used for decades if they are well cared for.

HISTORY OF THE HEIDSIECKS

1785 – HEIDSIECK & CO. founded by Florens-Louis Heidsieck and his three
nephews: Walbaum, Charles-Henri and Christian Heidsieck
1823 – death of Florens-Louis Heidsieck
1834 – HEIDSIECK & CO ceased existence

WALBAUM

1846: HEIDSIECK MONOPOLE founded by Walbaum

1930: Company taken over by Monsieur Mignot

1972: Company bought by G.H. MUMM; HEIDSIECK MONOPOLE & CO thus became part of SEAGRAMS

CHARLES-HENRI

1824: Charles-Henri died

1851: CHARLES HEIDSIECK founded by his son Charles-Camille

1893: Charles-Camille died, leaving the company to his son, Charles-Marie-Eugène; five brothers from the next generation became directors

1976: Merged with HENRIOT

1985: REMY MARTIN acquired a majority interest in CHARLES HEIDSIECK

CHRISTIAN

1834: HEIDSIECK founded by Christian (he died 6 months later)

1838: His widow married Monsieur Piper; the name PIPER-HEIDSIECK was born

1870: Company sold to Monsieur Kunkelmann

1986: The descendants of this family still control PIPER-HEIDSIECK

Charles Heidsieck
• • • • • • • • • • • •

For some time, Charles Heidsieck has been almost a Cinderella among champagnes, never quite recognized for what it was in spite of possessing some very alluring qualities. The current owners of the house, Rémy Martin, have reacted positively to this, and in spring 1988 the launch of a new Brut Réserve marked the culmination of a programme of investment which was set in action in 1985 when they bought the business from Henriot. Although I have always found the non-vintage blend of Charles Heidsieck enjoyable, there is no doubt that under the new packaging there is now a very grande marque taste.

Technically, Charles Heidsieck is beautifully equipped to the most modern standards and oenological operations are supervised by the very capable Daniel Thibault. An impressive cuverie of 154 stainless-steel vats was designed especially for the needs of the house and has been in place since 1981. Each vat holds 320 hectolitres, giving a total capacity of 50,000 hectolitres. The wines are fermented at between 17 and 19°C (63–66°F) and go through a malolactic fermentation. The aim of Daniel Thibault is to produce the "juice of fermented grapes" with the emphasis on purity of taste. Reserve wines are kept in glass-lined concrete vats and the blending vats hold 1,000 and 2,000 hectolitres. A centrifuge is used to aid precipitation before the cold treatment.

Charles Heidsieck own no vines but their purchases enable them to work with 105 different crus, an impressive palette with which to perform. In spring 1988 they bought the business of F. Bonnet, which has given them the management and production of ten hectares of Chardonnay at Oger. They also possess some of the most impressive chalk cellars in Reims, 2,000 years old and 20 metres underground. The temperature remains naturally at 9°C (48°F) and there is no doubt that these dark, silent, subterranean "cathedrals" are the ideal surroundings in which the second fermentation can take place and the wines mature. Remuage is both manual and automatic in gyropalettes, and between three to four years of stock repose in the cellars – the equivalent in bottles of more than 12 million. Annual sales are about 3.5 million bottles.

For many years, Jean-Marc Heidsieck was the personification of this house, with his charm and cultured manner. An intrepid traveller, he followed in the footsteps of his great-grandfather and founder of the house, Charles-Camille Heidsieck, otherwise known as Champagne Charlie. That gentleman managed to sell 300,000 bottles of his champagne in one year in the United States just before the Civil War broke out. Jean-Marc Heidsieck has recently retired, but he still welcomes his friends to Reims with a glass of the wine he helped to introduce to so many around the globe.

Brut Réserve NV: This new cuvée is the result of a policy of improvement, with better choice of grapes – more than 150 different top crus; better choice of juice off the press – only the "cuvée" is used (no vins de taille); improvements in the vinification, in one of the most modern cuveries of the region; better assemblage, with a greater proportion of reserve wines; and longer ageing, to wait for the best possible moment in the development and maturation of the blend.

The colour is gold – Charles Heidsieck do not like a wine to be neutral in shade or character. Made from a quarter Chardonnay and three-quarters Pinot Noir and Meunier divided equally, there are tiny bubbles, accompanied by a very fruity bouquet. The taste is full, round, ripe and nutty. It has the soft, cushiony style typical of Charles Heidsieck, with added class. There is enough weight for it to be champagne for food as well as an apéritif, but there is also marked freshness. A real success.

Brut Millésime 1982: A blend of one-third Chardonnay and two-thirds Pinot Noir, with a touch of Meunier. The colour is quite a pronounced gold and the bouquet has the full fruitiness we like in this marque. The taste is fat and rich, very succulent, with a flavour of brioche on the finish. The 1981 is very good, even with a saddle of hare!

Blanc de Blancs 1981: This is composed of Chardonnay from Chouilly, Cramant,

"Champagne à la coupe" can be a misleading sign in café windows, because when you go in and order your glass of champagne, what you are given is a flûte. In the Champagne region, ordering a glass of bubbly is nearly (but not quite!) as common as calling for a coffee or a beer.

Avize, Vertus, Le Mesnil, Villers-Marmery and Trépail. The colour is, obviously, more green here (no black grapes), with a nose showing just the right amount of ageing – toasty and hazelnutty. The taste delightfully combines freshness and maturity.

Brut Rosé NV: Very good mousse, medium depth, orangey pink, with a fruity smell. Tawny taste, very dry, even a bit "meaty", perhaps with a touch of liquorice.

Rosé 1982: A marriage between the Brut Millésimé and ten percent red wine from Bouzy, Cumières and Vertus from the same year, this has a similar colour and mousse to the Rosé NV but is more scented. Very fruity and elegant. At the end of 1987, the 1981 looked a little old to be drunk as an apéritif and needed to be served with food.

Cuvée Champagne Charlie: The 1979 vintage had come into its own at the end of 1987. A blend of Chardonnay and Pinot Noir, with a tiny amount of Meunier, it is the Chardonnay that comes out the most strongly. The wine is elegant with a great deal of finesse and a slightly nutty finish. It certainly needed this bottle-age – when it was first launched it was somewhat closed and "unmarried". The 1981 is on the market in 1988, half Chardonnay and half Pinot Noir. The colour is pale gold, the nose begins floral and leads on to an imposing taste of some vinosity. Already fine, it is sure to improve still further with a few more years in bottle, but will probably open out more quickly than the 1979.

The wine of Champagne Charlie is once more set to conquer markets from New Orleans to London, confident that extra effort and investment has more than paid off in the quality in the glass.

Heidsieck & Co. Monopole

No one would pretend that Heidsieck Monopole is the most fashionable of champagnes, yet those who neglect this marque do so at their own risk. Slavishly following fashion can be a somewhat limiting experience and is especially sad in the context of champagne, when there are so many tastes awaiting the adventurous wine lover.

Heidsiecks have been around for a long time, since 1785 in fact, if you go back to Florens-Louis Heidsieck and the original Heidsieck & Co. (see the family tree on page 100). One of his nephews, Walbaum, founded Heidsieck Monopole in 1846, and in 1972 the house was bought by G.H. Mumm, part of the Seagram empire. It thus benefits from the equipment and winemaking skills at Mumm, but contributes a formidable palette of vineyards and the special formula that produces a consistently fine non-vintage as well as one of the greatest champagnes made, Diamant Bleu.

The heart of the Heidsieck Monopole vineyards is Verzenay, where they own 21 hectares of Pinot Noir. They also own the Montagne de Reims' best-known landmark, the Moulin de Verzenay. Constructed in 1823 on a site known as Mont Boeuf, it is the only windmill you will see in Champagne. It was used as an

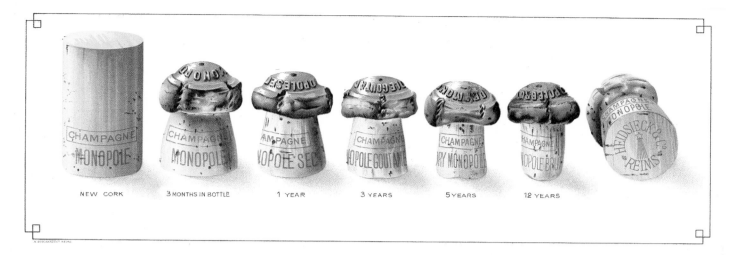

NEW CORK   3 MONTHS IN BOTTLE   1 YEAR   3 YEARS   5 YEARS   12 YEARS

observation post during World War I, and King Victor Emmanuel III of Italy and the French President, Raymond Poincaré, visited the site to observe enemy lines. At the end of August 1944, at the moment of the Liberation, the windmill was being used by the American Army. Now, in more happy days, the guardhouse, with its wonderful view and flower-filled garden, is used by Heidsieck Monopole for receptions.

The other 100 percent Pinot Noir vineyards owned by Heidsieck Monopole are 21 hectares in Ambonnay, three hectares in Bouzy, two hectares in Mailly and 0.5 hectares in Beaumont-sur-Vesle. Then there are 19 hectares of Pinot Noir in 99 percent-rated Verzy, 22.5 hectares of Chardonnay at Faverolles and 21 hectares of Pinot Meunier at Savigny-sur-Ardre – a grand total of 110 hectares, providing a third of the house's requirements.

Since 1985 the wines have been made at the modern cuverie at Mumm, but on the Heidsieck Monopole premises halves, magnums and "special bottles" are handled. The cellars extend for 70 kilometres at a depth of 15 metres in the chalk subsoil, and the temperature remains at a constant 12°C (54°F). For many years the chef de caves was Alfred Simon, a well-known figure in Champagne who still keeps an eye on matters, especially with his close contact with the vineyards. Annual sales are around two million bottles.

Dry Monopole NV: Made from 71 percent black grapes, both Pinot Noir and Meunier, and 29 percent Chardonnay, this is a straightforward, absolutely true champagne that I always like; extremely palatable.

Red-Top Sec and Green-Top Demi-Sec NV: These are popular in Germany and Switzerland, but I have not come across them.

Dry Monopole Brut Vintage: Made from 58 percent black grapes and 42 percent Chardonnay, this is powerful and definite tasting, strongly "grands noirs" – one always feels this is from a Reims-based house. It does not come out every other vintage – Heidsieck Monopole select the best. The wines last very well: I have enjoyed the 1979, 1975, 1973 (still excellent), the 1969 and the 1955.

Rosé Vintage: Made from 58 percent black grapes and 42 percent Chardonnay. A

A perfect illustration of the way corks change shape according to how long they have been in the bottle. A young champagne will always have a cork that is somewhat splayed out, while a champagne with bottle-age will have a cork that is narrow and straight. The British tend to go into ecstasies when they see the latter type of cork, assuming that the champagne thus has "landing age", but the Swiss, for example, will expect to see a really wide cork, thereby ensuring that the champagne will be very young and fresh.

deep attractive topaz. The 1979 shows maturity, but I find it a rich nectar, especially with food.

Diamant Bleu: This is the cuvée de prestige that was launched in 1967 with the 1961 vintage. Then, the bottle had a shape like an Indian club, but this changed to the current bottle, cut like a diamond, which was introduced in 1981 with the 1975 vintage. The cuvée is composed of 100 percent-rated crus, 50 percent Chardonnay and 50 percent Pinot Noir. It is a great champagne with a most definite taste; in blind tastings the panel is often divided, with half the tasters giving it top marks, the rest rating it far lower. I am in the former group. Whether it is "your" taste or not, any champagne lover can see that this is a sublime blend of power and finesse, beautifully balanced between force and seduction. In 1988 the vintage is the 1982, with a floral, almost mineral bouquet. The taste has a hint of flint and on the palate it opens out to sheer complexity, rich and yet austere at the same time. For me, it is pure class, very marked by the influence of Verzenay. The 1979 is utterly tempting, but I have a special affection for the concentration and enveloping velvet texture of the 1976. The 1975 and 1973 were also fabulous.

Try drinking Diamant Bleu with a "diamant noir", Brillat-Savarin's evocative name for a black truffle. It is a marriage made in heaven, but happily obtainable on earth.

Diamant Rosé 1982: In a transparent diamond-cut bottle, the 1982 vintage is the first, and very probably the last, vintage of this exquisite champagne. Only 15,000 bottles were produced, and it was launched in the United States, but the decision has been taken to abandon it to concentrate on the Diamant Bleu. One can only hope this will be reviewed, because the wine is quite superb. The beautiful pink colour leads to a nose of strawberries and a palate of freshness, great fruit and wonderful harmony. It would be a tragedy if this disappeared from the scene. Meanwhile, I shall console myself with as much Diamant Bleu as I can honestly procure.

Henriot
. . . . . .

Joseph Henriot must be one of the busiest men in Champagne: he is certainly among the most able. Apart from heading Veuve Clicquot in the Moët-Hennessy-Vuitton group, he also has his own family house – Henriot. This is no modern whizz-kid business: founded in 1808, Henriot has perfect credentials. The Henriot family can trace their origins in the region to the 16th century; they were always more vineyard owners than négociants. They prepared cuvées for other houses, but already had their own clients in the last century.

The great strength of Henriot lies in the vineyards at their disposal, 115 hectares with an average rating of 96 percent. The vineyards are now owned by the Moët-Hennessy-Vuitton group but their production is reserved for the Henriot marque. Chardonnay comes from Beaumont, Epernay, Le Mesnil, Oger, Chouilly, Vertus, Villeneuve, Avize and Voipreux; 60 percent of their vines are

on the Côte des Blancs. Pinot Noir comes from Verzenay, Verzy, Trépail, Aÿ, Mareuil, Avenay, Mutigny and Epernay. This covers 90 percent of the requirements of the house. Purchases are made according to the quality of the harvest and thus vary from year to year, with the emphasis on Chardonnay and Pinot Noir. When you travel around the Champagne vineyards you quite often see bold notices indicating the Henriot vines – the only other house to attempt the same visibility is Taittinger (Moët's little milestones are incredibly discreet). Henriot's wines are made in the Clicquot cellars under the same competent technical direction. Remuage is in non-automatic gyropalettes.

The aim of Henriot is to produce a champagne that has character, not merely a commercial brand. The house has the ingredients necessary for making a wine with individual taste and personality: vines, and stocks – Henriot has five years of them. More than a million bottles are produced each year and the principal export market is Switzerland, where Henriot has an excellent image. According to Joseph Henriot, "the Swiss like a wine that does not compromise". Germany is also a very good market.

It is worth listening to Joseph Henriot on the subject of his own house, as he has a unique view of the overall picture in Champagne and the financial stability to choose his own niche on the market. He considers that certain marques will remain unaffected by shifting fashions because their production will be

A collage made by a picker during the 1987 vintage, a suitable decoration for his tent! One can only assume the picker came from Lorraine, but he certainly associates champagne with celebrations.

deliberately limited and therefore their image will not be polluted by excessive marketing: the marque will be seen as "authentic", as a Rolls-Royce. It will be a cultural point of reference, as Baccarat glass, or Sèvres or Limoges porcelain. This type of marque will never be "trendy", but it will stand the test of time.

Brut Souverain NV: Usually more than half this cuvée is Chardonnay, marking the wine as very Henriot but essentially different from many non-vintage blends. As with all the wines, there are lovely small bubbles. The nose is fuller than the blanc de blancs, and nice and appley. There is a slightly "metallic" note and it can be full and a mite raw at the same time. The style is very dry but it is not a personal favourite.

Blanc de Blancs NV: (The word crémant is being removed from the capsule.) The lovely bouquet is of hedgerows, fresh and delicious. This is always a very pretty wine, an utterly enchanting apéritif, with a juicy finish.

Brut Souverain Vintage: Here the style is always very different from the non-vintage, with more Pinot Noir. The 1981 has a classic champagne nose, apple blossom and hazelnuts, and lovely balance. This vintage could certainly be kept a few more years.

Brut Rosé Vintage: Blended with red wine for the colour, Chardonnay is also sometimes added for perfect balance and the lightness desired by the house. The 1983 has a good tawny colour and a delicate, rather "hedgerows" nose. There is good fruit on the palate, with a taste of strawberries. It is fresh and young, elegant, but with some bottle-age should develop more personality.

Réserve Baron Philippe de Rothschild Vintage: Just as in 1850 the King of Holland gave Henriot the Royal Warrant, in our times Baron Philippe de Rothschild of Mouton Rothschild asked Henriot to make a special blend for him to serve at the château. The result is a complex champagne which can take bottle-age.

Cuvée Baccarat Brut Millésimé: This is the jewel in the Henriot crown, a really aristocratic champagne. The 1976 is composed of 55 percent Chardonnay from Chouilly, Oger, Le Mesnil, Villeneuve and Vertus and 45 percent Pinot Noir from Mareuil, Vertus, Le Clos L'Abbé (Epernay), Trépail, Verzy and Verzenay, all house vineyards. It has a wonderful, big, bready bouquet, rounded, with acacia elements. The flavour has some lovely vanillin and the balance is perfect. A superb champagne, which should be better known. With Joseph Henriot at the helm, it probably soon will be.

Jacquesson & Fils

I was always told never to start a piece of writing with a negative, but it matters little that Jacquesson is not a Grande Marque. Indeed, it is the living proof that a small, well-established house can produce champagnes of great quality which can stand up to the most intense competition. Quality cannot be judged on a brief encounter, with all the emotional instability that this entails, but on sustained performance over a credible length of time.

Jacquesson's historic documents give ample proof of their popularity with the great and famous, especially one notable customer who took it with him onto the battlefield. The champagne itself has a far gentler image, its conquests more the result of a seductive taste than a show of military force.

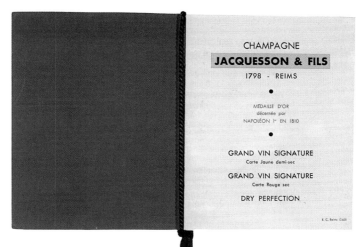

CHAMPAGNE
JACQUESSON & FILS
1798 - REIMS

•

MÉDAILLE D'OR
décernée par
NAPOLÉON I⁰ᵉʳ EN 1810

•

GRAND VIN SIGNATURE
Carte Jaune demi-sec

GRAND VIN SIGNATURE
Carte Rouge sec

DRY PERFECTION

The house of Jacquesson possesses this track record; Claude Jacquesson founded the marque in 1798. Subsequently, a German, Joseph Krug, worked for the firm, but he left and founded his own house in 1843. In 1867, the year of the Exposition Universelle, Jacquesson was selling one million bottles and enjoyed a visit from the Queen of Holland. Later, the house became the property of the great broker of the 1920s, Léon de Tassigny, who moved the firm from Châlons-sur-Marne to Reims, but in 1974 the Chiquet family became the new owners. They wisely made their headquarters in Dizy, to be near their vineyards and to enjoy the benefits of a lovely house and cellars. Today, young Jean-Hervé Chiquet runs the business, with a sure eye for quality and a determination to achieve his goals.

I have to say that the wines of Jacquesson are close to my heart in spite of their association with Napoleon, one of history's most belligerent players! He visited the cellars in 1810 (then at Châlons-sur-Marne) and cases of Jacquesson followed him on campaign; certainly, he enjoyed Jacquesson champagne at Wagram, and at the Tuileries on the occasion of his marriage to Marie-Louise. During his visit to Jacquesson, he gave the marque his Médaille d'Or "for the beauty and the riches of the cellars", and this gold medal still adorns the labels of their champagnes.

Sales are now a third of those achieved in 1867, but this enables the wines to have a "handmade" quality about them which is wholly beneficial. About 60 percent of the firm's needs are provided by family vineyards at Aÿ, Dizy, Hautvillers and Lagery, as well as 11 hectares at Avize belonging to the Tassignys, making a total of 22 hectares with an average échelle rating of 96 percent. The Chardonnay comes from Avize, Hautvillers and Dizy, the Pinot Noir from Aÿ and Dizy, while the Pinot Meunier is supplied by the five hectares at Lagery, south of the Ardre. The supplementary grapes that are bought in are nearly all black.

The cellars are impeccably run, with a family atmosphere – when I was last there, one man was disgorging magnums in the old traditional way, "à la volée", and using a small eight-nozzle dosage machine for the addition of the liqueur d'expédition. It reminded me of hand-bottling in Burgundy cellars more than 20 years ago, with the quiet calm that reigned, instead of the decibel level of today's fast-moving lines.

Blanc de Blancs: I consider this to be one of the most successful of the genre in the entire region. It is based on those splendid Chardonnay vineyards at Avize and thus Jean-Hervé Chiquet says it is the "easiest" wine for them to make. Undoubtedly, this is the main contributory factor in the finesse of the wine, with its fresh grass bouquet, somehow reminiscent of summer mornings in the country. It might well have three vintages in it: the 1984–83–82 blend was very successful, a lesson in the art of Chardonnay assemblage. It is always delicious and creamy, soft and supple, with the acidity so perfectly in balance that it slips down with the greatest of ease and the maximum of pleasure.

Perfection Brut sans année: This is usually a blend of 20 percent Chardonnay, 30 percent Pinot Noir and 50 percent Pinot Meunier, and the style is floral and soft, delicious and well balanced. It is a most gulpable champagne.

Brut Rosé sans année: The pink is obtained by adding 10–12 percent red wine (nearly all Pinot Noir) from Dizy, and this gives a beautiful jewel colour. There is often a taste of strawberries on the finish, which comes from the red wine (which itself has a taste more resembling raspberries in its earlier life). A recent tasting was of a wine of the 1984 and 1983 vintages, but the red was the product of 1982's harvest. It is an apéritif rosé or, with its strawberry taste, a splendid accompaniment to a dish of wild strawberries.

Vintage Perfection: This is always a delightful champagne. The 1982 had a smell of hedgerows, scented, easy, and typical of the attractive qualities of the year. It is the kind of wine that disappears all too quickly. The 1979 was a wine of great delicacy. Usually the blend is 45 percent Pinot Noir, 35 percent Chardonnay and 20 percent Pinot Meunier.

Vintage Signature: A special champagne millésimé, fermented in 75-hectolitre oak foudres, this comes entirely from Jacquesson's own vineyards: 50 percent Pinot Noir from Aÿ and Dizy and 50 percent Chardonnay from Avize. Going from the Perfection 1982 to the Signature 1981, you notice immediately a deeper, more complete and complex nose, and a long finish. It somehow combines being both soft and austere at the same time. There was also a 1979. Signature is always presented in the same shaped bottle as those found following a famous shipwreck, the remnants of a cargo of Jacquesson on board the sailing ship *Niantic* which burned while moored in San Francisco in 1851. Like so many similar ships, she had been abandoned by her crew, anxious to join the Gold Rush. A series of hotels and other buildings were built on the site of the beached vessel, with each excavation offering up remains of the still-effervescing cargo. The latest discovery was 60 bottles in 1975.

Old vintages, disgorged just before release: These very special wines should, on no account, be called "Recently Disgorged", a term registered by Bollinger, but they are champagnes "dégorgés tardivement" – disgorged later – on receipt of order and pre-despatch from the Jacquesson cellars. There have been two vintages sold in this way, the 1969 and the 1970. I tasted the undosed 1969 at the end of 1987 – it was disgorged just before we drank it! Unlike the 1970, it is a Blanc de Blancs which, apparently, was not regarded highly as a very young wine. Much later, the Chiquet family retasted it and found that it had altered dramatically for the better. Certainly, it exploded on the palate with youth and freshness, with its slight taste of lime and a very silky texture – it went down very well while talking in the office one early afternoon, but it would also be superb with foie gras. A year earlier I had tasted the 1970, disgorged on November 5, 1985 (so with a year of cellaring after dégorgement). This was glorious, with the tiniest bubbles, a smell of lemon and honey, and a rich, deep, heady taste – there were apricots somewhere, too. A truly great champagne. As an extra bonus, the label for the 1970, with its pastel blue, green and gold colours, is a joy to behold – a reproduction of that used on the 1842 vintage.

Krug
····

It is no secret that I am a confirmed "krugiste". In a changing world, where one is constantly reappraising values and beliefs in the light of experience and shifting ethical standards, Krug stands as solid and as reassuring as ever. This edifice to quality and consistently high standards remains a monument to our ideas of excellence and a bastion in our fight against mediocrity. We all aspire to be a little like the Krugs and their wine, to have intrinsic worth, to reach a level of achievement which others can respect and of which we ourselves can be proud. If, somehow, all this is not possible, one can drink their champagne, bask in their reflected glory, and become "krugiste".

To be a Krug is to combine the Protestant work ethic with inspiration and flair. It is also to have a somewhat mischievous sense of humour. The Krugs were both proud and quietly amused that their vintage champagne was served to Pope John Paul on his Aer Lingus flight from Shannon to Boston in October 1979. On an only slightly more serious note, they were also pleased that it might have been a small gesture towards ecumenism.

In fact, anyone drinking Krug, at any time, is contributing towards better understanding between men. For it would be impossible to entertain feelings of rancour or bitterness while drinking such exquisite nectar. The sole cause for dissatisfaction has only ever been shortage of supply. However, most of us are tolerant of deficient quantity when we know an "objet de luxe" takes years to make and when we are sure that principles will never waver in its making. With the Krugs this is a certainty, and it is to the credit of their parent company, Rémy Martin, that the family remains in complete control of winemaking and policy. It is confidence that has rarely been as well placed.

Jean-Joseph Krug, born in Mainz but naturalized French in that eventful year of 1848, founded the firm in 1843. He was followed by his son, Paul, with

··········

Henri Krug, winemaker extraordinaire, with his barrels, to which the firm remains faithfully attached. The first fermentation takes place in these old casks, a method that is tailor-made for the complex Krug style and the immense potential for longevity found in the wines. It is a moot point whether the bouquet is more heady in one of these empty casks or in a Krug champagne itself.

whom I have a particular affinity, for it was he who, in 1880, sold his Private Cuvée in England for six shillings the bottle. Given the high standard of that nostalgic name, it was not surprising that in 1891 he announced a price rise of five shillings the case, due to the rarity of wines of quality. Paul's son, Joseph II, was a passionate traveller (a character trait common in the great Champagne families) but, again, like so many Champenois, he was caught up in the turmoil of World War I and was wounded and taken prisoner during the battle of the Ardennes. In his absence his wife, Jeanne, supervised the making of the 1915, a landmark Krug wine composed entirely of black grapes as the Chardonnays could not get through to Reims from the Côte des Blancs. When Joseph returned after the war, his health had so suffered that it was feared he could not run the firm on his own, so his nephew, Jean Seydoux, joined him. This was a happy and long partnership and, in fact, Joseph did not die until the ripe old age of 97, which illustrates that with champagne at one's side it does not do to be pessimistic about one's life expectancy.

Joseph's son, Paul, began working in the business in 1935, joining his father and cousin Jean Seydoux. He became managing director in 1941 and Joseph retired in 1958. Paul led the Krugs into a new era. Although the family believe that everyone has their role in Champagne – the growers their vineyards, the négociants the blending and sale of their cuvées – they also think it prudent that a champagne house should control a proportion of its own needs. Between 1970 and 1972, therefore, the Krugs bought 15.87 hectares of vines, and they now have about nine hectares of Pinot Noir at Aÿ and six of Chardonnay at Le Mesnil-sur-Oger, including the 1.87 hectares of Le Clos du Mesnil. The vineyards are all rated 100 percent and represent about 20 percent of the requirements of the house. These are the "crus de base" for the blends but, in 1974, the Krugs also signed a long-term contract for a significant supply of grapes from Avize, one of the essential components of their grande cuvée.

Now, Paul Krug's oldest son, Henri, is president and head of the house and is responsible for making the wine. His brother, Rémi, is managing director, in charge of sales and promotions across the world; both have roles which admirably suit their characters. When it comes to the crucial decisions involved in blending the cuvées, all three take part in the tastings, and devotees of Krug will be happy to learn that there are a mass of young members of the family waiting in the wings. This direct continuity ensures that the "Krug taste" is preserved by palates that are positively impregnated with the house style and know what they require in a champagne.

About 500,000 bottles are produced each year, and their stock amounts to the equivalent of more than six years' sales, something of a record in Champagne. It can be imagined that the high stocks are not due to sluggish demand for Krug but to an insistence on ageing the wines for an exceptionally long time. This is a policy designed to suit the Krug taste, which begins by a first fermentation in 205-litre oak casks of an average age of 35 years. The reserve wines are kept in 40-hectolitre stainless-steel vats. (This is the reverse of the Roederer policy, which does not stop the two houses displaying a high level of mutual respect.) No particular effort is made to manipulate the malolactic fermentation – sometimes it can take place in cask, but usually it happens in bottle after the prise de mousse. As Krug bottles remain many years in their cellars before disgorging, the effects of this process have disappeared long before they would be noticed by the consumer. Perhaps this fermentation in wood helps induce the very small bubbles you see in Krug, although it is also a question of yeast and cellar temperature. Certainly, if you put your nose into a Krug cask, your senses are assailed by a scent of searing intensity, rather like a perfume from Guerlain!

It is easier to begin to comprehend the complexity of a Krug wine when actually tasting it.

Grande Cuvée: This is the Krug flagship, and 80 percent of their total production. The one I am drinking at the moment is composed of no less than 47 different wines chosen from eight vintages, which is something of an awe-inspiring logistical exercise. The grape variety composition will vary according to the cuvée, with Pinot Noir between 45 and 55 percent, Pinot Meunier 10–15 percent and Chardonnay 35–45 percent. It is not surprising that the wine possesses richness, depth and complexity in abundance, as well as enormous potential for ageing further in bottle if you like an even more "intellectual" taste. There is always harmony, elegance and finesse, with a totally brut character allied to suppleness. For those who remember the famed and fabulous Private Cuvée, the Grande Cuvée has more Chardonnay. But the other difference is that there was no input from Aÿ in the Private Cuvée, and wines from Aÿ develop more quickly than wines from other parts of the Montagne de Reims. I would judge that Grande Cuvée is at its peak sooner than Private Cuvée, which aged in a quite extraordinary manner, but it is also fair to say that no one has yet cellared Grande Cuvée for very long: it was only launched in 1978.

Krug Vintage: Obviously, the grape variety composition differs with the year, and Henri Krug is a master of enhancing certain qualities in a given vintage by judicious blending, just as the same process can compensate for those ingredients which are lacking in another year. The 1979, for example, was composed of 36 percent Pinot Noir, 28 percent Pinot Meunier and 36 percent Chardonnay, and there were 29 different growths in the blend. In early 1988 it was only just beginning to come into its own.

I have had the immense good fortune to taste many older vintages of Krug, either as "standard" vintage, when they were 7–15 years old, or as later releases, when they are labelled Krug Collection. The 1976 is extraordinarily successful for the year, when many wines were somewhat "top heavy". By brilliant blending, Krug managed to make a wine with a flowery bouquet and a crunchy fruit taste – a vintage for the sensualist who likes a bit of flesh on the structure. A blend of 21 different growths and the product of a generous crop, there is almost a whiff of warm apples about it.

The 1975 is truly classic and will last for decades. The 1973, last drunk in magnum in 1987, has enormous grace and delicacy – the Krugs compare it to

The vineyards of Le Mesnil-sur-Oger, including the Clos du Mesnil. Krug now own the famous walled Clos, once part of a Benedictine monastery. Planted entirely in Chardonnay, it has a very favourable microclimate due to its perfect situation, and wine from the Clos can thus stand on its own as a great unblended champagne. Very light netting (foreground) is put over the vines in September to keep the birds away from the grapes.

Below: Two of France's most gifted chefs, Alain Senderens and Alain Chapel, have collaborated with Rémi Krug to create wonderful marriages of taste between Krug champagne and food.

their 1969. The 1971 had great beauty at a comparatively young (for Krug) age, but the 1973 may well outlast it.

Going into the decade of the 1960s, at one tasting I felt that the 1969 had definite similarities with 1962, and not only in near-identical total acidity levels, but more recent tastings of the 1962 show that they are moving apart. The 1969 is a sheer Krug year, bouncy, with verve and attack, destined for supremely beautiful old age — if you can resist its middle-aged attractions. It smells of acacia, as is sometimes noticeable in white burgundy and California Chardonnay. The result of a blend of 24 different growths, the 1969 has a dosage of one percent, necessary in a year with firm acidity — although, surprisingly, the other vintage with the same dosage was the 1976, with far less acidity. Such are the mysteries of champagne blending.

The 1964 is a classic. In fact, I was so bowled over with it at a 1985 tasting that I subsequently bought a case at auction and am enjoying it to this day. It has a glorious new-bread smell (not to be confused with "yeasty"), just like walking past a boulangerie early in the morning, and slips down with the ease displayed by all perfectly balanced wines, sensationally elegant and harmonious. The 1964 is a blend of 23 different growths, with rather less Chardonnay than in most other vintages but a hefty 53 percent Pinot Noir, a proportion only equalled in 1961.

The 1962 is very special, and not only because it was the first vintage made by Henri Krug — a remarkable "first attempt". It is an astonishing blend of 28 different growths, with a total acidity of around nine grams per litre, which undoubtedly contributed to the extraordinarily youthful nature of the wine when I tasted it in 1985. Then, both bouquet and palate were fresh and young, with the bottle-age giving it a honeyed finish which was exquisite. At the end of 1987 I tasted it again, and then it had much less mousse. It was a pronounced gold colour, but the vintage was deep-toned right from the beginning. It had the flavour of a great still white wine, something like a mature Laville Haut Brion in type and weight — logically, it should have been more like a Montrachet, with 36 percent Chardonnay, plus 38 percent Pinot Noir and 26 percent Meunier.

The 1961 was the last vintage that Paul Krug made alone, before Henri joined him. At a 1985 tasting it looked older than another view of it at the end of 1987 — and the 1987 bottle had been disgorged many years before, which proves the idiosyncracies of old wines. At the more recent tasting the 1961 was lighter in colour than the 1962, with an amazing stream of insistent bubbles. There was the boulangerie nose and an incredible, vibrant taste — a great bottle. Twenty different growths made this wine, and it is interesting to compare the grape proportions with those of the 1962: the 1961 was much stronger in Pinot Noir, with 53 percent, plus 35 percent Chardonnay and 12 percent Meunier.

Krug 1959 is another brilliant example of the blender's art, when the burning summer sometimes defeated the champagne makers' attempts to create a wine of elegance. Krug 1959 has a gloriously ripe nose and is bone dry, elegant and ethereal. It has practically no dosage (0.5 percent), which may well be why it is not in any way heavy like some 1959s, which took on a rather beery character with age. This is a wine for the aesthete, who likes the fine bones of beauty, made more apparent with age. It would be perfect with fresh foie gras.

I find it difficult to describe the 1945 – it is almost too personal. Suffice it to say that it is, to this day, magnificent, nutty, complex, and full of strength and verve. Then there is the extraordinary honeyed 1928, with its high proportion of Meunier grapes (just to defy the rule book!), an unbelievable experience when approaching its seventh decade. I have not myself drunk the 1906, but a wine-loving friend, who enjoyed it in Scotland in 1958, pronounced it the most delicious champagne of his life.

Krug Rosé: First produced in 1983, it is (with Roederer) the palest of all the "pink" champagnes: a pale yellow colour, like the sun coming up shyly on a winter morning. It has the most intense, piercing, almost "tawny" nose – a Krug bouquet. Very dry, tight and austere, but with the richness that the addition of reserve wines can give, it packs a punch of sheer concentration and ends on a Pinot note. The composition is 50–55 percent Noir, 20–25 percent Meunier, with Chardonnay making up the rest, and the colour is obtained by blending in selected Pinots Noirs from Aÿ which have been fermented on the skins.

Clos du Mesnil: This walled Clos has existed in the village of Le Mesnil-sur-Oger since 1698. Until 1750 it belonged to the Benedictine monastery of Le Mesnil. It was bought by the family in 1971, but the vines were so old that the Krugs needed to embark on a progressive programme of replanting. So it was not until the 1979 vintage that Clos du Mesnil was judged ready to meet the world, a pure Chardonnay champagne from a gentle, southeast-facing slope. Naturally, the wines are fermented exclusively in small oak casks. The unique position of the Clos persuaded the Krugs to depart from their fundamental belief in the art of blending in order to produce great champagne.

The 1979 vintage produced 15,512 bottles, but the 1980 only 9,988 and the 1981 vintage 12,793. I found the 1979 rather closed when it was first released but at eight years old it was showing real harmony. The 1980 has good structure and acidity balance, and needs keeping for a few more years. Undoubtedly, they are fine Chardonnay wines, although I am still searching for that extra dimension that is Krug. Perhaps I will find it around the corner when the wines (and the vines) have attained greater age, thus at last proving that the Chardonnay is the most long-lasting of grapes – a tenet held by some but which tasting has never yet proved to me. Or else, I will remain convinced that the greatest of champagnes are the result of a blend of grape varieties and sites.

The Krug taste is both majestic and magisterial. Does its remarkable bouquet and flavour, personality and longevity, come from the small oak barrels, allowing the wine to "breathe" during fermentation? I think it has a very significant influence, but there is also the raw material, the attention to detail, the ageing, the handmade quality. And there are the Krugs themselves, with their adherence to a certain vision of their wine, the palate memory of five generations without a break, their lack of compromise. Above all, the "Krug taste" is an idée fixe, an obsession of the noblest kind.

Lanson
· · · · ·

The champagne scene would not be the same without the tall, imposing presence of the Lanson family. Victor Lanson was a particularly monumental figure in every sense: it was he who pronounced the immortal words, "A magnum is the perfect size for two gentlemen". One can forgive him for not knowing the right kind of champagne-loving women. Like Pommery, Lanson is now owned by the giant French food corporation BSN, but Pierre and Jean-Baptiste Lanson are still very much at the helm. It was their father, Victor, who also said, "I make wine for myself. What I can't drink, I sell!". As production of Lanson is now running at between five and six million bottles a year, it is obvious that the family itself, however willing, needs a little help from the rest of us, a task we are happy to undertake.

Even without historical documents on the Lanson family, unfortunately lost during the course of the two World Wars (yet another reminder that the Champagne region has always been in the firing line of European disagreements), the value of continuity via six generations in the company has been considerable. Between the wars, Victor and Henri Lanson had the vision and economic courage to buy large parcels of vineyard in all the best sites. The 1930s were not, ostensibly, the best time to buy anything, with depression more than a state of mind, but the shrewdest members of the wine trade, whether in Champagne or Bordeaux, took advantage of the low prices and put their faith in the future. Now, 25–30 percent of the needs of the house are provided by their own vineyards and the firm is sure of a solid quality base.

It is worth looking at the actual vineyard breakdown, because the spread and variety of the crus is beautifully balanced:

COTE DES BLANCS:

66 hectares

Grapes: Chardonnay

Echelle rating: 100 percent

    Situated at: Avize, Cramant, Oger, Oiry, Chouilly

MONTAGNE DE REIMS:

43 hectares

Grapes: 37 ha Pinot Noir
      6 ha Chardonnay

Echelle rating: 100 percent

    Situated at: Ambonnay, Bouzy, Verzy, Verzenay, tiny holding at Beaumont

---

VALLEE DE LA MARNE:

65 hectares

Grapes: 52 ha Pinot Noir
      13 ha Chardonnay

Echelle ratings:

Mareuil-sur-Aÿ 99 percent,

Dizy 95 percent,

Hautvillers 93 percent,

small holding at Champillon 93 percent

There are also some 16 hectares in the Aube, but the grapes are used in Lanson's subsidiary marque, Massé.

Six pressing centres, with traditional presses, receive the grapes, and the must then goes to Lanson's premises just outside Reims, where there is a fine "parc" and even a few vines. The firm started to replace the wood fermentation casks in 1959 and completed the process in 1970, having installed a large amount of stainless steel in time to cope with the mammoth 1970 harvest. Lanson do not put their wines through malolactic fermentation, partly because they think the accompanying heat to induce the process is unadvisable, and partly because they consider that it helps their wines to keep well and maintain their freshness on their travels around the world. They are confident that their reserves and the quality of their crus give the necessary "ampleur", or weight and fullness, to their wines. Reserves, which are all-important, have on occasion been as high as 30 percent.

The bottling line, completed in 1987, can manage 16,000–18,000 bottles per hour, but there is nothing lightning about the ageing period after the prise de mousse, which takes two years pre-dégorgement. Bottles are also stocked for six to eight months after disgorging and the addition of the liqueur d'expédition. Lanson had their first machine for automatic disgorging in 1967.

Black Label Non-Vintage: This is the big seller for Lanson, with more than 90

Jean-Baptiste (left) and Pierre Lanson, with an illuminated map of the Lanson vineyards. Most champagne houses have a plan of their vineyard holdings, with the press centres and buildings where pickers are lodged also marked. The Lanson family had the vision to buy vineyards during the depressed period between the two World Wars, and this foresight has stood the house in good stead.

percent of the total output. Made of 40 percent Chardonnay and 60 percent Pinot Noir, with some Meunier in the percentage of black grapes, it is always an easy, fruity style, perfect for those who fear manifestations of acidity. The nose is usually quite mature, due to Lanson's policy of not rushing the bottles out of the cellars, and sometimes the dosage can be on the high side – a "soft-landings" kind of champagne.

Vintage: I find these really show the quality of the house, and a vertical tasting of Lanson vintages is always a lesson in the characteristics of each year.

1982: 45 percent Chardonnay and 55 percent Pinot Noir produced a fruity, attractive wine which is thoroughly appealing.

1981: 46 percent Chardonnay, 54 percent Pinot Noir, and a wine of immense character. Wonderfully deep and very well balanced.

1979: 50 percent Chardonnay, 50 percent Pinot Noir. What a deliciously "easy" wine, just like the vintage! But the Lanson '79 took its time to show its real paces which, in 1987 in magnum, were impressive. It is a lovely, round, fruity wine, with a touch of fresh bread to it and a real fruit profile (always the aim at Lanson). I defy anyone not to fall for this one.

1976: 54 percent Chardonnay, 46 percent Pinot Noir. The high proportion of Chardonnay has contributed to making this more elegant and lighter than many 1976s.

1975: 45 percent Chardonnay, 55 percent Pinot Noir. (This was the time of the "piano-legs" shape bottle – or, in my case, magnum, when I last tasted it in 1987.) The wine has a really biscuity nose in the glass and the flavour a wonderful edge to it, which will soften and develop with more cellaring.

1971: 50 percent Chardonnay, 50 percent Pinot Noir. When last tasted, in 1987, it was still young, with a hazelnut, keen bouquet and elements of hawthorn. I liked the touch of austerity, which some might put down to the "drying out" process of age but which, for me, is just the style of the wine.

225 – 1980 vintage: This is Lanson's top champagne, made originally in the 1980 vintage to celebrate Lanson's 225th year of champagne-making and presented in a facsimile of their 1760 bottle: 55 percent Chardonnay, 45 percent Pinot Noir, selected from this smallish vintage, from five of Lanson's own 100 percent-rated vineyards at Avize and Cramant for the Chardonnay, and Ambonnay, Bouzy and Verzenay for the Pinot Noir. It has a really flowery, elegant nose, and is brut and perfect for a stylish apéritif.

225 – 1981 vintage: Again, this is extremely elegant, with great finesse and a lovely finish.

Noble Cuvée: Whereas 225 is all finesse, this other Lanson "de-luxe" champagne is more powerful, with a slighty higher proportion of black grapes. Again, in the 18th-century replica bottle, the first vintage was the 1979, although there was a non-vintage blend before this.

Rosé: Made from 40 percent Chardonnay and 60 percent Pinot Noir, with an addition of red wine for the colour, the topaz shade leads on to a definite taste, full of quite austere fruit.

Laurent-Perrier

Laurent-Perrier is undoubtedly the star of the post-World War II years, amazing in the rapidity of its rise. It is a brilliantly managed house, where hard work and flair have paid the kind of dividends one dreams about. The remarkable Bernard de Nonancourt has been the mastermind, and he has surrounded himself with one of the most competent teams in Champagne. When La Veuve Laurent-Perrier died in 1925, the house lapsed in dramatic fashion: it was hardly more than a marque when Marie-Louise de Nonancourt, sister of Victor and Henri Lanson, acquired it on the eve of World War II. Her son, Bernard, spent much of the war in the Resistance, and took over the firm in 1949. Then Laurent-Perrier was selling 80,000 bottles; now it sells 7–7.5 million, making it the most important family-owned firm in Champagne.

This is an extraordinary achievement, where vision is underpinned by solid structure. Laurent-Perrier own outright 80 hectares of vines, but their contracts with growers give them a total of 800 hectares with an average rating of 96 percent. This provides them with a massive choice on the Montagne de Reims and the Côte des Blancs; their cuvées are mostly composed of Pinot Noir and Chardonnay, with very little Meunier. These supply contracts and vineyards provide 87 percent of the house's requirements, giving them room for manoeuvre each vintage dependent upon its intrinsic quality. Laurent-Perrier like to say that "a good contract is worth more than a bad wine", which is typical of the good sense prevailing in the firm. They have a very close relationship with more than 1,000 growers, whose loyalty to the house is part of its success.

Bernard de Nonancourt, head of Laurent-Perrier and one of the most remarkable men in Champagne. When he took over the house in 1949, it sold 80,000 bottles; now it sells more than 7 million, making it the most important family-owned firm in Champagne. A dedicated chasseur in his spare time, his labrador is never far from his side – labradors seem to be the most popular dog among the hunting Champenois.

Alain Terrier, Laurent-Perrier's cellarmaster and chief oenologist, with different lots of grape juice in his laboratory. At this early stage the must is thick and murky, and it is difficult to believe that this unedifying liquid will one day be great champagne.

Behind the zooming sales and conquests of international markets, Laurent-Perrier remains a very traditional house. Twenty percent of the cuvées receive cork closures instead of crown caps for the second fermentation, remuage is entirely manual, and disgorging "à la volée" is still used in some cases. But Laurent-Perrier's exceptionally gifted cellar master and chief oenologist, Alain Terrier, oversees a remarkable "armoury" of temperature-controlled stainless-steel vats, with work arranged on four levels to use natural gravity instead of pumping. This kind of technical mastery can enable the house to make its high-selling rosé by the "saignée" method, with a vatting of 48 to 72 hours.

Laurent-Perrier was the forerunner in the development of a lighter, more elegant style, with the emphasis on finesse and freshness. This does not mean that the wines have lost their vinosity: they have definite character and the top cuvées are some of the best in Champagne. There is about all of them an aura of good breeding: Laurent-Perrier is a very "bon chic, bon genre" champagne. Families in France often acquire their Laurent-Perrier direct (a very important part of the house's sales on the home market), while abroad it is always "de bon ton" to offer it. Good taste evolves from a civilized approach to life – and a visit to Laurent-Perrier in sleepy Tours-sur-Marne, in the heart of the vineyards, would convert the most sceptical. Never has a giant business been as picturesque or as discreet.

Brut NV: I remember a time, more than 15 years ago, when I found Laurent-Perrier NV somehow slight and lemony. This is most certainly no longer the case. The bouquet is floral and nutty, very showy. The style is well and truly brut, and it has a real kernel of champagne flavour to it. An utterly satisfying example of what the region produces.

Crémant NV: This cuvée mystifies me somewhat. It is only available in France. I had a splendid bottle at the Reims restaurant Le Florence, when it was fruity and beautifully balanced, and lovely with both foie gras and a pot au feu de la mer of red mullet, salmon and sole; then, two months later, I bought a bottle in a shop in Epernay and it was crude, coarse and tasted of vin de taille. Given the formidable reputation of Laurent-Perrier, it seems a pity to jeopardize it in any way with cuvées that are less than perfect, whatever the commercial pressures of the French market.

Vintage Brut: The 1982 vintage sports a new gold standard label. The nose has an abundance of flowers (very 1982) and the taste is round and delicious. Some people consider it a little "sweet"; I think subsequent releases of this vintage may be a little drier.

Rosé Brut NV: When the "pink newspaper", the *Financial Times*, celebrated its centenary at the end of 1987, it chose Laurent-Perrier rosé to mark the occasion: the centenary logo appeared on the neck label of the traditional embossed "dump" bottle. The colour is a pretty pink-orange, the bubbles are tiny and there is a fresh appley smell. The taste is blossomy and fresh, ready to stimulate the appetite. There is vinosity behind the prettiness, and it seems drier than a few years ago, which is all to the better.

A fascinating advertisement for Laurent-Perrier, announcing the availability of Sans Sucre champagne, the true brut that the British, particularly, favoured. Royal and aristocratic customers are supplemented by Madame Adelina Patti, the opera singer, whose long career was no doubt helped by champagne (we know she also liked white Graves). The three vintages on sale were all very fine indeed.

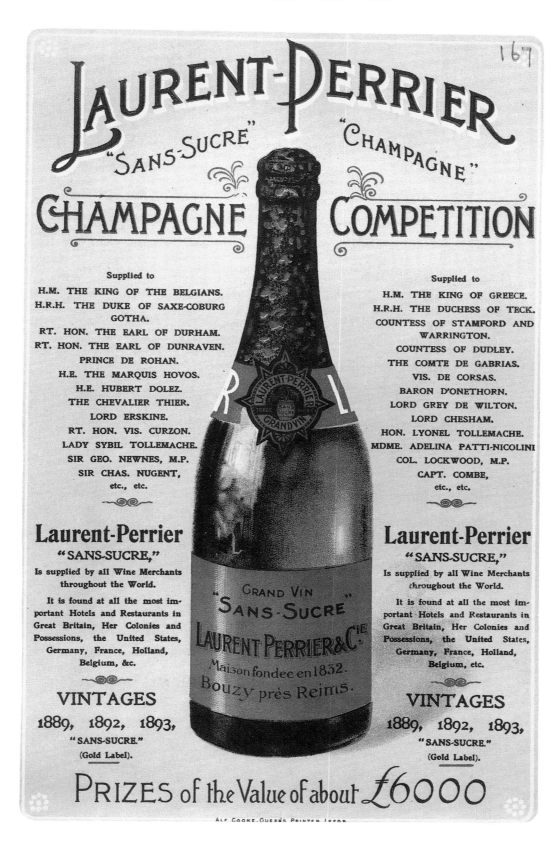

Every year, Laurent-Perrier awards the Prix Grand Siècle to a highly deserving individual or group, drawn from every conceivable aspect of life. Some of the winners have been Rostropovich for his help to dissidents in the Soviet Union, Lord Mountbatten for his presidency of the United World Colleges, Mrs Kennedy-Shriver for her work with handicapped children and the French Red Cross for its dedicated voluntary work. Perhaps champagne lovers everywhere should award Grand Siècle a special prize for enhancing our wine-drinking lives.

Ultra Brut NV: This is a wine with no dosage, and I can only say that with every cuvée Laurent-Perrier master this art to a greater degree. In 1988 the wine has a wonderful intense bouquet, with flowers but also added complexity. The taste is both classic and austere, *the* great champagne with oysters. I find it endlessly fascinating in the glass. Normally it has a strong Chardonnay influence and is based on a ripe year, necessary when there is no sugar to camouflage.

Millésime Rare: One of the most multi-dimensional vintage champagnes currently on the market. Outstanding years are kept sur pointes and released at a later date. Both the 1973 and the 1975 were simply marvellous in 1988, although Alain Terrier tells me that when the 1975 was young, its "musqué" character caused them problems. Actually, I am never averse to a little muskiness, but that is all history, and the wine is now a classic of the genre.

Cuvée Grand Siècle: Grand Siècle almost requires a book to itself. It is one of the greatest champagnes that exist, and its history and makeup deserve some study. But before the wine, the bottle: it is a replica of one that was blown in 1705 at the time of Louis XIV, the Sun King. I can only say that it is worthy of the wine inside it.

In February 1988, Laurent-Perrier organized for me in their cellars in Tours-sur-Marne an incomparable tasting of Grand Siècle cuvées, all disgorged just before tasting, and all in magnum except two, which I will indicate. It was the most intellectually fascinating champagne tasting of my life.

Grand Siècle is always a blend of three vintages, with the emphasis on the last vintage of the trio. In the United States, where the vintage seems to be inordinately important, it is sold with a date, and the last one I tasted was the 1979. The difference between the two cuvées is not as great as would be imagined, but I do think the European cuvée has the edge for complexity. The scope that a non-vintage cuvée can give a master blender in Champagne should never be underestimated.

Grand Siècle 1952/53/55: Bottled April 1956, sold from 1959. Nose slightly petrolly at first, like so many old wines, then becoming coffee scented. Taste of walnuts. Very round and immensely rich. Old champagne, but what an experience.

Grand Siècle 1961/64/66 (in bottle): Bottled May 1967, sold from 1970. A really mineral, almost salty nose. Finishes in a taste of warm bread – old, but much younger than the previous cuvée.

Grand Siècle 1966/69/70: Bottled April 1971, sold from 1975. A nose of hazelnuts and butter that is just beginning to melt in a pan. A marriage of elegance and richness, with a lovely nervy tension – like a racehorse raring to go!

Grand Siècle 1970/73/75 (in bottle): Bottled March 1976, sold from 1980. There is an immensely opulent character to this wine, which comes out of the glass to meet you. The finish is of both hazelnuts and walnuts, leading to a really honeyed flavour.

Grand Siècle 1973/75/76: Bottled April 1977, sold from 1981. Normally there is more wine from the most recent vintage in the blend, but this was the exception, given the special nature of the 1976 harvest which needed to be carefully counterbalanced by more orthodox years. There is a bouquet of clean linen (fanciful, but true), with a certain stoniness and classicism which I associate with 1975. The wine is a keeper, very solid and the most powerful and perfectly composed of the whole collection.

Grand Siècle 1975/76/78: Bottled April 1979, sold from January 1983. A touch of hawthorn on the nose; the taste is minerally, buttery, more mature than the cuvée above, ageing faster than some of the other blends.

Grand Siècle 1976/78/79: Bottled March 1981, sold from 1986. Another "clean-sheets" nose, something I find very pleasing. This cuvée has real finesse and a very lacy character – ideal apéritif champagne and totally seductive.

Grand Siècle 1978/79/82: Appearing on the market as we tasted. The nose is floral with toasty elements, the flavour as flowery as the 1982 vintage influence would suggest. To savour over the next few years – and more.

It almost goes without saying that the component parts of Grand Siècle are all 100 percent on the échelle. The grape variety blend is on average 50 percent Chardonnay, 50 percent Pinot Noir, but the proportion of each can vary between 40 to 60 percent according to the cuvées.

The exciting news for the future is that Laurent-Perrier will shortly bring out a new cuvée de prestige on which they have been working for several years. It will be a rosé, the vintage will be 1982 and the bottle will be the same as for Grand Siècle. The name (in spring 1988) has not been decided, but it is clear that the champagne will be very special: a rosé made with pressing and skin contact, vatting together Pinot Noir and Chardonnay.

Abel Lepitre/Georges Goulet

These two houses are owned by Les Grands Vins Chatellier, under the chairmanship of Félix Chatellier, who is also proprietor of Château Dauzac in Margaux. George Goulet was founded in Reims in 1867; Abel Lepitre has existed as a house since 1924. The two champagnes are now made very much in tandem, although their identities on each market are kept separate. Both enjoy the benefits of "crayères" cellars, although at the end of November 1987 the abnormal amount of rain meant that one had to paddle rather than walk through them. There is also another cellar on the outskirts of Reims, not as quaintly picturesque as the 1920 rustic-beams style of the buildings over the Gallo-Roman crayères.

Remuage is manual and the prise de mousse takes place in bottle sizes up to the giant Methuselah. The houses own no vineyards but buy from 20 different communes in the proportion of 60 percent Pinot Noir, 30 percent Chardonnay and ten percent Pinot Meunier. The Abel Lepitre marque is concentrated on France and French-speaking markets; George Goulet is better known in Britain and the northern countries. Sales of Abel Lepitre are 500,000 bottles annually, of George Goulet 200,000 bottles.

I have to say that of all the tastings made during the preparation of this book, this was where I found the least interesting wines. This is a pity, especially with regard to the crémant blanc de blancs which has always been a firm favourite of mine. In any case, this wine was phased out at the beginning of 1988, in view of the move away from the use of the word "crémant". In future, it will be a vintage blanc de blancs.

George Goulet 1982 (Crémant) Blanc de Blancs: This wine is essentially from the Côte des Blancs – Avize, Cramant, Le Mesnil-sur-Oger, Oger and Vertus – together with a little Chardonnay from the Montagne de Reims. The nose is slightly lemony, and there is freshness and good balance with acidity. It just does not seem quite as charming as in the past.

Brut NV: Composed of 55 percent Pinot Noir from the Montagne de Reims, 30 percent Chardonnay from the Côte des Blancs and 15 percent Pinot Meunier from the Vallée de la Marne. The just-disgorged bottle that I last sampled had a nose that was marked by the recent dosage and was thus rather coarse.

George Goulet 1982: The Chardonnay came through quite strongly here, although the cuvée contains only 15 percent from the Côte des Blancs. The wine is predominantly made up of 75 percent Pinot Noir from Verzenay, Bouzy and Louvois, together with ten percent Meunier. The nose is floral but the taste, at the end of 1987, was still quite sharp and green.

Abel Lepitre 1982: In magnum, this seemed very similar to the George Goulet from the same vintage.

Rosé 1982: A composition of 55 percent Pinot Noir and 30 percent Chardonnay, with the addition of 15 percent Bouzy Rouge. A full wine, not the most elegant, but good body.

George Goulet Cuvée du Centenaire 1982: 70 percent Chardonnay from Avize, Cramant and Le Mesnil-sur-Oger, with 30 percent Pinot Noir from Verzenay, Aÿ and Bouzy. The nose is more complete and complex, even musky and smoky. The palate is still young and this should be viewed again after a couple of years.

A particularly racy form of champagne promotion – a pair of garters with each bottle! Needless to say, this special offer was available in the unbridled days of the end of the last century, when champagne flowed with a will and gentlemen formed liaisons that were not always "comme il faut".

Mercier
• • • • •

This is a marque that really belongs to the French. If the average Frenchman had to name one champagne house, the odds are that it would be Mercier. That same man is probably only going to buy a bottle of champagne a few times a year, for a birthday or an anniversary: he is most likely to go to a supermarket or the shop on the corner and his choice will fall on Mercier. Since 1970, Mercier has belonged to Moët-Hennessy, but its identity has been kept strictly separate from its giant cousin. France takes more than 3.5 million bottles a year (about 85 percent of sales), while Great Britain absorbs more than 500,000 bottles, more than 12 percent of sales.

Mercier was founded in 1858 by Eugène Mercier, a master of the grand plan. He supervised the excavation of the vast cellars, stretching for 18 kilometres: in the 1950s, a car rally was held in them! Most visitors make the trip in an electric train and I have no shame in saying that is how I saw my first Champagne cellar. Eugène Mercier's greatest publicity coup was the construction of a giant oak cask, which he then had hauled to Paris, not without some damage to buildings and trees on the route, for the Exhibition of 1889. Today, Mercier has a hot-air balloon, carrying on a tradition started in 1900.

The house has 176 hectares of vines in production, which represents about 20 percent of its requirements. The vineyards are scattered over the entire Champagne region and there is a preponderance of Pinot Meunier. The other 80 percent of the grapes needed come from contracts with growers: it is worth noting that Moët & Chandon, Mercier and Ruinart between them buy about 25 percent of the total amount of grapes available on the market. Winemaking is supervised by the Moët technical team, but in 1987 it was agreed that the huge modern Centre Viticole de Chouilly should make the champagne. Stocks are the equivalent of 12.5 million bottles.

It may be fashionable to decry Mercier, but every time I am offered the non-vintage, in particular, I am impressed. This could be because I drink it more often in Britain than in France, where impressions are not as glowing. But the real test of unprejudiced wine opinion is a blind tasting, and here Mercier often comes out extremely well with a wide spectrum of tasters. Its secret is that it is blended to appeal to "le grand public", of which I am clearly a paid-up member.

Brut Réserve NV: (In France called Brut Non-Millésimé.) The non-vintage is always a very black-grape wine, the Meunier in it conferring a delicate scent and a soft taste. It is gentle, seductive and mouth-filling, and invariably satisfying. The French "version" tends to be coarser but still fulfils its role admirably.

Brut Réserve 1982: The colour is greeny gold and the bubbles are tiny; the bouquet is clean and fresh but fairly neutral. On the palate there is good fruit, but the finish appears to be slightly coarse and perhaps a bit sweet, to cover just that aspect. I always feel that, in Britain, the non-vintage is a far better bottle in terms of sheer enjoyment.

Brut Réserve Rosé 1982: Orange-pink in colour, the bouquet is richly Pinot and

Mercier's giant oak cask, with a capacity equal to 200,000 bottles, which 24 oxen hauled to Paris for the Exhibition of 1889. Publicity coups of this magnitude are rare even today. The intricate carving was carried out by the Reims sculptor Navlet – although whether the figure in the alcove approves is another matter.

the taste is round, ripe and grapey. This is very good mealtime rosé champagne, especially with pink lamb.

Extra Rich: (Sold on the British market; the French have Demi-Sec.) Greeny gold, with bead-like bubbles. Good strong, clean, winey nose. The taste is clean and fruity and very sweet. You have to have a sweet tooth to like this, but it is well made and not coarse grained.

Cuvée M33, Brut Vintage 1955: At Easter 1988, a very kind Bordelais friend gave me this mystery bottle. It came from cellars in Anjou and had obviously been very well kept. Apparently this was a one-off cuvée de prestige reserved for restaurants and certainly, when compared with the straight 1955 vintage, there was a distinct difference in breed. We cannot know how the assemblage was made up, but the wine was extraordinary. It was very pale for its year and had a lovely, short-lived crown of bubble when poured. The bouquet was intense, toasty, while the taste was of fresh brioche, slightly minerally on the finish.

The good news is that in 1988 Mercier are launching a new cuvée de prestige, the non-vintage Bulle d'Or. Reports are that it will be full, honeyed and hawthorn scented. If it is half as good as the Cuvée M33, we shall be in for a treat.

Moët & Chandon

The greatest mistake anyone can make in judging champagne is to under-estimate Moët & Chandon. In this case, Big really is Beautiful. Once any giant concern has decided on excellence, it is actually often easier for them to achieve it than for medium-sized operations. They have the money: thereafter, all they need is the will and the organization.

Moët have both, in superabundance. The evolution of the house should be made required reading for every student of business. One wonders if Claude Moët, who founded the house of Moët in 1743, had any idea of what he was starting. Succeeded by his son and grandson, it then passed to the latter's son Victor Moët and son-in-law Pierre-Gabriel Chandon. The house thus became Moët & Chandon and acquired the Abbey of Hautvillers and its vineyards – giving it almost divine right over the name of Dom Pérignon. Moët & Chandon acquired control of Mercier and Ruinart in the early 1970s and in 1971 merged with Hennessy. Diversification was relentless: Christian Dior, vineyards in the Napa Valley and Brazil, companies producing roses. Finally (perhaps that word is unsafe in the context of Moët), in 1987, Moët-Hennessy merged with Louis Vuitton, which already owned Veuve Clicquot and Henriot, giving the group immense development potential on a global scale.

In all the plethora of statistics that emanate from this most dynamic of houses, the two that I like most are that one in every four bottles of champagne exported comes from Moët & Chandon, and a Moët cork pops every two seconds somewhere in the world. As I pop so many of them, there must be areas where drinkers are not contributing their share.

Moët own 459 hectares of vines, 84 percent with a rating of between 90 and 100 percent. They are spread over the entire area of Champagne and are in all three grape varieties. There are 127 hectares on the Côte des Blancs, 119 hectares in the Grande Vallée de la Marne, 49 hectares in the region of Verzenay and 41 hectares in the Aisne – and plenty more besides.

But all this only provides about 20 percent of Moët's requirements in grapes; the rest come from the vast network of contracts that the group maintains with the growers. Sales in 1987 amounted to more than 25 million bottles, with almost 20 million exported and 5.5 million sold in France. Moët & Chandon represent 17 percent of the sales of all champagne houses, taking 7.6 percent of sales on the French market and 26 percent of sales abroad. Stocks are the equivalent of 87 million bottles (this includes actual bottles, reserve wines and wines in vat).

The socio-economic ramifications of such an enterprise are considerable. For example, Moët and Mercier together employ more than 2,300 pickers at vintage time, all lodged and fed in the company vendangeoirs. In the Moët, Mercier, Ruinart group, well over 2,000 people are employed full time in offices, cellars and vineyards. It has always been thought that any technical change in the winemaking process would see its most dramatic effects at Moët but, in fact, the research that they have led into "les billes", or yeast capsules, would ultimately have far more effect on space in the cellar than on personnel. Moët's 28 kilometres of cellars are now fully stretched, as all remuage is by hand, but the use of encapsulated yeasts on an industrial scale cannot be applied for several years.

This has been the aspect of Moët & Chandon's technical research that has interested so many concerned with champagne's future, but the group has always been at the forefront of research which, when developed, will benefit the whole industry. Investment has also gone into studying the application of in-vitro techniques to the vine and improving fermentation. Moët work with the Institut de la Recherche Agronomique (INRA), the CIVC, the Faculty of Science at Reims University, the food concern BSN and St. Gobain glass on ways to improve winemaking, the structure and shape of bottle that will best facilitate the descent of the sediment, and the taste of corks. The formidable Moët technical team includes Edmond Maudière (who also masterminded Domaine Chandon in Napa), Philippe Coulon and Dominique Foulon. If every winemaking region of France had a team of this calibre, there might well be greater consistency in quality overall.

Moët led the way into stainless-steel cuves and have always laid great importance on the choice of yeasts for the first fermentation so that it finishes cleanly and well, in spite of anti-rot treatments in the vineyards which have caused some fermentations to "stick". A centrifuge is not used for the débourbage (it takes too many elements away from the must), but after the alcoholic and malolactic fermentations it is used to give a completely clear wine which in turn then requires less sulphur – the SO_2 cannot combine with any impurities. The emphasis at Moët is on working with a clean, pure base, but never on removing too much from the raw material which would give a champagne with too neutral a taste. Moët's wines have character. Balance is also something they regard as vital – the balance between finesse and flavour, vinosity and lightness of touch.

This massive empire is presided over by Yves Bénard, who also happens to be mayor of his little village of Boursault. Moët buy the grapes from the 17 hectares of vines that belong to the Château de Boursault, once the home of La Veuve Clicquot and now lovingly restored to its ornate splendour.

Brut Impérial NV: (Called Première Cuvée in Britain.) Made from Chardonnay, Pinot Noir and Pinot Meunier. This is a house that is (rightly, in my opinion) not at all apologetic about using Meunier; when from good sites and blended well, it gives scent and softness to champagnes that are going to be drunk relatively young. Moët non-vintage always has a real "champagne nose", fine fruit and flavour and is emphatically "black grape" in style – although recent blind tastings have also elicited remarks such as "pretty" and "lemony", perhaps denoting a lighter influence.

Brut Impérial Millésimé: Made from Chardonnay and usually a higher proportion of Pinot Noir, with a small amount of Meunier, this is one of the most reliable of all vintage champagnes. It is also made to last, and there is nothing more reassuring than seeing a magnum of Moët vintage with some bottle-age on a

host's table. In 1988 we are enjoying the 1982, a fragrant, delicate, floral wine, with a most enticing taste and Moët's customary balance. There was a classic, hawthorn-scented 1981, more austere than the 1982; unlike virtually every other house, Moët did not do a 1979. I was particularly fond of the 1976, which was both creamy and heady at the same time. I enjoyed both the 1980 and the 1978 but neither is a "laying down" Moët. Other highlights have been the Silver Jubilee cuvée of 1977, released to celebrate Queen Elizabeth II's 25 years on the throne but which was, in fact, the splendid 1971 vintage, and a highly successful 1970 which aged beautifully.

Brut Millésimé Rosé: Usually made from 25 percent Chardonnay and 75 percent Pinot Noir that is partly vinified as red wine from Bouzy. This is always a rosé of deep colour and vinosity, which gains in bouquet and complexity with bottle-age and goes superbly with food, particularly pink lamb. The 1982 is topaz pink with a bouquet of raspberries and Pinot Noir. The taste is very red fruit, with redcurrants on the palate, but the style is more apéritif than most Moët rosés, due to the vintage character. The 1981 is big and cushiony, the 1980 not quite as impressive and the 1978 very strawberryish. The 1973 has gone well with strawberry soufflé and the 1970 was always good.

Jean-Rémy Moët commissioned Jean-Baptiste Isabey, the fashionable miniaturist of Napoleonic society, to design this elegant orangery and sunken formal garden opposite what are now the offices of Moët & Chandon in Epernay. The reflections in the long rectangular pool are real, and not the result of generous hospitality at the Trianon.

Mucha, the Czech poster artist, was much in demand at the end of the last century. He designed posters and menus for Ruinart, Moët & Chandon and Heidsieck Monopole, and his elongated ladies have become instantly recognizable.

• • • • • • • • • •

Dom Pérignon: 50 percent Chardonnay and 50 percent Pinot Noir (although this can vary ten percent either way, as in the 1982, which is 60 percent Chardonnay, 40 percent Pinot Noir) and all with a vineyard rating of 100 percent. At the sight of the dark, dump-shaped bottle, bronze-coloured foil and heart-shaped label, most wine lovers' legs turn to jelly! Dom Pérignon is certainly the cuvée de prestige with the highest profile. Put on the market in 1936 by the dynamic Robert-Jean de Vogüé, it was the first luxury champagne of modern times (although Cristal was the one first created). It was the 1921 vintage and it sailed to New York in the liner *Normandie.*

Behind the hype, Dom Pérignon is a superb champagne, maintaining constant excellence in spite of its enormously increased sales. It is worth noting that it can be a little higher in alcohol than Moët's other champagnes because the grapes that go in it come from the best, most sunlit sites. With age, Dom Pérignon takes on a totally seductive fresh-toast-and-coffee bouquet, one of the most intriguing scents in champagne. Magnums of the 1961, disgorged in 1981 on the occasion of the Prince of Wales' wedding, are undoubtedly one of the finest champagnes I have ever tasted, although the coffee-ish 1964 is not far behind. The 1969 is extraordinarily fine, and the 1976 is faultless – one could drink it for ever. At the moment, we ponder over the 1978 and the 1980, both of which make delicious "young" drinking. The next vintage will be the 1982.

Dom Pérignon Rosé: Known affectionately in the United States as DPR, the colour is sometimes obtained by the "saignée" process of vinification, rather than by blending in red wine. For example, the 1985 rosé was achieved by this method, as the colour in the perfectly ripe grapes that year was so perfect. Made from Chardonnay and Pinot Noir, the first vintage was the 1959 but it was produced exclusively for the Shah of Iran's entertaining. The first commercial vintage was the 1962, sold in 1970. I do not see it nearly as often as the blanc, but have always found it both delicate and full, with great length of flavour and elegance. The 1980 was 65 percent Pinot Noir, partly vinified as red wine from

Bouzy, and 35 percent Chardonnay. It is quite a deep pink, with dynamic bubbles charging up the centre of the glass and exploding on the surface like an erupting volcano. There is a very fruity bouquet of crushed strawberries and cream and a taste like strawberry cup – very youthful. I would love to keep this for another five years to see how complex it becomes.

Mumm

Mumm has always been better known and better appreciated in the United States than in Britain: in this instance, it is the "new" country that must teach the old about the civilized things of life! This very important link with North America predates by many years the Seagram ownership of the house. Mumm sent 420,000 bottles to the United States in 1877 and 1.5 million in 1902, its best year for that market. However, Queen Victoria was also drinking it, leading the way for British connoisseurs of champagne. Mumm is still in second place in the United States, behind Moët: no wonder Maurice Cense, Mumm's export director, describes those of his profession as "purveyors of happiness".

The house was founded in 1827 by two Germans, one of whom was Peter Arnold de Mumm. The Cordon Rouge marque, which has proved such a winner for the company, was launched in 1873. Unfortunately, the Mumms had been so busy selling successfully that they had not bothered to seek French nationality, so after World War I Mumm was confiscated and put up for sale.

There were several shareholders in the new ownership arrangements, one of which was Dubonnet. René Lalou, whose wife was a Dubonnet, ran Mumm until 1973 and gave his name to their top cuvée. Mumm was taken over by one of the shareholders, the giant Seagram, in 1972, and the group also embraces Perrier-Jouët (run very separately in Epernay) and Heidsieck Monopole. The Chairman of Mumm is Alain de Gunzburg, the son-in-law of Seagram's founder, Samuel Bronfman. Mumm is a truly international champagne, poured in liberal quantities in New York nightclubs, top Paris restaurants and hot African hotels – ask for Cordon Rouge, and a bottle of beribboned Mumm will appear.

Mumm own 218 hectares of vineyard throughout the Champagne region, but particularly at Avenay, Mailly, Bouzy, Ambonnay, Vaudemanges, Aÿ, Avize, Cramant and Chambrécy. This supplies about 20 percent of their needs. The rest comes from the usual sources of supply of grapes, with the emphasis on Pinot Noir and Chardonnay. Current production runs at about 9.5 million bottles a year and stocks to three years of sales. Mumm is the largest company in Reims.

The cellars are excavated galleries, not the crayères found in some parts of Reims, and took 70 years to prepare. Eighty percent of production undergoes remuage in gyropalettes, but the cuvées de prestige are still handled manually. Winemaking is overseen by the technical director, Monsieur Carré, who told me that what he looks for in champagne, its raison d'être, is vinosity and character. This is hardly surprising, considering that he was once with Krug. He works with 70–80 crus each year, and as there are 1,253 vats there is clearly a good deal of

Britain, the US and West Germany are the main export markets for champagne, taking 19.2, 15.8 and 10.5 million bottles respectively in 1987. The principal houses, by volume of sales, in the UK are:
Moët & Chandon
Lanson
Marne et Champagne (the huge firm that specializes in own-label wines and myriad marques)
Mumm
Laurent-Perrier
Duval-Leroy (a large firm specializing in buyer's own brands)
Veuve Clicquot
Bollinger
Mercier
Piper-Heidsieck
Britain and West Germany are big markets for own-brand champagnes, especially in the supermarkets. At the same time, Britain is a traditional market for the top grandes marques, whereas the US favours the big, long-established houses.

The principal houses in the US, by volume of sales, are:
Moët & Chandon
Mumm
Perrier-Jouët
Taittinger
Piper-Heidsieck
Louis Roederer
Veuve Clicquot
In West Germany, the leading brands are:
Moët & Chandon
Pommery
Veuve Clicquot
Charles Heidsieck
Lanson
Laurent-Perrier
Piper-Heidsieck
Heidsieck Monopole
Mumm
Louis Roederer
With all these figures it should be remembered that the situation is by no means immutable, and a dynamic push by a champagne house can have an immediate effect on the positionings.

Left: An 1895 poster by Realier-Dumas for Jules Mumm, who was the son of the founder of G.H. Mumm but left to start his own business. Although his labels were eye-catching, the house did not survive: G.H. Mumm now own the marque, which is rarely used. The lady in the poster seems to be sipping rather gingerly from her coupe.

Far left: Tito's poster for Mumm in 1921, linking the red sash of the President of the Republic and the Cordon Rouge of one of the world's best-known champagnes.

selection within each cru: "I have to temper the pride of the Chardonnay, moderate the mettle of the Pinot Noir and calm the nervousness of the Pinot Meunier". Coming from a Frenchman, this is a perfectly normal description of the challenges of blending.

Cordon Rouge Brut NV: Made up of 45 percent Pinot Noir (for structure, character and power), 25 percent Chardonnay (for finesse, lightness and elegance) and 20 percent Pinot Meunier (for freshness and frankness), the Mumm recipe is finished off with ten percent reserve wine. At a recent blind tasting of many good champagnes, I put Mumm top for its sheer drinkability and appeal to all wine lovers. It has a delicate nose and is a lovely apéritif champagne, but the taste is good and definite and could stand up to most foods.

Cramant de Mumm Blanc de Blancs NV: This was formerly the lovely, tongue-twisting Crémant de Cramant, but as the word "crémant" is being dropped by all the champagne houses a new formula had to be found. The wine is 100 percent Chardonnay from the village of Cramant on the Côte des Blancs. Whatever the name, the champagne is mouth-wateringly crisp and enticing, perfect as an apéritif and with a mild cheese soufflé.

Cordon Rouge Brut Vintage: Usually about 70 percent Pinot Noir, 30 percent Chardonnay; the 1982 is infinitely pleasing, with a wonderful, ripe-fruit, nutty bouquet and a full, round, mouth-enveloping flavour. This is opulent, expansive and showy wine – champagne is one of the few things in life in which showiness is a virtue. Magnums of the 1979 stay in the memory and the 1976 was very creditable.

Cordon Rosé 1982: The base is the vintage Cordon Rouge blended with about ten percent red wine from Mumm's vineyards at Bouzy. The pink rose on the neck of the bottle must have a subconscious influence because I often think this wine is "rosy" in taste. There is very good fruit on the 1982: it seemed a little sweet when first launched, but now it is soft and ripe and easy. I prefer a little more austerity to give ultimate class to a rosé but this is a very pleasant, commercial style. The rose comes from the Japanese painter Foujita's *La Petite Fille à la Rose*: apparently, when the wine was served for the first time at the Elysée Palace, the guests all wanted empty bottles to have them signed by the artist.

Mumm de Mumm: This is a new cuvée for the house, made from 50 percent Pinot Noir and 50 percent Chardonnay. It is a little lighter and more supple than Mumm's other prestige cuvée, René Lalou, as about 20 percent of the Pinot Noir comes from the Marne Valley near Epernay. It has excellent depth and flavour.

René Lalou: Launched in 1969 and usually half Pinot Noir, half Chardonnay, this is excellent champagne for meals, the kind that takes you from oysters to lobster to strawberries. There is really classy vinosity and length on the finish. The 1979 needed time to come into its own but is now showing beautifully. The 1982 has a green-gold colour and a bouquet that is brut, austere and yet broad, with elements of hawthorn. The palate is full with great depth, a round and ripe champagne. Remember that the dump-shaped bottle will not fit into a cylindrical wine cooler, so you need to keep it cold in an ice bucket while dining.

Bruno Paillard

I remember once asking Bruno Paillard what he thought was important about his house. "What is important is that we exist!", he replied. Which was the answer I deserved because this young firm, entirely owned by Bruno Paillard (who is himself "young"), was only created in 1981 and thus goes against a stronger trend towards giant groups, mergers and takeovers in the champagne world. Bruno Paillard is one of the relatively few houses in Champagne founded since World War II and joins a select band of personally, or family-owned, "maisons" operating at national and international level.

But Bruno Paillard is very far from being a newcomer to the champagne scene. His family have long been vignerons in Champagne with, in the past, strong connections with Pommery. He first worked in his father's brokerage business from 1975 to 1980, selling only in France, before setting up his own broking firm in 1981 specializing in finding wine for customers abroad. However, he keeps this activity rigorously apart from his own Bruno Paillard champagnes – although, obviously, those sales help finance the establishment of stocks so essential to quality. In a young house, sales have to be balanced against stocks: at the moment, nearly 300,000 bottles are sold a year, with about 90 percent going to the export markets.

In 1987, Bruno Paillard bought in from 29 different villages, representing the production of approximately 40 hectares. Forty-five percent comes from the Montagne de Reims, 35 percent from the Côte des Blancs and the Sézannais, and 20 percent from the Marne and the Aube. Overall, he buys in about 38 percent Chardonnay (divided between the Côte des Blancs and the Sézannais), 40 percent Pinot Noir and 22 percent Pinot Meunier. The champagnes are made in his new "cellars", a model of thoughtful and practical design, outside Reims along the Epernay road. With cellars above ground, it is vital to have perfect temperature control, and this has been achieved with the most sophisticated machinery which gives only a quarter of a degree variation all year round. Everything is spotless and ordered and, with the automation, only three people, as well as the chef de caves, work on the premises. Since 1987, all the remuage has been done on computer-controlled gyropalettes; otherwise the traditional tried and tested methods are followed. Bruno Paillard is an advocate as well as a practitioner (which is not always the same thing) of low dosages. The wines go through a malolactic fermentation.

A young house aiming for top quality sometimes has to make painful financial sacrifices. Bruno Paillard did not sell any 1984, a decision which cost him more than one million francs and certainly braked sales. But he considered (rightly) that, lacking the considerable reserves of old-established houses, the herbaceous quality of the 1984 wines would show through all too clearly. This is the kind of adherence to quality that can give you confidence in a house.

The style of Bruno Paillard champagnes reposes on elegance, but not without complexity and vinosity. The house makes a speciality of vintage wines sold with the date of disgorging. They are highly successful, although I have tasted far too many great "old" champagnes, kept for a considerable time between dégorgement and consumption, to agree that this practice necessarily causes excessive oxidation or maderization. Nor does disgorging shortly before consumption always produce fresh wines – the character of the vintage and, of course, its age, also play their role. But, conversely, disgorging just before drinking can, in some cases, seem to turn vintage characteristics on their head. Bruno Paillard's own taste favours drinking his champagnes one to four years after dégorgement, providing the cellarage is ideal. All these wines leave the cellars two to three months after disgorging.

In 1987, I tasted a range of Bruno Paillard vintage wines with varied disgorging dates, and found the exercise fascinating.

1981, disgorged January 1986: A really "bready" nose, very young and lively. A taste of pears and apples – nothing to do with the pejorative peardrops! Such freshness of flavour would beautifully "cut" a rich pâté.

1981, disgorged July 1985 (tasted a few months later): The *tiniest* of bubbles, coming up the centre of the glass in white clouds as they hit the surface. The taste is creamy and hazelnutty, getting richer all the time on the palate.

1979, disgorged September 1985: A really scented bouquet, with breed. Masses of flowers on both nose and palate. Totally different from the 1981. Wonderfully "feminine", with a touch of vanilla and blossom.

It has to be said that the very marked difference in taste between the 1981 and the 1979 is greatly due to the grape variety proportions. The 1979 has more Chardonnay, marvellously successful in this year. The 1981 has much more Pinot Noir because this was better in this vintage. (Like most champagne houses, Bruno Paillard's "assemblage" varies from one year to another for the vintage wines, hence the different labels each year to emphasize this, but the non-vintage recipe is always the same.)

1976, disgorged February 1986: A young, delicate nose which steals up on you. Lemon vanilla. It is not at all the overripe, "fat" style found in some 1976s, but where the vintage does come through is in the wonderful, long, fat finish. Great complexity of flavour – many layered.

1976, disgorged December 1986 (tasted a few months later): Wonderfully fresh and gulpable. Marvellous throughout a meal, and especially with salmon trout!

1975, disgorged January 1986: Excellent, classic, "together" 1975 nose. Still very young and bouncy. Well-knit, presents itself one-dimensionally at the moment. A very Paillard wine.

1969, disgorged May 1987: This was hardly darker than the other wines – Paillard champagnes are always an appealing greeny, hay gold. It had a really wonderful pungent, heady nose: immediately one saw that this was going to be the controversial wine of the tasting, with the troops mostly dividing as the English "for", the French "against". The taste was almost salty – not orthodox. I love its richness and complexity – really interesting champagne, but for meals, not as an apéritif.

Vintage makes up about 15 percent of Bruno Paillard sales, with the Brut Non-Vintage just under 60 percent, the Crémant Blanc de Blancs eight percent and the Rosé about 18 percent. Of the three, the Crémant 100 percent Chardonnay is my clear favourite. It has a beautiful, keen, almost piercing nose — fresh mountain flowers. Very good acidity balance and the hazelnuts of the Chardonnay. It lingers on the palate in a fresh, bouncy way. In April 1988 Bruno Paillard launched his Blanc de Blancs 1983, disgorged in January 1988. There is a lovely almond blossom bouquet and a delicious fresh, lively flavour and finish. It will be perfect towards the end of 1988.

The Rosé, made by blending in red wine, has a soft, strawberry nose and good strawberry persistence, the result of about 85 percent Pinot Noir and 15 percent Chardonnay. On the palate, there is good zip and attack, but a soft centre, slipping away with ease. The Brut Non-Vintage, made up of about 40 percent Pinot Meunier, 30 percent Chardonnay and 30 percent Pinot Noir, has a fuller, rounder nose than the Crémant, but is still keen — a Paillard hallmark. It is a bit coarser grained than the Crémant and finishes on one note. But, that note is high — top C, or D for Dégorgement?

Joseph Perrier
• • • • • • • • •

Joseph Perrier is now the only champagne house of any importance in Châlons-sur-Marne, and it makes a perfect excuse to visit this bustling town, where the burghers eat well and drink copiously. After all, the town was once called Chaalons en Champagne. The ambience is set at Joseph Perrier by the beams in some of the cellars, giving a delightful country air to the place. But more than a nod to modern requirements is shown in the new cuverie of gleaming stainless steel, completed in spring 1983 in time for the big vintages of 1982 and 1983.

Joseph Perrier was founded in 1825 and named after its founder, but the firm was sold to the Pithois family in 1888. They still own it, with Georges Pithois the chairman and his nephew, Jean-Claude Fourmon, the managing director. Joseph Perrier own 20 hectares of vines, Pinot Noir in Cumières, Damery and Hautvillers and Pinot Meunier in Verneuil, giving a third of the firm's requirements. The cellars have an excellent level of humidity (enough, but not too much, even in a very wet winter) and conifers are planted above them to maintain the exact humidity desired. At Châlons, the cellars have been excavated horizontally, transforming the old Roman quarries. Thus the arches are rounded, whereas in Reims, where the cellars have been excavated from above, they are pointed. One of the sights of the Joseph Perrier cellars are the Jeroboams and Methuselahs undergoing the prise de mousse; later they are disgorged "à la volée" and the dosage is done manually.

The malolactic fermentation is always carried out. Reserve wines are kept in demi-muids, wooden casks with a capacity of 600 litres, as well as in the traditional champagne "pièces" of 205 litres. Sales are 625,000 bottles a year.
Cuvée Royale Brut NV: Usually composed of one-third Chardonnay and two-

thirds Pinot Noir and Meunier, with more of the Meunier. The mousse is always very fine and the taste is rounded and well made, even when there was 1984 in the blend. I have, however, thought that the non-vintage is less consistent than in the past and I hope it can recapture its previous high level of performance, which used to be so evident in blind tastings.

Cuvée Royale Brut Blanc de Blancs NV: The most recent cuvée I tasted, in 1988, contained a good deal of wine from the 1981 vintage. The nose was very complete and hawthorny. It was a lovely wine, although there was not much mousse on one occasion, even when tried in different glasses.

Cuvée Royale Brut Vintage: This is a wine that I have often much admired, notably the 1975 which has been excellent for many years. The 1982 is 50 percent black grapes (35 Pinot Noir and 15 Meunier) and 50 percent Chardonnay. There are very good small bubbles and the bouquet is slightly lemony, fresh and floral. It is delicate wine, ready to drink, with a delicious aftertaste of peaches. The 1979, 1976 and 1973 were also successful, and 1971 in magnum was memorable.

Cuvée Royale Brut Rosé NV: The pink colour is obtained by the addition of red wine from the Joseph Perrier vineyards at Cumières. I often find this rather coarse and it is not my favourite wine of the house.

Cuvée du Cent-Cinquantenaire: First created in 1975, this is an almost equal

The headquarters of Joseph Perrier in Châlons-sur-Marne, by far the most important champagne house in the town (although Laurent-Perrier now have cellars there). Châlons-sur-Marne was once Chaalons en Champagne – it was probably changed between 1650 and 1700 to link the river Marne with the town. The old label shows how important Sillery was at one time.

blend of Chardonnay and Pinot Noir. It is always a marriage of several vintage years: the last one I tasted was a blend of 1979, 1976 and 1975. It had a pretty gold colour and a taste of digestive biscuits, those peculiarly British biscuits made with wheatmeal which tend to crumble on impact. The wine was looking older than the straight 1975 in magnum.

A new cuvée de prestige is planned.

Perrier-Jouët
• • • • • • • •

Perrier-Jouët are one of the most prestigious houses in Champagne, perfectly marrying size with style and emanating breed with every bubble. This is due in part to the formidable array of vineyards they possess, but also to wine leadership of unalloyed experience and good sense. Although Mumm took a majority shareholding in 1959, and both houses later fell under the control of Seagram, Perrier-Jouët have kept a very separate identity, probably helped by the fact that they reside in splendour on the Avenue de Champagne in Epernay.

The house was founded in 1811 by Pierre-Nicolas-Marie Perrier, who had married Adèle Jouët. The premises where you will still find the firm were bought in 1813; the first shipment went to Great Britain in 1815 and to the United States in 1837. The second part of the 19th century saw great consolidation, expanding sales of brut to the British and the acquisition of superb vineyards, above all at Avize and Cramant: Perrier-Jouët were really the first to recognize the great virtues of Chardonnay in a cuvée. As the Belle Epoque began, to which Perrier-Jouët almost lay claim, more than a million bottles were being produced.

The grand total of Perrier-Jouët vineyards is now 108 hectares, with an average rating of 95 percent. Essentially they are at Mailly on the Montagne de Reims for Pinot Noir, in the Marne Valley with Pinot Noir at Aÿ and Meunier at Dizy, and Pinot Meunier at Vinay and Orbais l'Abbaye. The fabulous Chardonnays came from 29 hectares at Cramant and ten hectares at Avize. This covers 30 percent of Perrier-Jouët's requirements; their other needs are supplied by purchases of grapes in the three main regions of Champagne. About three million bottles are produced every year, and about four years of stocks are kept in the cellars.

There are stainless-steel vats of 220 hectolitres for the first fermentation and in another, older cuverie, there are vats of both stainless steel and lined concrete. The malolactic fermentation is effected at Perrier-Jouët. Cane sugar is used for the liqueur de tirage, and the prise de mousse takes place in the large-sized bottles, with automatic poignetage during this process. Ninety-eight gyropalettes, controlled by computer, do the remuage in seven days. Because the special cuvée Blason de France comes in an unusual bottle shape the gyropalettes cannot do the remuage effectively, so it is done by hand.

The essential element in the Perrier-Jouët style of wine is the continuity in those who blend the cuvées. They know what they want, and have both the vineyards and the tasting experience to achieve it. When Charles Perrier, the

founder's son, mayor of Epernay and superb salesman, died, the house went to his nephew, Henri Gallice. In 1917, control of Perrier-Jouët passed to Louis Budin, who was related by marriage, and since 1959 his son, Michel Budin, has been at the head of the house. He is the guardian of tradition and quality at Perrier-Jouët, and it would be difficult to find anyone more imbued with the subtleties of blending and the knowledge of what each village and cru can produce. Michel Budin is backed by a solid technical team, led by the cellarmaster André Baveret, which takes infinite care at every stage of the champagne process. A typical example of Perrier-Jouët philosophy is the decision not to make a blanc de blancs champagne. They only like to work with the grands crus in Chardonnay, and the introduction of such a cuvée would take away grapes now used for other wines. If the cuvée became successful, "we would have to go to the Sézannais". Clearly, only perfection will do at P-J.

Grand Brut NV: Usually about 70 percent black grapes (40 percent Pinot Noir, 30 percent Meunier), 30 percent Chardonnay. It has a lovely nutty nose and is always very floral on the palate – a real giveaway in blind tastings. If you like hazelnuts and flowers in a wine (and I do), this is the one for you.

Vintage Brut: Made up of about the same proportions of grapes, tasting always indicates more Chardonnay than there actually is, probably due to the very high quality of the blancs. The 1982 has a delicate nose, with lovely forward fruit, as

Some of the Perrier-Jouët staff in the days when being photographed was a very solemn procedure, not even enlivened by the two bottles of champagne. It is not known in what capacity the dog was employed, but it, too, looks suitably subdued by the occasion.

The elegant town house in Epernay belonging to Perrier-Jouët, with its classic forecourt, shutters and long windows. Not all the buildings on the Avenue de Champagne are so felicitous – there are many "Victorian piles", of dubious beauty but redolent of wealth.

always with P-J. This is accentuated on the palate in the 1982 vintage. Excellent acidity balance – with a little more bottle-age, the bouquet will be more pronounced. Already it is a beautifully behaved apéritif, and in February 1988 had filled out enough to be delicious with venison and juniper berries. I have also admired, and seen disappear, the 1979, 1978, 1976, 1975 and 1973.

Blason de France: I consider this one of the most underestimated (because it is often unknown) cuvées de prestige on the market. The whole effect of the presentation is "antique" – dump bottle, silver foil and label with "old" lettering. It started life as vintage – the 1976 was the last – with the non-vintage cuvées appearing in 1984. The contents, 40 percent Pinot Noir, 20 percent Meunier and 40 percent Chardonnay, are from vineyards with a rating of 98 percent. The wine has a marvellous "minerally" nose, with elements of lime flowers. There is a lovely, long, lemony finish, and the P-J beautiful balance. This is really classy champagne, with something to say.

Blason de France Rosé: (The rosé was never vintage.) Made from a similar base as the Blason blanc, the colour is obtained by blending in 14–15 percent Pinot Noir from Bouzy. The last cuvée I tasted had a slightly tawnier colour than the bluer Belle Epoque Rosé, but it could have been an older blend. There were hints of raspberries, but the nose was not pronounced. The taste was a little old and flat, which leads me to believe that this cuvée is best when first released.

Belle Epoque: Called Fleur de Champagne in the United States, the cuvée was launched in 1970 (the vintage was 1964) and has gone on to become the most important cuvée de prestige to appear after World War II. It is not merely the bottle – the enamel-painted anenomes were first created for Perrier-Jouët by Emile Gallé in 1900 in his Nancy workshop – it is also the taste. The composition of the cuvée is a vital 50 percent Chardonnay based on Cramant, and 50 percent Pinot Noir (sometimes with a small amount of Meunier), with a vineyard rating of 98–99 percent. The 1982 vintage, when tasted in 1987, had a light, floral nose and was youthful, fresh, delightful. It needs time in bottle to develop complexity, although many who order it are not seeking that particular quality. I will bide my time, because I know where it is going – to greater heights of interest. The 1979, tasted in 1987, had a wonderfully rich, almost white Burgundian nose – that is the Chardonnay singing through. It was biscuity, with great richness and marvellous complexity on the palate. The finish was round and emphatic – superb wine. Other highly recommended vintages are 1978, 1976 and 1975, which Perrier-Jouët characterize as "different from the others" in its vintage features. In this case, "different" must mean classic. One of the great bottles of 1988, for me, was a Jeroboam of 1973 Fleur de Champagne drunk in Miami – it was sheer perfection.

Belle Epoque Rosé: This is basically Belle Epoque with the addition of 14–15 percent Pinot Noir from Bouzy for the colour. Here the famous flowers are fired onto a transparent bottle. Launched on the 1976 vintage, the cuvée is always outstanding. The 1982 has a taste of crushed strawberries and a long finish with a touch of cassis. If you want delicacy and finesse in a rosé, go no further.

Decidedly, the Belle Epoque lives on. We should be forever in debt to Perrier-Jouët for capturing its essential esprit in liquid form.

Perrier-Jouët menu cards, perfectly illustrating the gaiety and largesse of the Belle Epoque. One has the feeling that at this time a magnum was always better than a bottle.

"Champs Elysées" is a cellar sign: the cellars of many champagne houses are so huge that the alleys are given street names for easy identification.

Philipponnat

Philipponnat is one of those "secret" champagnes that are quietly "adopted" by wine lovers and then served as a delightful discovery. Thus the name gets whispered from connoisseur to connoisseur and the coterie of aficionados grows into a band of followers. The present Philipponnat company in Mareuil-sur-Aÿ was created in 1910 by Pierre Philipponnat, and in 1935 he purchased the Clos des Goisses vineyard, which played a significant role in drawing attention to the company. Michel Collard-Philipponnat and his son Dominique run the firm which, in April 1987, was bought by Marie-Brizard, opening up development possibilities in France and abroad.

Philipponnat own 12 hectares of vines with an average vineyard rating of 98 percent. They are all at Mareuil-sur-Aÿ and the surrounding area and are made up of 80 percent Pinot Noir and 20 percent Chardonnay. This fulfils 25 percent of the house's needs, with supplementary grapes coming from all three varieties. Production runs at 450,000 bottles a year, so Philipponnat is what the French call "confidentiel" – a "private" marque for those in the know. Methods are traditional, as befits a small house.

Royale Réserve Brut NV: Made up of 60 percent Pinot Noir, ten percent Pinot Meunier and 30 percent Chardonnay, the nose is floral, the taste full – occasionally, it can be a bit coarse.

Royale Réserve Brut Rosé NV: In a clear bottle, this comes wrapped in silver paper to protect the wine from the light. The base wine is as for the straight non-vintage, with the addition of Pinot Noir from the Clos des Goisses. The colour is pale topaz pink, the mousse "soft". There is a delicious, heady bouquet of wild strawberries, so intense that you can smell it as the champagne is poured. It is really a lilting scent, followed by an ethereal, floaty, utterly mouthwatering taste. This is one of the very best apéritif rosés and probably the greatest bargain in this department. It is pure pleasure.

Royal Réserve Brut Vintage: Usually a blend of 65 percent Pinot Noir and 35 percent Chardonnay, the 1981 is made up of wines from 30 villages. The wine is stylish with good depth of flavour. I have a particular affection for the 1976 (a "monstrous" year, says Michel Collard-Philipponnat), which showed exemplary balance.

Cuvée Première Blanc de Blancs: The 1980 has a delicate bouquet, the Philipponnat balance and lovely flavour on the finish. It is the kind of wine from which it is difficult to separate oneself.

In February 1988 I had a sneak preview of the Grand Blanc 1982, due out later in 1988, replacing the Cuvée Première. 1982, of course, was a wonderful year for the Chardonnay, and here there is all the finesse one would expect. It comes in a clear bottle and the blend is similar to the previous blanc de blancs.

Clos des Goisses: The discreet presence of Clos des Goisses can be felt in some of the classiest "watering holes" in France and abroad, but the market is never going to be swamped by the unique product of the five and half hectares overlooking the

Marne river. Part of the Clos is very steeply sloped and faces due south, which is a tremendous asset in sunless years, but in sunny vintages the flatter land behind the slope provides the balance necessary to ensure that Clos des Goisses is never too heavy a champagne. The soil is chalk under 50cms of loamy topsoil. As with many quality wines, the emphasis is on intensity of flavour, not overt power. The grape composition is 70 percent Pinot Noir and 30 percent Chardonnay.

1982: Tasted in February 1988, and without any dosage. It had a lovely blossomy bouquet and ultra-fine flavour. In another year or two the true depth will open out.

In October 1987 I tasted the following vintages:

1979: The nose is young and floral rather than complex at this stage. On the palate the wine is wonderfully lively, full and blossomy. Undoubtedly, the 1979 is having a charmed youth.

1978: The bouquet is immensely full, reminiscent of hawthorn blossom. There is a keen bite to the taste and the wine is beautifully fresh. The 1978 is probably hovering between being the "French taste" (young) and the "English taste" (mature) – in any case, it is at the point where I like it very much.

1975: This is another hawthorn nose. It is still very fresh, with a soft, gentle finish, opening out into more flowers. A highly appealing wine.

1971: The bouquet is hazelnutty and deep. The taste has become round, showing age and richness, far more suitable for drinking with food than as an apéritif. It would be perfect with foie gras.

To produce champagnes like these you have to be something of an artist. But creative talent abounds in the Collard-Philipponnat family. Michel Collard-Philipponnat is a pianist and he conducted the Epernay Symphony Orchestra for 30 years. His son, Jean-Philippe Collard, is one of France's foremost pianists. Never has the marriage between wine and music been so harmonious.

Michel Collard-Philipponnat using pliers to ease the cork out of an old bottle of champagne, ably supported by son **Dominique.**

Right: The centrepiece of the feast – traditionally called the cochelet – for the pickers at the end of the vintage is the "tarte" specially decorated for the occasion. During the harvest itself, the dish that is most appreciated is the potée champenoise, a soup with meat and vegetables on the side.

• • • • • • • • • • • •

Piper-Heidsieck

Of the three Heidsieck champagne firms, this is the only one to be still family controlled and not part of a large group, although, confusingly, the family are not Heidsiecks. The d'Aulan family control a large majority of the shares: the maternal great-grandfather of the company's present chairman, Marquis François d'Aulan, was a partner of Henri Piper (who married La Veuve Heidsieck) and he inherited the business when Henri Piper died in 1870. The rather complicated Heidsieck "family tree" is set out on page 100. The d'Aulans are a distinguished family (the previous Marquis was a hero of World War II) and the present Marquise, Sonia d'Aulan, is Austrian and the grand-daughter of Comte Czernin, the last Foreign Minister of the Austro-Hungarian Empire.

Piper-Heidsieck own no vineyards but have long-term contracts with a great number of small growers which assure consistency of supply. They buy both grapes at vintage time and also "vins clairs", or still wines, the following spring. Their purchases are 70 percent black grapes (both Pinot Noir and Meunier) and 30 percent Chardonnay. The vinification cellars are modern, bristling with stainless-steel vats which each contain 20 cuvées. Malolactic fermentation is not practised at Piper, where a centrifuge after the first fermentation removes the bacteria which would induce it. Interestingly, the pH is often the same in champagnes that have gone through malolactic fermentation as in those that have not, as tartaric acid is in some cases added to those wines that undergo the process. However, as the composition of the acids is not the same, the wines do mature in different fashion, and a champagne that has not been through its malolactic fermentation will appear more austere when young than one that has.

Remuage is entirely by gyropalette, even for magnums. It has been totally automated and computer controlled since 1978; the programme has to be changed according to the character of the year as deposits vary, some being more easy to move than others. The prise de mousse takes place in the larger bottles up to Jeroboam size. At Piper, bottles destined for the British market are kept a little longer than for other countries, both sur pointes and after final corking. This is in deference to national taste, and also with regard to the more sharp malic acidity.

Piper have one of the best transvasage, or decanting, lines in Champagne and many firms use these facilities when they have large orders for quarter-bottles. The lines are so quick and efficient that the decanting process from bottle to quarter no longer tires the wine as it once did – witness the fresh quarter-bottles now served on some airlines. They may not be aesthetically pleasing, but the quality of the champagne inside is usually beyond reproach. The secret is in the speedy bottling and equally rapid consumption.

Sales of Piper-Heidsieck are five million bottles a year: two million in France and three million on the export markets. Average stocks cover three to four years of sales. The style Piper are seeking is fresh and elegant rather than round and ample.

Brut Extra NV: Although paler in colour than the vintage, the non-vintage nevertheless has more black grapes, 85–90 percent Pinot Noir and Meunier, usually in equal parts, and 10–15 percent Chardonnay. The wine has a pronounced nose, almost pungent, and fine mousse. The taste is full and quite rich, a mite coarse, needing bottle-age to soften and for the acidity to mellow.

Brut Vintage: 65–70 percent Pinot Noir, 30–35 percent Chardonnay. The wine has both grapeyness and verve, combining liveliness with body, if you can give it bottle-age. Michel Lacroix, Piper's directeur des caves, considers that the ideal time to drink their vintage is four to six years from the vintage date, but eight to ten years often suits my palate best. In 1988, the 1979 (which has an unacceptably short cork) has a rich gold colour, tiny bubbles (not very strong) and a delicate nose. The acidity is still there and it finishes a bit abruptly. But it was excellent with Chinese prawn wun tun and chilli and garlic sauce, which might have crushed a softer wine. The 1982 (which has a better cork) has a pale green colour and tiny bubbles. The bouquet is good and champagney and the taste lemony and stylish – much more balanced than the 1979, with a lovely fruity finish. I feel 1982 is a year that suits the method of no malolactic fermentation better than others.

Rosé Brut Vintage: 75–80 percent Pinot Noir (of which about 20 percent is vinified as red wine) and 20–25 percent Chardonnay. The colour is "oeil de perdrix", medium-depth pink and the shade that most people think of when they order a rosé champagne. At the end of 1987 I drank the 1979 with venison and a miroir aux fraises des bois – a glazed wild-strawberry mousse: probably only a rosé could manage that combination. There was an added "frisson" to the

• • • • • • • • • •
A rather dashing array of Piper-Heidsieck labels. The label for the Champagne Rare Vintage is a reproduction of a design by Fabergé in the second part of the 19th century.

The glamorous side of
Champenois life, when
the heads of houses
must be present at
glittering receptions
and star-spangled
galas – on this
occasion, the Marquis
(right) and Marquise
(second from left)
d'Aulan of Piper-
Heidsieck.

The glamorous side of Champenois life, when the heads of houses must be present at glittering receptions and star-spangled galas – on this occasion, the Marquis (right) and Marquise (second from left) d'Aulan of Piper-Heidsieck.

occasion because I understood (on the proverbial grapevine) that the Queen was enjoying the same wine more or less simultaneously on her 40th wedding anniversary. The 1982 (another short cork) was a bright ruby pink, with tiny bubbles and Pinot on the nose. It was very brut, with fruit on the middle palate but a short finish. It is soft enough for an apéritif, but it also went well, in Sweden, with marinated salmon (gravadlax), even managing to tame the accompanying sweet mustard sauce.

Brut Sauvage Vintage: 60–65 percent Pinot Noir and Meunier, divided about equally, with 35–40 percent Chardonnay. The wines used in the blend come from favoured sites because there is no sugar in the dosage: topping up after disgorging is only with exactly the same wine. The cuvée launched in 1980 was a non-vintage. The 1979 was the first vintage (with very short cork) and, in 1988, it had a deep gold colour and a lovely bouquet, deep and honeyish. The taste was honeyed, rich, full and of great quality, with a biscuity flavour. We tasted it at just under 15°C (60°F), which was on the warm side, but I find this suits totally brut wines. The 1982 (another very short cork – inexcusable in such a fine wine) had infinitesimal bubbles and was gold-green in colour. The bouquet was of acacia, the taste austere and yet rich and honeyed. The finish states emphatically that it is great champagne. It would be superb with beluga caviar, although this is a combination I have not yet tried.

Champagne Rare Vintage: This is Piper-Heidsieck's cuvée de prestige, first launched to celebrate the 200-year anniversary of Florens-Louis Heidsieck founding the original firm of Heidsieck in 1785. It is composed of 60–65 percent Chardonnay and 35–40 percent Pinot Noir from the 100 percent-rated villages of Avize, Cramant, Ambonnay, Aÿ, Beaumont, Bouzy, Louvois, Mailly, Puisieulx, Sillery, Tours-sur-Marne and Verzenay. The beautiful bottle is a splendid reproduction of an 18th-century hand-blown example in Piper-Heidsieck's museum. The heavy bronze foil is applied by hand using a French technique, "stagniolage", which was practised during the last century. The label, too, comes from the second part of the 19th century, when the original was designed by Fabergé. In 1988, the 1976 was excellent, with a lovely fruity taste, great youthful exuberance yet firmness and definite taste. It was just the right moment to drink this first vintage of Champagne Rare. The 1979 (with a good cork) has a green-gold colour and a lovely smell of may blossom. It is already soft and ready, but its nutty acidity gives it plenty of ageing potential – first-class champagne.

On May 6, 1785, at the Petit-Trianon, Florens-Louis Heidsieck presented Queen Marie-Antoinette with a bottle of his champagne: Queens are still drinking Piper-Heidsieck.

Pol Roger

Is it really an accident that the "two Christians" reign over perhaps the happiest house in Champagne? To arrive and be welcomed at Pol Roger is to experience a certain well-being: easy, warm and in no way smug. The family have a knack of spreading happiness, whether it is by their charm and hospitality, or by their champagne which, unerringly, gives immense satisfaction and pleasure. If I were asked to sum up the Pol Roger philosophy, I would say that it gives joy. It is a joy to drink, a joy to give, and a joy to know those who make it.

The two Christians are Messieurs de Billy and Pol-Roger, great-grandsons of the founder, Pol Roger. (When Monsieur Pol Roger died in 1899, his Christian name was added to the family surname, which became Pol-Roger, although the house and the wine have remained unhyphenated.) The apparent serenity of Pol Roger, of course, belies the considerable industry of the two Christians. Between them they slice up the world, preaching the gospel of Pol Roger from England to Korea, from Singapore to Australia. They are truly French, with their élan and their panache, but they are also firmly rooted in the Anglo-Saxon tradition, with rock-solid qualities of reliability and integrity. Equally at home with politicians and statesmen, pâtissiers and ambassadors, they do not merely respect history, they are usually around when it is being made.

The Pol-Roger clan are Epernay people, devoted to their town, to its surrounding vineyards, to their work, their elegant homes and their hobbies. A Pol Roger champagne brims over the glass to greet you, tempts you into having a better time just because you have made its acquaintance. But its prettiness is underpinned by the sheer application to work that you find in all the best champagne houses – the true grit behind the froth.

Pol Roger own 75 hectares of vines, with particular emphasis on the region in and around Epernay, in villages such as Mardeuil, Chouilly, Pierry, Moussy, Chavot-Courcourt. Cuis. Grauves and Cramant. These supply about 45 percent of the needs of the house, with the rest coming from grapes from the three

The two Christians, Messrs. Pol-Roger (left) and de Billy (right), who together run the prestigious family firm, Pol Roger. It is a perfect blend of cousins who have but one aim: quality.

Centre: Sir Winston Churchill watches his favourite horse, Pol Roger, named after his favourite champagne, before a race. The win announced by the telegram sent by Sir Winston to Odette Pol-Roger would surely have been celebrated in bubbly.

Bottom: The Pol-Roger connection with Sir Winston is far from over. Christian de Billy travelled from Epernay to present a cheque to the National Trust agent responsible for Chartwell, Churchill's home in Kent, so that new trees could be planted to replace those lost in the devastating storm of October 1987.

principal areas. Contracts with independent "vignerons" ensure that these vineyards are cultivated in the best possible way, with advice and support always available. Production is about 1.3 million bottles a year, backed up by nearly six million bottles in stock, giving a reassuring margin of about four years of supply in the cellars. There is plenty of room for them, too: 25,000 square metres of chalk galleries on two levels, while the depth of 30 metres gives a constant temperature of 9.5°C (49°F). Remuage, by four remueurs, is still on traditional pupitres, but bottling and disgorging lines are briskly modern.

The family consider that contact with the vineyards is essential to the final quality of their champagne. At vintage time, especially, they are "sur la route", standing by the pressoirs and seeing what they have to work with in the months that follow. Later, in quieter moments, some vignerons are invited to "la chasse", while those who do not hunt are also remembered and enjoy a lunch instead. Although Pol Roger was founded in 1849, it was not until 1955 that the family started to buy vineyards; before, they had thought that growing grapes was not their métier. Apart from buying established vineyards, they also exchanged some of their own property for vine-growing land, which has far greater value than a cereal farm.

The two Christians taste with their heart – "ce sont des assemblages de coeur". Ample technical assistance comes from the directeur des caves, James Coffinet, as Champenois as the family itself. One has the impression that they all know what they want in a champagne and with quiet, careful teamwork they go about achieving it.

The first bottle of Pol Roger ever exported was to England, although now the English have to share with 105 other countries. During the course of a dinner in 1944 at the British Embassy in Paris, Winston Churchill met the glamorous Odette Pol-Roger and became Pol Roger's best-known roving ambassador (and customer!), for he fell in love with the product on the spot. When the Council of Europe received him in Strasbourg, Pol Roger was ordered for the occasion, and his favourite champagne had a tendency to follow him wherever he went. His preferred vintages were the great 1928, the 1934 and the 1947, which were specially disgorged for him and despatched at suitable intervals. In fact, he drank the 1947 until the end of his life, showing a predilection for a mature taste in champagne.

I am sure he would also have liked the 1959 I tasted a few years ago. It had a lovely fruity, old nose of quince and honey, and the taste was gentle and soft, like a sweetish lolly. The long, lingering finish is what all lovers of old champagne search for. The 1973 is, to this day, a simply splendid wine, an incredible treat if you come across it – and we had the good fortune to stumble upon a cache in Haute-Provence recently. The young wine waiter told us that the French would not buy it, suspecting anything other than the current vintage, so we benefited from this misapprehension and found it the perfect reviver on a series of steamy days. The 1975 is a classic, set for a truly great old age, but glorious at any time of its life. The 1979 has enormous flirty charm, a totally appropriate millésime from which to select the special, royal-blue-labelled cuvée which Pol Roger brought out for the marriage of Prince Andrew to Miss Sarah Ferguson in 1986.

Vintage Brut: The 1982 is a Pol Roger vintage as we love them, a pure expression of quality and seduction. It is made up of 18 crus from the Epernay region, 60 percent Pinot Noir and 40 percent Chardonnay. The black grape gives depth and roundness, filling the mouth and staying long on the palate, the Chardonnay gives vivacity and a lightness of touch which is all Pol Roger in style.

Réserve Spéciale P.R. 1982: It is fascinating to compare this, which is something of a rarity, with the Vintage Brut. It has a little more body than the "straight" vintage wine and the composition is 50 percent Pinot Noir and 50 percent Chardonnay from six different crus at 100 percent échelle. The effect is sustained flavour in very elegant form.

Blanc de Chardonnay 1982: For a complete change of emphasis, but still with that Pol Roger charm, there is nothing more alluring than this Chardonnay – delicious, light, and refreshing to the palate. It lives up to its pedigree origins from the best crus of the Côte des Blancs: Cramant, with its touch of firmness, Le Mesnil and Oger, with their scent, Avize, playing a silky role in the middle, and Cuis.

Pol Roger Brut Sans Année: Known to devotees as White Foil, for obvious reasons. It is composed of the three grape varieties, and the cuvée I am currently drinking contains three vintages – there is always a minimum of two. That lovely floral bouquet is immediately familiar to regular drinkers of P.R. – it opens out to you, with notes of acacia and honey. I find it a totally and utterly "more-ish" champagne.

Rosé 1982: This is based on a classic cuvée of 75 percent Pinot Noir and 25 percent Chardonnay, with the addition of Bouzy Rouge. It has a really attractive, medium-shaded colour of a salmon-pink rose and is beautifully soft, with an abundance of ripe fruit – even a hint of peaches. I find Pol Roger rosés are delicious when young; seize them in comparative youth to enjoy them at their best.

Cuvée Sir Winston Churchill: This was first launched in 1984 with the 1975 vintage, made only in magnums. The event, appropriately enough, was held at his birthplace, Bleinheim Palace, in a happy family atmosphere of much affection. Lady Soames spoke with charm and simplicity of her father who, no doubt, would have appreciated the generous quantities of "his" wine which flowed on that summer day. Pol Roger made this Cuvée in his honour, always with the idea in their minds of what he would have liked. I think he would have mightily approved, especially if he could have cellared some of these magnums, as they are only now coming into their own.

Pol Roger are deliberately discreet about the exact composition of the Cuvée, but it is an alliance between the Chardonnay and the Pinot Noir. It was blended to reflect the spirit and indomitable character of Sir Winston himself – it is a tribute to the great man and his links with France, and the Pol-Roger family. The 1979 Cuvée was made in bottles and magnums and, at eight years old, was ready to drink. It has a nose reminiscent of roasted hazelnuts and a ripe, smoky, fruity taste, with very good acidity balance. For the future, we can look forward to the 1982 and then the 1985.

Churchill used to say: "I am easily satisfied with the best". No wonder he was so attached to Pol Roger. And no wonder his passion is shared by pockets of distinguished and knowledgeable wine lovers in all corners of the world.

Pol Roger's offices in Epernay, their elegance totally in keeping with the wine. Flags greet their visitors – a warming touch and a custom followed by many wine châteaux and domains in France.

Pommery & Greno

The imposing main
entrance to Pommery.
The totally
flamboyant, Victorian
Gothic style offices and
cellars dominate
Reims; Madame Veuve
Pommery built these
grandiose monuments
to success and solidity
as a compliment to her
many British
customers.

Pommery is, quite simply, one of the most glittering inheritances in Champagne. Its vineyard holdings are virtually priceless. To make Pommery is both an honour and a responsibility: the raw material is so splendid that the slightest imperfection in technique would be lèse majesté. Happily, with Prince Alain de Polignac to direct winemaking, Pommery rests easily on its throne.

As with many great champagne houses, there is a widow at the heart of the story. The house was founded in 1836 by Narcisse Greno, but Louis Alexandre Pommery joined him in 1856. When he died two years later, Madame Veuve Pommery took over. She had the foresight to open an agency in London as early as 1861, and during her travels in Britain she became very fond of the Victorian Gothic style of architecture. It is always said that she built the amazing series of "Scottish baronial" edifices that house Pommery today as a compliment to her British customers. She was among the first to see the potential of dry champagne with her Pommery Nature 1875. These wines needed longer storage than the sweet cuvées: hence the need for immense cellars. After the Franco-Prussian War, she bought 60 hectares on the Butte St-Niçaise which dominates Reims: the area included 120 Gallo-Roman chalk pits. These were levelled and linked with 18 kilometres of galleries in the chalk. The result is some of the finest cellars in Reims, which remain at a temperature of 10°C (50°F) all year.

But the Widow Pommery was also industrious on the personal front, for in 1879 her daughter Louise married Prince Guy de Polignac, one of the oldest

noble families in France. The Polignacs owned Pommery until 1968, when the company first appeared on the Stock Exchange in Paris. In 1979, Xavier Gardinier, who already owned Lanson, took control of Pommery, but in 1984 he sold both houses to the French food processing group BSN. The legacy of the Polignac's long association with Pommery is marked by the continued presence of Alain de Polignac.

There are 300 hectares of Pommery vineyards, with an average rating of 99 percent. In fact, all the vines are in the 100 percent class with the exception of the 15 hectares in Reims itself. From the classification point of view this puts them at the top of all the champagne house holdings. Chardonnay is planted in the vineyards at Avize, Cramant, Sillery, Reims and on three percent of the Aÿ holdings, while Pinot Noir is produced at Verzenay, Bouzy and Aÿ. On average, the Pommery vineyards represent 35 percent of the house's requirements and all their top cuvées (the vintage wines) are made from their own grapes. Purchases are made in all three grape varieties. Production is 5.7 million bottles a year.

Pommery are equipped with a massive modern installation of stainless-steel cuves and their wines go through the malolactic fermentation. Remuage is entirely by hand, although Pommery may experiment with gyropalettes in the future. They are firm believers in carrying out the prise de mousse in every bottle size, from halves to Methuselahs and Salmanazars; from the Jeroboam upwards the cork and metal clasp is used rather than crown caps. Dégorgement takes place in the deep cellars, which is rare – normally this is done in a ground-level cellar, or hall.

The winemaking philosophy of Alain de Polignac is incisive and as clean cut as the taste of the champagnes themselves. He sees his wine as brut, with finesse – all the character must come from the assemblage. The dosage must thus be as neutral as possible, with the vintage wines and cuvées de prestige containing less than the non-vintage to allow the grands crus to express themselves. He enters into minute detail to achieve the pure taste he wants – even the distance between the press and the vat where the juice clarifies is studied and the débourbage must last 12 hours. A champagne expresses itself through the crus, the assemblages and the time allowed for ageing.

Ultimately, Alain de Polignac wants his Pommery to be ethereal rather than vinous. He has certainly succeeded in lifting the whole quality of Pommery in recent years, in bringing out the breed of those incredible vineyards and in putting his house in the forefront of the truly classy champagnes. While I think the uncertainty of the 1970s must have had an effect on the consistent quality of the wines, the '80s have seen a remarkable renaissance at Pommery.

Brut Royal NV: 60 percent Pinot Noir and Pinot Meunier, 40 percent Chardonnay. A small part of the component wines comes from the Pommery vineyards, the rest from purchased grapes. I have a particular fondness for the Brut Royal because I drink it regularly at London's Garrick Club, a place intimately linked with convivial gaiety. Immediately you put your nose in the glass, that great, unmistakable bouquet of top-class champagne assails the senses – almost a slightly bready nose, with a hint of austerity in the fruit because it is truly dry. The bouquet is particularly pronounced in the slightly older stocks shipped to the UK. The taste is crisp and fine and rests most easily on the palate.

Rosé Brut NV: Made from about 75 percent black grapes, 25 percent Chardonnay, the colour is obtained by skin contact after pressing. The shade is a definite pink and the bouquet shows finesse. It is a really champagney style (as all Pommery), quite firm and big enough to go with food. Dry, but very fruity – excellent wine.

Vintage Brut: At 50 percent Chardonnay, 50 percent Pinot Noir, all rated at 100 percent and all from the Pommery vineyards, this has to be one of the most distinguished vintage champagnes on the market – and it is. (UK shipments are usually a vintage behind the rest of the world.) There is a palette of choice before us at the moment, because these champagnes keep. The 1983 will mature well; already it is a delicious apéritif, with acacia and hawthorn on the nose, finishing very clean on the palate because it is so brut. The 1982 is very floral, eternal spring! The 1981 is not very Pommery in that the Chardonnay did not express itself as much as usual, but it is wonderful with food. The 1980 is lively and pretty, very Pommery, whereas the 1979 is lovely easy drinking. I liked the 1976; however, Alain de Polignac's favourites, for their sheer Pommery expression, are the 1975 and the 1973. I would not quarrel with that.

Cuvée Spéciale Louise Pommery: This is 60 percent Chardonnay from Avize ("drier and metallic") and Cramant ("round and fat") and 40 percent Pinot Noir from Aÿ (discreet), rated, naturally, at 100 percent and from the Pommery vineyards. The cuvée is named to honour Louise Pommery, who is credited with bringing into the world (which meant Britain at the time) the first brut champagne in 1874. More than a century later we can enjoy the exquisite 1979, the first Louise, which always appeals to me because of its sheer class, shining out whether sipped appreciatively at dinner or puzzled over at a blind tasting. The 1980, which I last drank one morning in early 1988 with Gérard Boyer, is full, with a lovely balancing acidity. The next vintage will be the 1981.

Cuvée Spéciale Louise Pommery Rosé: This magnificent champagne is newly (spring 1988) launched. It comes from the 100 percent-rated crus of Pommery's own vineyards: Avize and Cramant for the Chardonnay, Aÿ for the Pinot Noir. The colour is obtained by pressing and skin contact. The 1980 is a delicate pale pink, topaz shade, almost like a cat's eye, with glinting yellow lights. The bubbles are tiny and there is an incredible bouquet of wild strawberries and mellow fruitiness. The flavour is wholly original, the least banal rosé champagne you will ever taste – my husband thinks it is the best rosé he has experienced. The wild strawberries also appear on the palate but with subtlety and breed. We served it not too cold, at 10°C (50°F), so as to savour the wonderful nuances.

Pommery is certainly the "inside track" champagne of the late 1980s. Although I do not really empathize with this expression, being something of an outside tracker myself, I do recommend ordering it the next time you are faced with the delicious dilemma of choosing your champagne.

Louis Roederer

Addicted as I am to Roederer, it would be additionally satisfying to say that I share the taste of their late Imperial Majesties, the Tsars of Russia. But it would also be inaccurate, as they drank their Roederer very sweet indeed. What I do share is their confidence in this great family firm, which has been making fine champagne since 1776. Unfortunately, my personal consumption of Roederer is not yet sufficiently important for me to request a special style of bottle for my own use, which is what Alexander II was inspired to do in 1876. He disliked the way his champagne was served with the bottle wrapped in a linen cloth because he felt that his guests could not tell that the wine was specially selected for him. So henceforth his champagne came in clear crystal bottles, and Roederer Cristal, the first "cuvée de prestige", was born.

Naturally, the Russian Revolution in 1917 destroyed this lucrative market for Roederer, leaving them with unpaid bills and a great deal of sweet and sticky stock. In fact, there was no Cristal produced between 1914 and 1924. They began to make it again in 1925, with a bottling, or "tirage", of 20,000 bottles. But an old-established house such as Roederer knows about the roller-coaster pattern of international sales. Historical perspective is easy to achieve when you can say that in 1985 one's house passed the sales figures for the year 1872, and now hover around two and a half million bottles!

Roederer champagnes have one of the more marked styles of all the houses, and the guardian of this heritage is Jean-Claude Rouzaud, grandson of Madame Olry Roederer, a formidable Champagne widow who safeguarded Roederer's great reputation for quality. In fact, many of the most wondrous champagnes of my life were the Roederer vintages of the 1950s and 1960s, in Cristal, straight vintage and rosé (which was sold with a year at that time).

The remarkable economic strength of Roederer comes from their vineyard holdings: 180 hectares, of which more than 130 hectares are classified 100 percent, and averaging 98 percent overall. Prosaic as it might seem, you need economic strength to make fine champagne, and it gives this family firm a towering advantage in the quality stakes. With 70–80 percent of their needs coming from their own vines, the solid base is undeniable. The spread of vineyards is also well-nigh ideal, with 55 hectares in the Montagne de Reims, 50 in the Vallée de la Marne and 75 in the Côte des Blancs. Body comes from Verzenay and Verzy, fruit from the Pinot Noir at Louvois, Cumières, Hautvillers and Aÿ, while finesse, freshness and subtlety come from Chouilly, Cramant, Avize, Le Mesnil and Vertus. During the vintage, 600 pickers work in the Roederer vineyards, with accommodation, food and liquid refreshment provided. The pressing centres are at Verzenay, Aÿ, Avize and the Petite Montagne. Like Krug, Roederer are important buyers at Leuvrigny in the Vallée de la Marne, as well as at Festigny and Villers-sur-Châtillon.

Jean-Claude Rouzaud is an oenologist trained at Montpellier (with Yves Bénard, the Chairman of Moët & Chandon – a powerful pair) and one of the few I

The "Champagne Widows" are a phenomenon in the region. The most famous was undoubtedly La Veuve (The Widow) Clicquot, but in our times it was Madame Lily Bollinger. Less well known were Madame Veuve Pommery, Madame Veuve Laurent-Perrier and Madame Olry Roederer. When their husbands died, these women not only assumed responsibility for their firms but often expanded their holdings and sales. In view of this special history, it is a pity that there are not more women in the champagne trade today.

have known who has admitted to making a mistake. I always felt that some vintages of Cristal during the 1970s were not quite of the stratospheric quality that this wine can reach. With total candour he told me that, in the 1970s, he was convinced that great quality in champagne could be achieved at the same time as high yields. He has now revised this opinion, drastically reduced the amount of fertilizer used in the vineyards, pruned more severely and cut yields – and Cristal has once more gone into orbit. The policy is also draconian as far as sorting "on the vine" is concerned in order to avoid rotten grapes: during the 1987 harvest, the enormous quantity of 1,500 kilograms per hectare was rejected among the black grapes in the Roederer vineyards.

Perfection in the cellars is also the aim. Attention to detail is what contributes to quality: a bottling system guaranteed to avoid all oxidation, chaptalization with cane sugar and not beet, avoidance of filtration at very cold temperature, which tires the wine, and a gentler process of a longer (up to a month) but less brutal temperature change before bottling. The policy towards the malolactic fermentation is flexible – in 1985 there was none, in 1986 it was effected partially and in 1987 it was again avoided. So the intrinsic character of the vintage is taken into account and there is no overall "blanket" rule. Remuage is by hand, with some experimentation in gyropalettes, and vintage wines leave the cellars after about five years of ageing, non-vintage after three and a half.

But the essence of Roederer, what gives it that special taste so recognizable to devotees, is in the reserve wines, a total of more than 7,000 hectolitres lovingly

The official warrant from the Imperial Russian Court granted to Champagne Louis Roederer in 1908 put the seal on the house's astounding success in this market. For Roederer, the Russian Revolution was a disaster – no customers and mountains of unpaid bills.

A trio of Roederer
labels, living up to
their Imperial past.

kept in great wood foudres in an air-controlled room at a maximum temperature of 12°C (55°F). The foudres are treated to remove the tannin, which would be a disaster for champagne. To put one's head into an empty foudre and experience its intense scent, rich, intoxicating and estery, is to know why Roederer tastes as it does. The foudres, with an average capacity of 40 hectolitres, contain still wines from the different villages, their names proudly displayed on the outside. A Roederer non-vintage will have 10–20 percent of these reserves in its assemblage, made up of at least three different vintages. The other reserve "liqueur" wines are kept in small casks and represent 1,200 hectolitres; these are a real selection of a true tête de cuvée of the grape varieties. No one will touch these liqueur reserves for four years – and the incredible scent they leave in an empty cask indicates the synergy that this protracted ageing produces between foudre and wine. Jean-Claude Rouzard believes that the heart of the Roederer taste lies not only in the blend of the grape varieties, the crus and the best reserves, but also in these liqueur wines.

So the Roederer recipe could be described as casks, stock, and ageing the finished champagnes for up to six months after disgorging, before they leave the cellars. But how to describe that taste?

Brut Premier: In its new, smart gold attire (one is permitted a fleeting moment of nostalgia for the old, discreet script of the Extra Quality), this is made up of approximately 66 percent Pinot Noir and 34 percent Chardonnay. It always has an imposing bouquet, rich, full and fruity. The taste is fruity, round and structured, with a long finish on the palate. It is a champagne of weight of flavour, not sheer weight.

Life at Louis Roederer in the 1920s: the grapes from the wide spread of vineyard holdings are pressed; the juice is then collected from the pressing centres and brought to Reims; and finally, when the long process of champagne making is complete, the cases are despatched to thirsty customers all over the world.

Blanc de Blancs Millésimé: Usually made with only four atmospheres, this comes from their own vineyards, with the addition of others which can be cultivated or controlled by the house – they have, for example, an important exclusive contract in Cramant. It is always refreshing, sometimes with an almost Chablisien nose, but can last well, as I have proved with 15-year-old beauties from my own cellar.

Vintage Brut, or Brut Millésimé: These wines follow the grape variety proportion of the Brut Premier, but the wine, of course, comes from a single year. They are champagnes to lay down, with incisive taste and great acidity/weight balance. The 1979 was perfection at eight years old and the 1981 already had intense bouquet and flavour in early 1988.

Rosé Brut: Made nowadays without year, but there were some incredible vintages in the 1950s and 1960s which gained a fantastic tawny concentration in ageing. The 1971 was also memorable. This is one of the few rosé champagnes made by pressing and skin contact, and the blend is 80 percent Pinot Noir, 20 percent Chardonnay. It is, with Krug, the palest of the rosé champagnes, a yellow topaz colour, a wine with an intensely classy taste and a smell of wild strawberries when young.

Cristal: Here the blend is 50–60 percent Pinot Noir, with a minimum of 40 percent Chardonnay, sometimes rising to 50 percent. All the grapes come from Roederer's own vineyards, but the crus chosen vary from year to year. One of the true signs of Cristal is its underlying lacy character, persistent and lingering. Again, there were some magic vintages in the 1960s and I loved the 1970. I know that, where the 1970s are concerned, my favourite vintages do not concur with the personal preferences of Jean-Claude Rouzaud. He favours 1974 and 1977, whereas I adore the almost walnutty 1975, the soft, ripe 1976 and the exceptionally beautiful, aristocratic 1979. It is early days for the 1981, with its keen, hazelnut bouquet and great potential for ageing. The 1982 was just making its way onto the market in early 1988; it has a silky seduction and a "noisette" nose deriving from the Chardonnay – something of a special Cristal. Ahead of us we have the harder, classic 1983 and the undoubtedly stunning 1985. When storing Cristal, do not remove the yellow cellophane from the clear glass bottle: it filters 98 percent of any ultraviolet rays to which it might be exposed.

Cristal Brut Rosé Millésimé: First produced in the 1974 vintage, this is a rosé champagne made from skin contact and, with 70 percent Pinot Noir and 30 percent Chardonnay, an interesting comparison with the Brut Rosé. The 1976 is splendid, but the 1974 was extraordinarily successful for the year. Cristal Rosé cellars well for those who like a more mature taste.

Roederer Rich: This is the only non-brut champagne I really like. At three percent dosage it is not sweet, but it does have richness of body and a bouquet and flavour of caramel. It goes beautifully with the mince pies at Christmas.

Roederer will forever spell magic for me, for so many of its bottles have become inextricably intertwined with my life. There is no help for it: I am fanatical about Roederer champagne!

Ruinart

• • • • • •

It is perhaps indicative of the whole forward-looking attitude of Champagne that the oldest continuously trading house in the region launched, in 1987, a new range of wines intended to conquer new markets and reawaken those that are slumbering. In one sense, the history of Ruinart has turned full circle. Dom Thierry Ruinart, a Reims priest and well-known scholar, was a friend and confidant of Dom Pérignon, and he provided the knowledge for his nephew, Nicolas Ruinart, to found the house of Ruinart in 1729. Perhaps, then, it is only fitting that Ruinart has belonged to the Moët-Hennessy group (enlarged in 1987 to Moët-Hennessy-Louis Vuitton) since 1963, thus uniting the two ecclesiastics. Nicolas Ruinart had begun his working life in the linen trade and he, like businessmen of today, found it helpful to give champagne as presents, so the change in his career was easy. Successive Ruinarts proved very adept at selling, juggling equally well the contrasting markets of America at the time of President Jackson and Russia under Tsar Alexander II.

Ruinart have one of the greatest Gallo-Roman "crayères", or deep chalk cellars, together with Veuve Clicquot, Pommery, Charles Heidsieck and the old part of the Taittinger premises. They are classified as a historic monument and were greatly used during World War I, when André Ruinart ran the business from a raft floating in the flooded gallery! Now, however, Roland de Calonne presides over annual sales of 1.2 million bottles from offices which could more accurately be described as a most elegant town house.

Ruinart own 15 hectares of vines at Sillery, mainly Chardonnay, representing about 20 percent of their needs. Obviously, judicious buying is necessary, and this is where being part of an important group is more than helpful. Ruinart might be only five percent of that group, but they have access to the very best raw material and can draw from 200 crus, including all the best sources.

Since 1984 there have been great changes in the range of wines offered by Ruinart, but old traditions and policies have been strictly maintained, as seen by the ratio of annual sales (1.2 million bottles) to stocks held (5.5 million). The house has recently been less shy about proclaiming its long history and fabulous wines, which can only be a desirable move if it enables more people to discover them. Undoubtedly, people with "innate taste" knew about Dom Ruinart, but now they are invited to look at the "R" de Ruinart range – they are wines for those who drink champagne regularly. Slowly, the "R" de Ruinart champagnes will find their way onto all markets – a treat in store for the United States which, up until now, has only made the acquaintance of Dom Ruinart. Along the way, something had to go, and that was the Tradition Non-Vintage, of which I was very fond – but pastures new can be stimulating!

Ruinart have, of course, the image of being a "Chardonnay house", with the splendid Dom Ruinart Blanc de Blancs flying the standard. But the unusual use of the Chardonnay is in the Dom Ruinart Rosé, where it makes up 80 percent of the blend and thus presents a very different profile to most pink champagnes.

Ruinart only produce brut champagnes. Gyropalettes are partially used for the "R" range, never for Dom Ruinart.

Dom Ruinart Blanc de Blancs: The interest in the 100 percent Chardonnay composition of the wine is that the origin is not only the Côte des Blancs but also the Montagne de Reims, which gives depth to the blend, especially from the northeast-facing slopes of Sillery where Ruinart have owned vineyards for more than two centuries. As a result, Dom Ruinart ages well, and the 1973 and 1975 are still superb. The 1976 is fruity with good character, but the 1979 surpasses it, with its keen, floral nose and taste of hazelnuts. It is an utterly classic, complete wine, in the very top category. The first Dom Ruinart produced was the 1959.

Dom Ruinart Rosé: Here you find the fascinating blend of 80 percent Chardonnay with 20 percent Pinot Noir. The colour is obtained by adding red wine from Bouzy. Again, there is Chardonnay from the Montagne de Reims in the assemblage. Ruinart describe their rosé champagnes as "carminé", but that might give an impression of being too dark. In fact, the colour is just right, taking an intermediate position in the vast and confusing range of tints one sees in these pink "danseuses". The 1979 (with modified label) has a red-fruits nose, which superimposes itself on the Chardonnay perfume. It is both fresh and mature at the same time, which means that it is ready to drink. The 1978, tasted a year earlier, had a pink-grapefruit colour and a pretty, delicate aroma, with austerity and true brut character mixing with the strawberry flavours: an elegant wine, with an enticing finish. This is the kind of rosé champagne that can be drunk "en apéritif". The 1975 is superlative.

"R" de Ruinart Rosé Non-Vintage: This is quite different in character, made with 80 percent Pinot Noir and 20 percent Pinot Meunier and no Chardonnay at all. Bouzy rouge provides the colour. Immediately one notices the Pinot Noir, almost vegetal smell, with more emphasized red fruits. It is a champagne of depth and flavour, ideal with food – even pink lamb.

"R" de Ruinart Brut: 25–30 percent Chardonnay, 30–40 percent Pinot Noir, 30–40 percent Pinot Meunier. I tasted a cuvée with 20 percent Chardonnay, and here there was a very Pinot Meunier nose, perfumed and soft, leading to a very supple, attractive taste. The cuvée following this was going up to 30 percent Chardonnay, so there are, as always, variations between "lots" according to the vintages available for the blend. A very "all-purpose, all-moments" champagne. I have stocks at home, and find it keeps very well.

"R" de Ruinart Vintage, or Millésimé: 30 percent Chardonnay, 70 percent Pinot Noir, but the 1982 had 40 percent Chardonnay and 60 percent Pinot Noir. There is no Meunier in the blend. The bouquet of the 1982 is ultra floral; this is a great wine, with perfect balance. A very successful vintage, more seductive than the quite powerful 1981.

Although this book is exclusively about great champagne and not about the still wines of the region, Ruinart's Chardonnay Blanc de Blancs, Coteaux Champenois, is for me by far the best of the genre. It has an excellent, grapey nose and a nutty, fresh taste – I find it delicious with fish soup.

Salon

• • • •

Salon remains something of a mystery in the champagne world, tiny, rare and tasted by a mere handful of people. It is not an old house: on the contrary, it was founded in 1914 (hardly a propitious time) by Eugène-Aimé Salon. It was a hobby for him, financed by other business activities and, like many hobbies, it became a passion. Eugène-Aimé Salon wanted to make a single-growth, single-grape-variety champagne, using Chardonnay from Le Mesnil-sur-Oger. This is the very antithesis, of course, of what most champagne is all about: astute blending of grapes, villages and crus.

However, as demand increased, he had to buy in grapes from other growers in Le Mesnil, but he only produced vintage champagne in the years that merited this status. Salon became the house wine of Maxim's during the 1920s: the two decades of the '20s and the '30s were the heyday of Salon. Besserat de Bellefon bought Salon in 1963 and now both are owned by Pernod-Ricard. Thus, management is in the hands of Jean-Jacques Bouffard of Besserat de Bellefon, and the wine is made by oenologist Jean-Louis Dohr at Le Mesnil. There is now only one hectare of vineyard, which goes into Besserat de Bellefon when there is not a Salon vintage. This hectare represents about 20 percent of the house's needs: the remaining grapes needed come from a cooperative at Le Mesnil with 20 members. Their vines are nearly all on the slope, with only a few near the forest. Annual sales are about 40,000 bottles.

There is no malolactic fermentation at Salon, which explains in part why the wines need bottle-age. The first fermentation takes place in vat: then the wine is matured in wooden demi-muids (casks), before the "tirage", or bottling, which lasts from October to the following spring. This is significantly different to normal procedure in Champagne, and more suitable for a wine that has not been through a malolactic fermentation.

About 15 years ago I tasted many old vintages of Salon, but I think those notes are hardly relevant today. However, in February 1988 I did a fascinating tasting of three Salon wines in Champagne, and followed this up with the tasting of the 1964 two months later. For the session one evening in Reims, the wines were disgorged in the morning: they had been kept sur pointes. None of these wines had any dosage.

1979: A pale colour, a feature of young Salon wines. Great freshness on the nose, bouquet of fresh hay that has just been cut, often to be found in Chardonnay. Strong taste of hazelnuts on the palate. Clean, clear and concise. There is a certain lack of dimension that you can find in young blanc de blancs, but the wine is very stylish.

1969: Pale. Slightly reductive nose, initially like some white burgundies, but on contact with air more like the "petrol" of old Riesling. Others thought it was like a vin jaune on the nose. Clean, lanolin taste. A style one either likes or not – I do. In the empty glass, a distinct smell of walnuts.

1964 (in magnum): The best part of this wine is its sublime bouquet, complex, intriguing, deeply fascinating. The palate has not the same dimensions but could develop them in time. It is still very young and, of course, straight from the cellar, in perfect condition. Undoubtedly a Salon that will make a splendid old bottle – it just requires more layers of flavour on the finish.

1947: This was, naturally, darker in colour than the other wines. The nose was of apricots and prunes, very honeyed. The aftertaste almost resembled sherry, especially with oxidation. It should be drunk fairly quickly after pouring to get the full fruit impact, which is quite wonderful.

Secret Salon – the most elusive wine in Champagne. I am still firmly of the belief that mono-grape champagnes rarely have the same complexity as blends of grapes and myriad crus, but there is no doubt that Salon, with age, develops qualities all its own. If you wish to see how Le Mesnil Chardonnay ages, this is the way to do it – but wait at least 25 years before opening the bottle.

Taittinger

If Taittinger have built up their empire in the post-World War II period, it is very much because they are a house that mirrors our times: dynamic, highly aware of how best to promote their image and keenly attuned to modern tastes – like Claude Taittinger himself. Some elements of the past remain: they are a family firm (quoted on the Paris Stock Exchange, but the majority of the shares are in the hands of the Taittinger family), and quality is not sacrificed to efficiency. Taittinger are very at ease with high technology but retain tried and tested methods when deemed necessary. But they are after their quarry, notably the American market. They are hot behind the heels of the Big Three in the United States, Moët, Mumm and Perrier-Jouët, and the very astute business minds at Taittinger undoubtedly have other goals in sight.

The foundations of the house are among the oldest in Champagne: Jacques Fourneaux established his marque in 1734. After World War I, Pierre Charles Taittinger bought the Château de la Marquetterie at Pierry near Epernay, now the house's centre in the vineyards, on the site where Frère Oudart once worked on the production of sparkling champagne, both during and after the life of Dom Pérignon. In 1931, Pierre Charles Taittinger took control of Fourneaux, and the family bought the 13th-century Maison des Comtes de Champagne. The cellars for the Comtes de Champagne (the wine this time), originally excavated as crayères in the Gallo-Roman era, are under what was St-Nicaise Abbey, destroyed during the French Revolution. There is also another, much larger cellar where the main part of Taittinger's champagnes are made.

Taittinger are important vineyard owners, with 250 hectares in 30 growths at Pierry, on the Côte des Blancs, on the Montagne de Reims, in the Aube and Sézannais. Pierre Taittinger had had the great good sense to buy vineyards in the depressed period between the two World Wars – those who did the same thing in Bordeaux also found it paid off handsomely. However, more than half the purchases of vines were made in the 1950s. All three grape varieties are

Claude Taittinger in his book, Thibaud Le Chansonnier, Comte de Champagne, recounts how his hero discovered the Chardonnay grape in Cyprus when returning from the Crusades in 1240. He enjoyed the wine from the vineyards around Limassol and brought home cuttings to plant in the chalky soil of his properties in Epernay and Sézanne. So we have Thibaud to thank for this most costly of grapes that contributes so much to the finesse of champagne. (Thibaud was a poet and musician as well as a soldier and diplomat, hence the sobriquet "Le Chansonnier".)

represented but a good half are Chardonnay, which is a high proportion. Taittinger's own vineyards supply about 50 percent of their needs. Sales are now running at four million bottles a year, with 15 million bottles giving them three and a half years of stock.

Automatic remuage (computer-controlled gyropalettes) is used for all Taittinger champagnes except the Comtes de Champagne. With their cuvée de prestige, everything is traditional, down to the cork and metal clasp closure for the second fermentation. The prise de mousse is done directly in all sizes of bottles up to the Methuselah.

It is sometimes quite difficult to winnow information from Taittinger. There is a certain wariness not found in other houses – but then the Taittingers are a very political family and politicians are more suspicious than most of us! As Philippe Court, managing director of Taittinger, puts it, "we sell a dream". But

• • • • • • • • • •

A map drawn up in 1790 shows the vineyard holdings, press centres and where the pickers were housed and fed in the early days of what is now the house of Taittinger. The foundations of the house go back to 1734, when Monsieur Jacques Fourneaux of Reims established the firm that the Taittinger family acquired in 1931.

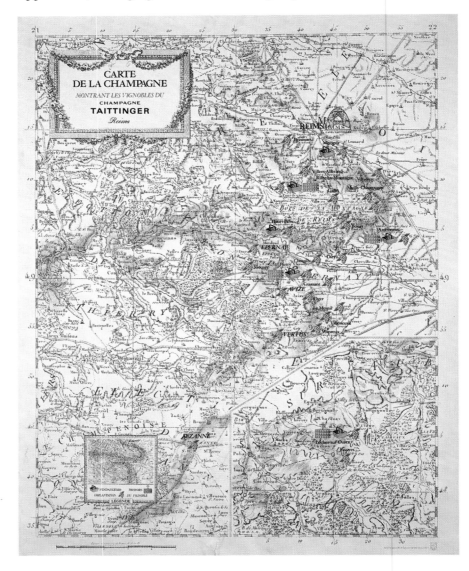

they need not be frightened of the real world where their champagne is concerned, because there are no dark secrets to hide.

Taittinger themselves see their champagne as being very marked by Chardonnay, easy drinking, with finesse and elegance. They have perceived that the style needed now is for lighter wines and have tailor-made their champagnes to fit. But they are not just going for the apéritif style – after all, they sponsor the Prix Pierre Taittinger, which attracts top chefs from all over the world. Gastronomy is a plank in their sales platform.

Brut Réserve NV: 60 percent black grapes with 40 percent Chardonnay. Taittinger are looking for a taste that is brut but round, as the market likes supple wines. Usually they achieve this end, although I do sometimes chance upon bottles that are a mite green and rather charmless.

Brut Vintage: 60 percent black grapes with 40 percent Chardonnay. Here, there is definitely more age on the wine and consequently much more interest. There is more breed than in the non-vintage and the Chardonnay is much in evidence. Of the 1979, 1980 and 1982, I opt narrowly for the last, largely because it was such a

St John the Baptist in his niche in what was the crypt of St-Niçaise Abbey, now part of the old Taittinger cellars in Reims where their prestige cuvée, Comtes de Champagne, is made. There is almost something holy about the quiet, cool crayères: one senses a miracle at work.

great Chardonnay year. The 1979 is quite gold in colour with a very ripe smell, Chardonnay influenced. It is rich, lovely and mature, both floral and nutty – I liked it very much at the beginning of 1988. The 1980 is also golden, the bouquet is nuttier, the taste rounded – food champagne now, as it tastes older than the 1979. I admired the 1976 and 1975 a few years ago. The 1970, tasted in 1988, had a gentle bubble and a lemony scent and taste. It was full and yet with marked lemony acidity, enjoyable but needs drinking.

Vintage Collection: 60 percent Pinot Noir and Meunier, 40 percent Chardonnay and the same cuvée as the brut vintage. The artist-designed bottles were launched on the 1978 vintage, and were followed by the 1981: there were no brut vintage Taittinger wines in those years, as they were small harvests. I have happy memories of the contents of the 1978, the "gold" Vasarely bottle. By far the most beautiful bottle is the André Masson "coating" for the 1982 vintage – highly symbolic of the climatic cycle in Champagne and devastatingly blue. The wine (just in case we forget it) is wonderfully stylish. The lovely gold colour and very strong mousse lead into a full, hazelnutty taste, with a blossomy Chardonnay finesse. This is exceptionally classy champagne, one of the most seductive on the market as I write and the epitome of elegance.

Remember that these Collection bottles, with their painted covers, take longer to chill than usual.

Comtes de Champagne Blanc de Blancs: The bottle shape is from the time of Frère Oudart, the recipe is 100 percent Chardonnay from the best areas of the Côte des Blancs. The first vintage was the 1952, launched in 1957 when blanc de blancs champagnes were very rare. Drinking this cuvée is always thrilling, although I could wish it was less wincingly expensive. Comtes de Champagne transcends the criticisms of limited dimension that can usually be applied to blanc de blancs: but then, although it is mono-grape, it is not mono-cru. It is a wine of immense breed and I would place the 1976, 1975 and 1973 among the greatest of all champagnes I have drunk.

In January 1988 I did a fascinating tasting in London of three Comtes wines, each with a decade between them:

1981: On the market in 1988. It has a warm, very blossomy Chardonnay nose: you can get this very varietal smell when the champagne is young because, later, secondary aromas take over. It is liltingly delicious, with a soft and ripe sweetness at the finish. It goes on unfolding on the palate, which means it has potential for longevity. But with the Comtes, don't exaggerate the ageing if you wish to catch it at its apogee: eight to ten years seems about ideal.

1971: Pale lemon colour. Slightly petrolly smell but a wonderfully fruity taste, both peachy and greengagey. Round and luscious, with a simply lovely long aftertaste. What a treat.

1961: Deep colour. Almost a botrytized "Sauternes" smell – or Manzanilla. Foie gras wine; old, reminds me even of an old Graves. Almondy finish.

I have it on good authority that the 1966 is lively and "en pleine vie".

Comtes de Champagne Rosé: Made by the maceration/skin-contact method. 100

percent Pinot Noir from Bouzy and Ambonnay and a vineyard rating of 100 percent. The first vintage was the extraordinary 1966, launched in 1972: Taittinger gave up doing a "normal" rosé champagne at a time when most houses were turning from vintage to non-vintage, thereby going against the general trend. The labels are a lovely Brazilian topaz colour.

At the same London tasting at the beginning of 1988, I faced up to two vintages of this fabulous wine:

1976: Bluey-pale pink. Lovely, really fragrant nose. Gloriously "sweet" in the Pinot Noir sense (*not* dosage). It was heavenly in the chill light of a January morning, but it would be spectacular with cold salmon trout – perhaps on a luxury picnic.

1970: An orangey colour, it smells very Burgundian. This is a real *wine*, with really ripe fruit. It would be splendid with pink lamb: a champagne rosé to take very seriously indeed.

On another occasion I have appreciated the 1979, with its deep bluey-pink, bouquet of real breed and concentrated taste. There is the fragrance of the hedgerows allied to an excellent firm taste. The 1975 is outstanding, and 1981 is the vintage coming on stream in 1988.

You can drink Taittinger at Glyndebourne and the English National Opera. Alternatively, you can reach for your best CD recording and open a bottle at home. Both are experiences to savour.

Veuve Clicquot Ponsardin

No other champagne has quite the same visibility as Veuve Clicquot. That yellow label is instantly recognizable, even when glimpsed from afar. It is the champagne we love to call by its diminutive, The Widow, or the affectionate Gula Änka of Scandinavia. It is the champagne of nostalgia, of family reunions, Christmas parties and hesitant débuts into an adult world. But it is also the marque that has now woken up to its full potential in today's market, equipping itself to meet current demands and prove, as the house has always done, that quantity can be married to the very highest quality. From the dynamic direction that Clicquot is now taking, one would think that The Widow herself was back in control.

The house was founded in 1772 by Philippe Clicquot Muiron, but its main activity was in textiles and banking. Clicquot's son, François, married Nicole-Barbe Ponsardin, and after she was widowed at the age of twenty-seven, she took over control of the company. She always had the aid of very able men, both in sales and wine making, and one of them, Comte Edouard Werlé, was rewarded by becoming a partner – the Werlé name is still on the Clicquot corks and labels. Madame Clicquot herself had experimented with ways to clarify her wines, and together with her chef de caves, Antoine Müller, she developed the system of remuage sur pupitres. The house passed through the Werlé family to that of Comte Bertrand de Mun and then the de Vogüés. In 1987, Clicquot, already

Madame Clicquot was the most astute, empire-building woman of her day, so it is more than appropriate that her house should sponsor the Veuve Clicquot Award for the Business Woman of the Year. The Widow must have been one of the first to realise that to expand is to export, and so she would have been pleased with my personal contribution to the effort. When I arrived on a Peloponnese beach in the summer of 1987 with some personally imported Clicquot, the boy in charge of the primitive refrigerator looked at the label and exclaimed, "This is the best, isn't it?" – surely the ultimate in brand recognition and a very fitting accolade to a great house.

Madame Veuve
Clicquot, whose
presence still seems to
dominate Champagne.
She was a dynamic
director of sales,
forever seeking new
markets, and she
invented the first basic
system of remuage sur
pupitres. More than a
century after her
death, she remains an
example to
businesswomen
everywhere.

owned by the luxury luggage company, Louis Vuitton, merged with Moët-Hennessy, to form the largest single force in Champagne. Clicquot is now headed by Joseph Henriot.

Clicquot own about 260 hectares of vineyard, with an average on the échelle of over 95 percent, but with more than 160 hectares 99–100 percent. All three grape varieties are grown, and the vineyards are in villages such as Avize, Cramant, Aÿ, Bouzy, Ambonnay, Verzenay, Le Mesnil-sur-Oger, Oger, Verzy and Villedommange. This covers about 30 percent of Clicquot's requirements, with the rest coming from grapes grown over about 800 hectares, planted in all three varieties. Total sales are about 8 million bottles a year. At the end of 1987, there were 32 million bottles in stock at Clicquot.

Clicquot have some of the most impressive crayères cellars in Reims. The sense of history that imposes itself as you walk through them is perhaps enhanced by the poignant reminders of World War I – the headquarters of a French general with a niche for his field telephone, the natural stage of chalk where the soldiers used to put on productions to amuse themselves while incarcerated in those damp depths. In these 25 kilometres, there was a military hospital during the Great War.

The stunning quality of Clicquot wines now is in part due to Jacques Peters, oenologist, chef de caves and future technical director of the house. His approach, integrity and winemaking abilities are immediately apparent. There has undoubtedly been renewed investment in equipment and a tightening up of

Bottles about to be
labelled at Veuve
Clicquot. This
operation is almost
always mechanized
now, although some
cuvées de prestige have
such complicated
labelling that it has to
be done by hand.
Presentation is vital in
marketing champagne:
it must always live up
to its reputation as a
true luxury product.

An old wooden press belonging to Veuve Clicquot. The vertical press is still widely used throughout the Champagne region and has proved its worth in every sort of vintage. However, horizontal presses are already installed in some large concerns, and more innovation and modernization is on the way.

the little details that make the difference between good and remarkable champagne. Clicquot now has a little less alcohol than a few years ago, the non-vintage a little less reserve wine, and certainly less oxidation picked up at the moment of dégorgement. The result is an added freshness which in no way diminishes the lovely depth of flavour to be found in Clicquot champagne. The malolactic fermentation is effected and dosage is now strictly limited: with the non-vintage, they aim for 11 grams per litre of residual sugar, the vintage nine (the 1983 has eight), while the Grande Dame 1979, a real tête de cuvée if ever there were one, only had six.

For the future, there will be more vats in stainless steel and a new pressing centre at Vertus is planned: Clicquot already have 12 vendangeoirs and 40 pressoirs, both traditional and horizontal. Remuage is manual for La Grande Dame, in gyropalettes containing 381 bottles for the other qualities.

At the moment, Clicquot is very much the darling of the Europeans, who have lapped up the wine with the utmost confidence for longer than most of us care to remember. The British agent takes care to keep the wine for six months after landing before sale, because that is how the natives like their Clicquot. But America, something of a sleeping giant where Clicquot is concerned, has suddenly woken to its charms, with the help of some efficient promotion. After all, the house is only reclaiming its rights – at the end of the last century, Clicquot had 35 percent of the American market.

Brut NV: 50 percent Pinot Noir, 20 percent Pinot Meunier, 30 percent Chardonnay. This is always a deeply satisfying wine, with the black grapes coming through and giving great bouquet and length. I usually buy the non-vintage in 2 or 3 case lots and keep it for a year or two: my friends then think it is

The bed on which Napoleon slept when he stayed at the house of Monsieur Ponsardin, the brother of Madame Clicquot, in Reims in 1814. The town had had an unhappy visit by Russian troops, but certainly Veuve Clicquot ultimately benefited, because their wine became known and very popular in the land of the Tsars.

• • • • • • • • • •

very classy vintage. The quality has been consistently fine for the past five years. Even when there had to be some 1984 in the blend, it was undetectable: hardly surprising when I learnt that 48 percent of reserve wine was used at the time, a financial sacrifice that certainly paid off in terms of image protection.

If you like fruit, full flavour and a certain voluptuousness, this is the non-vintage for you.

Demi-Sec NV: With the same grape proportions as the Brut, the wine is greeny-gold with tiny bubbles. The taste is both lemony and sweet, which prevents it being mawkish. There is some elegance and laciness, but it does not approach the sheer class of Roederer Rich, easily the best champagne in this category.

Brut Vintage: About 65 percent Pinot Noir, 35 percent Chardonnay (the latter has been increased a little recently). The 1982 is one of the most delicious Clicquot vintages I have known, utterly captivating, combining the fruit and charm of the year with the characteristic Clicquot explosion of flavour on the palate. It also seems to be the only wine where the new little "tabs" designed to help remove the foil really work, a minor aspect of technology which does not appear so unimportant when one is trying to open dozens of bottles for a party. Nota bene other houses, whose efforts in this direction have been largely ineffectual. The 1979 and 1976 Brut Vintage were very satisfactory, while the 1975 was outstanding.

Rosé Brut Vintage: Made from Pinot Noir and Chardonnay and usually blended with 12–15 percent red wine from the Clicquot vines at Bouzy. Clicquot reputedly made the first rosé champagne in 1777, Pommery the second. The 1978, blended with 12–13 percent Bouzy rouge, has become rather vegetal: it was always very dark in colour. The 1979 is paler and more attractive in shade, and much more elegant, with finesse and more style. The 1983 (with a low dosage of eight grams per litre) has a glowing deep topaz colour, quite different from the dark colour of the 1978. There are tiny bubbles and a fruity, blossomy, really winey bouquet. The flavour has elements of strawberry but with more finesse than previous vintages, without sacrificing the Clicquot body.

La Grande Dame: 62 percent Pinot Noir, 38 percent Chardonnay, and entirely from vineyards that originally belonged to Madame Clicquot. This is a superb cuvée de prestige, one that really complements food and has the balance to benefit from bottle ageing. The 1975 is a great vintage. The 1979, right from its launch, showed in stunning fashion in blind tastings. At the end of 1987, it had a lovely pronounced champagne nose and was wonderfully austere and taut with flavour, and yet full and all-enveloping at the same time. The 1983 has the tiniest of bubbles and a greeny colour. The bouquet is black grape and very winey, the taste strong and definite with a touch of hawthorn. Although young, the flavour is mature, obviously due to the high ripeness of top vineyards. This is incisive champagne for a grand dinner.

Colour coding for the Clicquot labels, but the showy orange for the non-vintage is still probably the most recognizable champagne label of all.

CHAPTER EIGHT

VINTAGES PAST
AND PRESENT

There are, naturally for such a northern vineyard area, significant differences between vintages in Champagne. This is mitigated by blending the wines of several years for non-vintage champagnes. Occasionally, there is a year when Nature is really unkind, and this can pose problems of stock. Quality is maintained by having large reserves of older wines on which a house can call to "bridge the gap", but they have to be integrated with care to preserve balance.

There has always been disagreement between lovers of young and "old" champagnes, although there are devotees who appreciate both styles of wine, matching the vintage with the moment. If you are ever faced with a really old champagne which has lost its life but still retains its flavour, it is not forbidden to add a drop or two of a good, young non-vintage champagne to inject a little vivacity into the old lady – somehow old champagnes are feminine rather than masculine, I find. This is preferable to a practice followed by one of the Grand Old Men of the British Wine Trade I had the pleasure of knowing during my early days in the trade, who used to add a dash of bicarbonate of soda to failing old champagnes!

It is interesting to compare our tastes now with those prevailing around 1863, as expressed by Shaw in his *Wine, The Vine, and the Cellar*. He suggests drinking the "good vintages" at five or six years old, others at two to three years old, which would probably correspond to the non-vintage wines we drink today. However, he suspects that many people would like to drink their champagne earlier, but those who appreciate "a true old, firm, creaming champagne" should practise the art of laying down some bottles. Nowadays, as champagnes are so much better made and are more technically sound than vintages of the past, you could safely keep your "grands millésimes" for eight to ten years, rather than just five or six, whatever your tastes.

André Simon, in his *History of the Wine Trade in England*, Volume III, gives some lovely vintage notes for the start of the 17th century. What is amusing is

The windmill at Verzenay is the best-known landmark on the Montagne de Reims. The only surviving windmill in Champagne, it was used as an observation post during World War I. The mill belongs to Heidsieck Monopole, whose Diamant Bleu is marked by the special Pinot Noir character of the Verzenay vineyards. The rich green of the vines at harvest time is in striking contrast to the denuded scene in winter.

"Comet vintages" are the years when a notable wine coincides with the appearance of a comet. 1630 was a "comet year"; so, apparently, was 1858. But the most celebrated is 1811, the year of the Great Comet. It is fascinating to speculate what the vinous result might have been had Halley's appearance in 1986 been as spectacular as forecast.

that they read just like the vintage reports I am sometimes asked to write for wine magazines. For example:

1600 Cold and rain in September; fairly large yield; poor quality.
1601 Severe spring frosts; small vintage, but excellent quality.
1602 Excessive heat in July followed by cold weather; very little wine made. Or:
1604 Early vintage; started mid-September; very large quantity of wine made, but of poor quality and selling at 15 livres; the wines of Aÿ the only exception as regards fine quality.

1605 Spring frosts reduced the quantity of wine made; vintage amounted to barely a third of the previous one, but the quality of the wine much superior; Aÿ wine sold at 40 livres and upwards.
1606 Disappointing vintage commenced very late, and not quite over on All Saints' Day.
1607 May and June were very cold; the smallest vintage on record, but the wine excellent.

One could go on, but I dare to suppose that, even for those with the finest cellars, it must be somewhat academic. It is worth noting, however, that 1630 was a "comet year".

Moving into the realms of the possible, even if hardly probable, Shaw states (and I venture to quote him, since I have not tasted any of them) that there was not one fine year in Champagne between 1846 and 1857, both magnificent, which seems a longer-than-average run of bad luck. He recommends 1834, 1846, 1857, 1858, 1861 and 1862.

Professor George
Saintsbury greatly
admired the Krug
vintage of 1865,
*"which memory
represents as being,
though dry, that
'winy wine', as
Thackeray describes
it, which Champagne
ought to be, but too
seldom is."*
(*Notes on a Cellar-
Book, 1921*)

The Cardiff wine merchant, S. D. Churchill, in *All Sorts and Conditions of Drinks*, circa 1893, makes the following assessments:

1865 Superior quality; very vinous.

1866 Bad.

1867 Mediocre.

1868 Very good, elegant, and lighter than the 1865s.

1869 Passable.

1870 Good. [Maybe better than this, but the Franco-Prussian War made it difficult for some producers.]

1871 Mediocre.

1872 Fairly good.

1873 Bad; acid.

1874 One of the finest vintages of the century, if not the finest.

1875 Passable.

1876 Mediocre.

1877 Mediocre; acid.

1878 Good; fine; light.

1879 Complete failure; yield small.

1880 Very good; lighter than the 1874s.

1881 Passable.

1882 Mediocre; acid; immature.

1883 Mediocre; acid.

1884 Fine, elegant wines; highly appreciated by all connoisseurs.

1885 Mediocre; resembling the 1883s.

1886 Some good wines, with abundance of vinosity; but for the most part, the vintage was under suspicion, which time has not so far lessened.

1887 Fairly good; light.

1888 Passable.

1889 Very good, and worth buying at present prices.

1890 Ordinary quality.

1891 Passable, but very dear.

This is a total of 27 vintages, of which eight were judged excellent, very good or good; nine were passable, ordinary or fairly good; seven were mediocre; and three

Far left: Winter pre-pruning, or tidying up the vines, can be a chilly business. The vineyards at Rilly-la-Montagne, on the northern slope of the Montagne de Reims, are particularly exposed to winds.
Left: Picking is always done by hand in Champagne – mechanical harvesters are banned. Smoking is permitted in the vineyards, but not in the cellars!

"The two best
vintages of the
'nineties were those of
1892 and 1899 as
regards quality, but
the most remarkable
vintage of the decade
was 1893. The heat of
the summer was so
great and lasted so
long that many wells
dried up and there
was a great shortage
of water, so much so
that, at the time of the
vintage, at Cramant,
anybody with a horse,
a cart and an empty
cask, who would go to
the Marne and deliver
at the pressoir a cask
of Marne water to
wash and cool the
presses, could go
home with his cask
full of new wine in
exchange, no money
passing: water was as
valuable as wine."
(The History of
Champagne, André
Simon, 1962)

were bad or a "complete failure". Clearly this proportion of poor vintages led to the necessity of the major houses keeping good stocks.

As a comparison, it is worth recalling Henry Vizetelly's impressions of the same vintages. He was a pioneer of the illustrated press and published translations of Zola, which led him into a certain amount of trouble with the law. He was also a considerable gastronome, frequenting the fashionable London literary restaurants of the 19th century around Leicester Square. Vizetelly says a really grand vintage in champagne normally only occurs once, and never more than twice, in ten years. During the same period, though, he admits that there will generally be one or two other "tolerably good" vintages. He comments that in grand years the crop, besides being of superior quality, is usually abundant. He lists the grand vintages as 1802, 1806, 1811, 1818, 1822, 1825, 1834, 1842, 1846, 1857, 1865, 1868 and 1874 – which makes 13 grand vintages in 80 years! Other good vintages: 1815, 1832, 1839, 1852, 1854, 1858, 1862, 1864 and 1870.

Happily, now, we enter a new era, when the rate of good to superb vintages was very much more impressive. The 1892 was magnificent (Professor George Saintsbury in his *Notes on a Cellar-Book*, 1921, recommended Pommery, Krug and Roederer), 1893 only slightly less so (Clicquot, Moët, Ayala). There was nothing special between 1894 and 1897, but 1898 developed very well. My husband, David Peppercorn, drank an 1898: Moët's Cuvée for the Coronation of Edward VII in 1902, but disgorged and imbibed in 1956 by the first Champagne Academy visit to the region. It was, apparently, a youthful revelation. The 1899 was stunning (Saintsbury selected Clicquot as the best).

Not to be outdone, 1900 was nearly as good, and the 1904s were famous. 1906 was almost as splendid (Saintsbury praises the Krug Private Cuvée), while 1911 was excellent, perhaps the finest vintage since 1874. I have never tasted a 1904, a 1906 and a 1911 together, but my husband compared the three vintages of Pommery in 1956 and pronounced the 1911 the best – certainly superb at that time. 1914 was very commendable, in spite of the presence of enemy soldiers in the region; the good 1915s were vintaged by prisoners of war and soldiers on leave. At the beginning of 1988 I had a lovely bottle of Bollinger 1918, a vintage I knew not at all. The wine was medium-depth gold and the taste concentrated, and perfect with filets de sole normande. The 1919s had a reputation for quality and elegance.

1920 was very good indeed, while 1921 was exceptional – Veuve Clicquot is probably the finest surviving example. 1923 was virtually as good, with Clicquot excelling again. 1926 was good, and then came the quite remarkable 1928 – nowadays, the Clicquot and the extraordinary Krug, tasted even more recently, are the kings of the castle. Apparently the Pol Roger, at 30 years old, was marvellous. The 1929s almost equal the previous vintage, but perhaps have not lasted as well.

Into the next decade, both 1933 and 1934 were very good – with Pol Roger '34 a favourite of Churchill's. 1937, however, was the star. Again, I have good memories of the Clicquot, which have been gloriously rekindled as I worked on this book – the wine was pinky-amber in colour, showing a lovely haze of bubbles when poured out, and with a honeyed, tawny, intoxicating taste.

Of the war years, 1943 was the best, but I have to move on to 1945 in this decade for personal tasting experience. It is a great, long-lasting vintage and, for me, Krug reigns supreme. It is still an extraordinarily vigorous champagne, and I only hope I can emulate its style! The two other fine examples have been Charles Heidsieck and Roederer. 1947, the result of a perfect summer, was almost as lovely, and here my favourites are Moët, Mumm and Clicquot (the last two in magnum), all drunk at the end of the 1970s/beginning 1980s. My husband says that, at 12 years old, Roederer was the pick of the whole bunch – one would love to run *that* tasting again. In fact, I did taste Roederer '47 in 1986 and it was pretty impressive, although I do not think the storage was ideal. 1949 was another beautiful vintage, with Pol Roger and Pommery the stars.

I cannot recall ever having tasted a 1952, although the vintage has a good reputation. My husband gives glowing reports of the Krug. 1953 was a delightful vintage: favourites are Clicquot, Bollinger and Roederer. Perhaps 1955 is the high spot of the decade – my finest recollection is of the Krug. Then we had to wait until 1959; Pol Roger is my most recent memory, although there were some lovely bottles of Roederer, including a stunning Rehoboam. There were also some quite heavy wines due to the long, hot summer, but the brilliance of the Krug assemblage avoids this characteristic.

As always with 1961, the inclination is to put it right at the top because of Bordeaux's reputation in this vintage but, although very good, you can usually do even better now with other vintages in the 1960s. I would immediately give Dom Pérignon 1961, disgorged in 1981 (and last tasted very recently), as the glorious exception: it is fabulous, toasty, elegant wine. Krug 1961 is also splendid, a rich, meal-time champagne. Less recently, a magnum of Roederer Rosé and Clicquot were milestones. I have dreamlike memories of Roederer and the superstar Cristal – but those memories need reviving!

1962 is a very good vintage, although it has not come my way as often as others in the decade. Krug is still a great experience, and Cristal was lovely too long ago. Today, 1964 certainly has the edge over 1962. Again, Krug is quite outstanding, but then so are magnums of Diamant Bleu, Heidsieck Monopole's largely unsung prestige blend. Cristal used to light up my life.

1966 is undoubtedly a fine vintage, although I do not see many now. Krug, of course, lives on and, until quite recently, Charles Heidsieck, both in bottle and magnum, was consistently delicious. Roederer hit the bullseye, especially with Cristal. Nor do I see many 1969s nowadays, but Dom Pérignon, gloriously elegant as ever, stands out. There was also an extremely pleasant Alfred Gratien Crémant, and the Krug has magnificent verve and attack.

The 1970s were really extraordinarily attractive wines, although they seem to be disappearing from the scene now. By far the two best examples of the vintage I have tasted recently have been Bollinger Blanc de Noirs Vieilles Vignes, almost a meal in itself, and Jacquesson, disgorged in 1985, a honey of a wine. Moët and

The "punt", the hollow in the base of champagne bottles, is not to deprive us of the equivalent measure of the wine; it is to help distribute the pressure of the contents over more surface area, thus reducing the stress on the bottle. It is also, of course, extremely useful when storing champagne, because the neck of one bottle fits neatly into the punt of the bottle in front – or below, if stacked vertically "sur pointes". The only exception is the bottle designed for Roederer Cristal, which has no punt.

Bollinger Année Rare are also very fine. I was extremely enamoured of Cristal when it was a decade old, but it has since faded from view, if not from memory. Taittinger's Comtes de Champagne Rosé is now almost Burgundian – and quite terrific.

1971 has proved to have elegance, and this is well illustrated by Cristal, an incredibly seductive Roederer Crémant which we have been drinking up until recently, and by a thoroughly satisfying Moët. Almost as I write, Taittinger's Comtes de Champagne Blanc de Blancs is wonderfully fruity and round – peaches and greengages – with a lovely long finish. Roederer Rosé was all tawny concentration five years ago, and Krug survives in style, as does Gosset.

For some reason, few expected the invariably charming 1973s to last particularly well, but Krug and Dom Ruinart Blanc de Blancs are proving them very wrong. Other favourites, superb now, are Clicquot, Laurent Perrier's Millésime Rare and Gosset. Not so long ago, Bollinger Tradition RD, disgorged in 1983, and Taittinger Comtes de Champagne Blanc de Blancs were excellent, as was Moët Rosé with some pink lamb, and a Jeroboam of Belle Epoque.

1974 was a non-starter for virtually everyone, but Roederer Cristal Rosé was marvellous with spun sugar and strawberries, as concocted by The Four Seasons restaurant in New York. Yes, I know it breaks all my rules about champagne with "le dessert", but this time it worked!

Vintages for Our Times

For detailed tasting notes, see under the individual houses in Chapter VII.

1975 One of the classic vintages of recent years, perfectly set for long life, if you are so inclined. The wines are full of flavour and individuality, firm but fruity, and utterly distinct in character. The balance and composition are impressive, and the youthful austerity which some did not understand has given the vintage the essential "nerve" so necessary if you wish to age champagne. I have not yet tasted one tired example. Recent "pick of the bunch": Bollinger RD.

1976 An extraordinary vintage, picked very early after an exceedingly hot summer. Some wines lacked balance, and needed to be blended with the utmost intelligence. When this has been done, there are some remarkable wines, such as Krug, Roederer, Pommery, Bollinger RD, Diamant Bleu and Taittinger's Comtes de Champagne Rosé.

1977 There is absolutely no need to linger over this unfortunate vintage, when Nature contrived to throw virtually everything at the Champagne region.

1978 A tiny vintage, but the late summer produced some good wines; however, only a few houses declared it a vintage. I always thought Moët was the best – not forgetting the excellent Dom Pérignon.

1979 This is a perfectly splendid vintage, when quantity married with quality. Some people judged that it would not last, but those champagnes that impressed from the beginning continue to do so – just look at Krug, Pol Roger, Dom Ruinart Blanc de Blancs, Bollinger Grande Année, Taittinger, Gosset, Roederer Cristal and Jacquesson Perfection for a start!

The vineyard slopes at Aÿ are gently undulating and beautifully exposed to the south. Predominantly Pinot Noir, the vineyards here produce wines that can be softer and more forward than those from other parts of the Montagne de Reims.

Veuve Clicquot's cellars are among the most impressive in Reims, making use of the chalk crayères originally excavated in Gallo-Roman times. Seemingly endless galleries lead to cavernous "halls": in World War I, when life went underground in Champagne, these cellars were used as a military hospital.

1980 Last-minute sun saved the vintage, but it was still small in quantity, and very few houses "declared". Moët was one of the honourable exceptions.

1981 The vintage turned out to be the smallest since 1978, which was a great blow to the Champagne region. However, the quality is very good, with Taittinger's Comtes de Champagne Blanc de Blancs liltingly delicious. Also recommended: Moët, Roederer, Ruinart, and Krug with, unusually, 50 percent Chardonnay.

1982 This is the vintage we had all been praying for. It was a dream year for the Champenois. A cool but frost-free winter was followed by a long, warm summer and then perfect conditions during the harvest. The result was an abundance of grapes that gave the equivalent of 295 million bottles. Rarely have I been more excited by the arrival of a new vintage. Every tasting seems to confirm that yet another house has made a splendid wine. Whether it is Clicquot, Pol Roger, Moët, Deutz or Gosset, you are in safe hands. And the Blanc de Blancs of Roederer and Pol Roger are remarkable. All this is merely to whet the appetite, for there is much more to come.

1983 A second consecutive abundant harvest. The last time there were two outstanding years in a row was in 1857 and 1858! 1983 produced approximately 300 million bottles, and the decision was taken to increase from 150 kilos to 160 kilos the amount of grapes required from which a hectolitre of must is pressed, thus effectively "creaming off" the best wine from this fine harvest. A reserve of about 25 percent of the total yield was held back for future market demand: in as northerly a wine region as Champagne, one cannot expect every year to be a 1983 or a 1982. The Chardonnays had great finesse and the Pinot Noirs were impressive. There will certainly be vintage champagnes in 1983, although some houses will go from 1982 to 1985.

1984 This was the year we did not want: a late harvest, starting around October 8, due to the late flowering and poor weather conditions in September. Rot was a problem, so quick picking, careful pressing and longer débourbage were necessary. Low alcohol, normal acidity, but the wines have a herbaceous taste. They have to be blended very carefully, and most houses used a far greater proportion of reserve wines than usual in order to give a better final result to their non-vintage champagnes. 196 million bottles were produced.

1985 The vintage that mystified everyone! A month before the harvest, people were predicting a total production of 110 million bottles. In fact, the superb sunny weather in September and October enabled the grapes to swell and ripen in perfect conditions, and the result was a total production of nearly 152 million bottles. The beautiful late season even permitted a rare "second harvest" at the end of October, when bunches could be picked that had been unripe when the vendanges opened on September 30. There is no doubt that the quality of the wines is excellent and there is sure to be a quantity of vintage wines in due course. However, it should not be forgotten that the severe weather in early 1985 did cause an estimated loss of ten percent of the vineyards, so new vines were planted in spring 1986 to come on stream in 1989.

1986 After a hard winter and very late budding, the vines had to endure alternately high and low temperatures throughout the spring. In spite of this, and the effects of the 1985 winter frosts, there was a good showing of embryo bunches of grapes. But from June 10 the sun appeared and installed itself for the summer. There were luxuriant leaves and Nature caught up on its late start, as it so often does in the vineyards. Flowering took place rapidly and evenly around June 25. The setting of the Chardonnay was perhaps upset by the rapidity of development, with a higher than usual incidence of non-pollination and malformation, but the two black grapes developed well. Any variation in quality throughout the Champagne region is more often due to one week of wet weather in late September, just before the 60,000 grape pickers begin to harvest (the use of harvesting machines is banned). Some 259 million bottles were made.

After tastings of the still wines in April 1987, there is no doubt that the quality of the Chardonnays is very fine. They have finesse, harmony and a hazelnut character in the Grands Blancs. Unfortunately, the flowering affected the quantity. The Pinot Noirs are a little thinner than in some years, lacking volume and power in certain cases. Quality in the Marne Valley was excellent, but in the Montagne de Reims, those growers who were careless in their anti-rot treatments suffered the consequences. There are some good Pinot Meuniers from the crus where the variety is traditionally grown.

Louis Roederer say they will probably make 20–25 percent of their total production into vintage wine, but I would think that much depends on the market and stock situations prevailing at the time as to whether 1986 becomes a universal vintage.

1987 Spring 1988 was probably the right moment to assess the 1987 harvest from a quality point of view, especially after extensive tasting of the vins clairs, or still wines. The good news is that all the wines taste clean and frank, whether Chardonnay, Pinot Noir or Pinot Meunier. Undoubtedly, the high yield in the Chardonnays has reduced character somewhat and the wines finish a bit short. Of all the crus, the Ambonnays taste the most impressive. However, overall, there does not seem much potential for longevity, so it would be surprising if many houses opted for a vintage in 1987.

Given the climatic scenario for the year, it is a miracle we have the quality that we do. The flowering did manage to survive an unpropitious start, but then rain set in between July 15 and August 17, exposing the vineyard to grey rot. There was more rain between August 24 and September 7, together with low temperatures and morning fog. Luckily, there was an Indian summer between September 8 and 22 which accelerated the delayed ripening. The rain did not entirely desert the region, but happily it was followed by fine, cold weather.

The extraordinary conditions made for regional differences, reflected in a staggered start to the vintage. Picking began in the Aube on September 28, but elsewhere grapes began to be gathered between October 5 and 10, depending on the grape variety and vineyard location. The harvest resulted in almost a million casks, or close to 264.5 million bottles: a very useful quantity for making non-vintage wines and keeping the reserves topped up.

". . . and the very best I ever had was a Perrier-Jouët. . . . It was a wine of the great vintage of 1857, and was supposed to have formed part of a parcel originally shipped for Queen Victoria, and designated 't.c.' that is to say très coloré. When I bought it, May 1884, it was . . . of a deep amber colour, and nearly but not quite still, though not at all ullaged. . . . It was so majestical that one was inclined to leave it quite alone, and drink it like a slightly sparkling liqueur [rather than] try if the immense dormant qualities of it could be waked up."

(Professor George Saintsbury in Notes on a Cellar-Book, *1921)*

CHAPTER NINE

THE LIFE OF CHAMPAGNE

What is it to be a Champenois, to view life through a champagne glass, to be the possessor of one of the world's luxury items? Undoubtedly, the bubble permeates almost every aspect of life in the region. Business and social activities revolve around it, and whole lives are devoted to its service. Above all, champagne is seen as inextricably linked to the glory of France. It flies the flag for its country on every conceivable occasion, be it inaugurations or anniversaries, cultural events, trade fairs or industrial triumphs. Bordeaux belongs to the British, Burgundy to the Burgundians, but Champagne belongs to France. It represents everything for which France is famous: esprit, élan and glamour.

The life of a Champagne grower is like that of any other farmer of grapes, only more angst-ridden, due to the extreme northerly situation of the vineyards. Perhaps that is why their collective historical memory is so acute. Who in Champagne can forget the four bad, or small, harvests of 1907, 1908, 1909 and 1910, culminating in the Champagne Riots of 1911? Only the Irish have longer memories. Now, of course, a Champagne grower is comfortably, if not very, well-off, which has brought its own socio-economic problems. The mentality is still to store wine, like a squirrel, for a "rainy day" (this has a literal sense, too), but unfortunately wine is a perishable commodity, and there is far too much exceedingly good potential champagne wasting away in growers' cellars.

It is difficult for any farmer to see the larger, global picture. In Champagne that remains the role of the men of the champagne houses, who must marry their responsibilities as producers and large buyers of grapes, winemakers and salesmen par excellence. Many Champagne families have been fulfilling this role for generations and a breed of truly dynamic, outward-looking, cosmopolitan Champenois has evolved, the envy of business communities everywhere. Perfect examples of the genre are Yves Bénard, managing director of Moët & Chandon, and Jean-Claude Rouzaud, managing director of Louis Roederer. They studied oenology together at Montpellier University, and both have extremely astute

financial brains. They swing from decisions involving huge international investment to remaining in constant contact with their vineyards and those who work them. Jean-Claude Rouzaud is always on hand in the Roederer vineyards during the harvest; Yves Bénard is mayor of Boursault, the Marne Valley village where Madame Clicquot had her grandiose château.

Then there is Bernard de Nonancourt who has, since World War II, built up what was then the tiny firm of Laurent-Perrier to the vast concern it is now. His mother was a Lanson, and there is no one more Champenois than this imposing man. He has the great financial vision to stage-manage an operation that went from selling 80,000 bottles of champagne in 1949 to well over seven million bottles today. In case anyone should think this is a dangerously large bubble which could burst, Bernard de Nonancourt is also very much "un homme de la terre", and Laurent-Perrier's wine requirements are solidly underpinned by 800 hectares of vines either owned or under contract to them.

Claude Taittinger is the head of a dynamic house where runaway success has come in the last 50 years. With Pol Roger, it is the only entirely family-owned firm of real size that still bears the name of the people who run it. The Taittinger family also own hotels and are deeply entrenched in political life, but Claude Taittinger has somehow found the time to research and write the life of Thibaud Le Chansonnier, Comte de Champagne – which is only fitting since, in 1933, his family bought Thibaud's 13th-century home.

Joseph Henriot has made the transition from family business to corporate man in triumphant fashion. He now heads Veuve-Clicquot Henriot within the Moët-Hennessy-Vuitton group, and a gust of fresh air is sweeping through the house of the venerable Widow. There are also young lions such as Bruno Paillard, with his unbending insistence on quality at all costs (and it *does* cost for a recently formed house), who are firmly rooted in the region and deeply committed to its long-term welfare.

There are, too, connections with other wine areas in France. The remarkable Jean-Michel Ducellier runs both Ayala in Champagne and that excellent Haut-Médoc 3e cru, Château La Lagune. Félix Chatellier, Président-directeur-général of Champagne George Goulet and Abel Lepitre, is also the owner of Château Dauzac in Margaux. The de Vogüé family, of Moët and Clicquot, have one of the finest domains on the Côte de Nuits, while the Chandon de Briailles tentacles stretch to the Côte de Beaune. The Loire connection, of course, is also traditionally strong – Alfred Gratien with Gratien & Meyer in Saumur, Bollinger with Langlois-Château, Taittinger with Monmousseau and Bouvet-Ladubay, Piper-Heidsieck with Vivency.

New generations come into the champagne business but, here, the son of the house does not necessarily sweep into a privileged position – he must serve his apprenticeship first in true, doughty Champenois style. The last time I lunched with Christian de Billy of Pol Roger, his son had just joined the firm, "but he will not be meeting customers yet". There is not much chance of young heads being turned in Champagne. Occasionally, someone comes from outside who brings

One of the most
hospitable tables in
Champagne is that of
Christian and Marie-
Hélène Bizot of
Bollinger. They are
generous in sharing
with their guests their
love of old champagne
– and old Bordeaux,
too.

business acumen allied to a desire to understand the region and the intelligence to do so – Jean-Jacques Bouffard, the Président-directeur-général of Pernod-Ricard's two houses, Besserat de Bellefon and Salon, is a prime example.

This special breed of men live and breathe champagne, but they are also civilized complete Athenians, with a wide variety of interests and passions. They are unmistakably French, but citizens of the world, travelling with their eyes and hearts open, ready to embrace any aspect of another culture that appeals to them. I have a feeling that the middle-aged to older generations are more imbued with this frontier-less education than the younger members of the champagne trade, but this is observable in every field and in every country nowadays. The difference probably springs from the fact that when transport and the pace of life were slower, the Champenois first set out to study and learn the language in England, or America, or Germany, and then went on extended trips, spending weeks at a time abroad. They often stayed with agents and friends, even customers, becoming more familiar with the national scene, taking part in activities other than selling wine. Consequently, they know many countries intimately and understand the various national mentalities, all of which is invaluable in judging and meeting the demands of a market. The new, youthful breed of Champagne businessman flies in and out of a capital city in a day, runs through balance sheets and sets sales targets equally well in French or in English, but is perhaps not as much at home as his parent when invited to spend a weekend in the English countryside, where the conversation might turn from restoring the ancestral roof to hunting and his host's dogs.

But perhaps I am being too hard. After all, no one more exemplifies the successful businessman today than Rémi Krug, an almost frighteningly

When Moët entertain
in Epernay it is at the
beautiful Trianon, with
its elegant white
buildings, sunken
garden and orangery.
(One of the first guests
at the Trianon was the
Empress Josephine.) A
succession of
champagnes is always
served, starting with a
younger vintage, then
perhaps a rosé, and
finally a venerable
Dom Pérignon.

Solid and reassuring
amid its vineyards, this
19th-century house is
the headquarters of
Bollinger in Aÿ. The
cellars lie alongside
and continue down
Aÿ's sleepy streets.

Solid and reassuring amid its vineyards, this 19th-century house is the headquarters of Bollinger in Aÿ. The cellars lie alongside and continue down Aÿ's sleepy streets.

energetic dynamo in his forties, whose engaging manner belies his shrewdness and flair for doing exactly what is right for his house. Rémi's fluent, easy chat in French, English (and Italian) wins him instant friends everywhere, and yet this is no mere public relations exercise – he is there to sell Krug, to see that it is perfect and, if not (heaven forbid!), to know why.

There is no doubt that champagne needs personalities. As mergers become the order of the day (the Champenois seem to prefer this word to "takeover"), it would be a pity if they became submerged beneath a welter of "company men". Throughout the history of champagne, the reputations of the houses have been made by a combination of quality wine and the larger-than-life characters who have sold it. It is not a product that lends itself to the "faceless" salesman. A house must have an identifiable persona, both at the home base and also among its agents abroad. In this way, the family firm has an outright advantage over the big combine, even if the financing side is sometimes difficult without outside investment. For a vast concern, the trick is to retain a personal style, not just a team of corporate clones.

Looking at the home life of the Champenois, one immediately comes up against a difficulty. When, exactly, can you be sure to find them at home? They drive to Paris' Charles de Gaulle airport at the drop of a hat – some, like Jean-Claude Rouzaud of Roederer, have their own planes. The autoroutes have opened up the region of Champagne in quite extraordinary fashion, especially when compared with the long, tortuous drive there 20 years ago. Now a Champenois will drive to Paris for a meeting, or for the theatre and dinner afterwards. Belgium, Germany and Switzerland are all close, and it is a mere hop across the English Channel. Soon the last part of the autoroute from Reims to

Taittinger's 18th-century Château de la Marquetterie at Pierry, just outside Epernay, is one of the loveliest properties in Champagne. It was on this site that Frère Jean Oudart, cellarer at the Abbey of St-Pierre-aux-Monts, worked at making perfect sparkling champagne: we know that the older Dom Pérignon visited him at Pierry.

• • • • • • • • • • •

Laon will be finished, linking the Champagne capital to Calais in a way that should encourage even greater numbers of thirsty visitors. As yet there is no Train Grande Vitesse from Paris to Champagne, but there is hardly any need – the train already glides along the Marne Valley at great speed.

You stand most chance of catching the Champenois in their lairs in the early part of February, when they are settling down to some serious tasting of the vins clairs, the still wines that make up the cuvée. This vital part of the whole champagne process, the blending, or assemblage, needs a team of regular and experienced tasters. In many houses this means the owner, or directors, and the resident oenologist/chef de caves (cellar manager).

Tasting is usually done in relative silence, punctuated by the occasional sharp criticism, cry of recognition as someone comes across a familiar cru, or sign of approval as something particularly good of its kind comes along. This takes place in the laboratory, clinical and white, and usually without extraneous odours. Occasionally, an oenologist will taste using black glasses, which can fix the mind wonderfully, but this is only an exercise and not a real instrument of tasting for the assemblage.

The head of a champagne house, especially one with vineyards, has to mastermind the finances of farming, of holding huge stocks, and of working out future potential sales of a product that takes years to make. Compare this with a Beaujolais house, which will virtually turn over its entire stock within the year! Inevitably, planning meetings, and sessions with the bank, take up a good deal of time. Then there is the whole marketing policy of champagne, so important with a product where image is all – well, nearly all, for we champagne lovers are also very interested in what is inside the bottle. Promotion and advertising are

When dining in a restaurant, a Champenois man will make minute enquiries as to how a dish is prepared before making his final choice. Henri Krug obtained a full description from Gérard Boyer at Les Crayères of a verjus sauce for his fish before giving it his approval. Such interest would be unlikely in an Anglo-Saxon milieu, and even in Paris most men spend as little time as possible ordering food before they get down to the real business of the meal.

essential weapons in the fight for sales, and the Champenois are a keenly observant bunch, alert to new trends, the activities of their competitors and the emergence of new, promising markets.

They also have a very varied social life, and pursue their interests with the same verve and enthusiasm as their sales goals. Many Champenois are collectors – Jean-Marc and Nadine Heidsieck and Bruno Paillard of contemporary painting, Christian and Chantal de Billy of beautiful porcelain and silver tastevins from the region (which do not have the same indentations as the Burgundian version), Michel Budin of furniture and glass from the Belle Epoque, Christian Pol-Roger of old cars. Quite a few people also collect old wines – Bordeaux, burgundy and, increasingly, vintage port.

Not all pursuits are so sedentary. Many Champenois are great sportsmen – "grands chasseurs" – in the true tradition of their region. (Charles-Camille Heidsieck, on a business trip to the United States in 1860, sent to France for his best gun so that he could impress the Americans and thus make himself and his champagne better known.) If you lunch with Christian de Billy, you are more than likely to eat pheasant shot by your host. The two Grand Bernard of Laurent-Perrier, Messrs de Nonancourt and de la Giraudière, are also expert and knowledgeable shots, with an overlapping interest in conservation.

The Champenois love eating and, in spite of their region not possessing the gastronomic reputation of, say, Burgundy or the southwest, many of them are formidable gastronomes. This, combined with their warm, easy hospitality, makes them ideal hosts. A Champenois home is the place to relax and enjoy oneself. If it is a small, informal lunch or dinner, the hostess will serve you herself. When there are more of you, a charming girl might bring out the courses, and for the more formal occasions, there is usually a man with white gloves. Sometimes, as when dining at Roederer, that person is also the chief remueur. This is always reassuring, as it means he will have "nosed" the wines, and you are sure that every champagne served will be in perfect condition.

Dining with Rémi and Cathérine Krug, you will probably also have the pleasure of the company of their youngest daughter, Camille. Grande Cuvée and cheese soufflé (with Rémi and Cathérine arguing over the relative merits of a "runny" or more solid texture), is followed by a roast, accompanied by some serious claret – two of Rémi's sisters have not married into Bordeaux dynasties for nothing. The first is Cos d'Estournel 1966 (surprisingly light, but very elegant), and then a superb Palmer 1962, vibrant and heady. Life can be more cruel than this.

At the home of Christian and Chantal de Billy, Pol Roger 1982, a very ethereal substance, leads into 1958 Château La Mission Haut Brion, which is so good that I guess it to be the 1962 – yet another example of this property making "off-vintages" that defy credibility. The choice of claret is no accident. For years the Woltners, who used to own La Mission before the sale to Haut Brion, sold Pol Roger in France; when you dined in Graves, you could expect P.R. as an apéritif, so the two-way traffic paid dividends for everyone.

Marie-Hélène and Christian Bizot specialize in surprises. Theirs is quite one of the most wine-loving homes in all Champagne. They have a real sense of how to compose a meal, and when they meet a fellow lover of old wines, the cellar doors open. First, a fondant au Gruyère, as melting as the name suggests, served with a slightly bitter green salad, is beautifully matched by Bollinger RD 1976. Perhaps, above all champagnes, Bollinger is for food, solid and confident enough in itself to be a wine rather than "just" a champagne. It is champagne for those who have no truck with apéritifs, but require one wine, preferably one that sparkles, that will go with every course.

But as you are with the Bizots, you do not have to content yourself with a solitary star from the Bollinger firmament. Out comes a venerable old bottle and, surprisingly, the champagne is not as dark in the glass as might be expected – just a warm, glowing gold. Christian says it is 1914, a famous vintage, picked as the guns thundered along the valley of the Marne. You take it as that, and enjoy its ambrosial qualities. A simple question about the cork allows us all to examine it more closely and, lo and behold, it is not a 1914 at all, but a neglected 1918, a forgotten year of some irregularity. It does not change the taste. Christian wonders how it could have emerged from the pile. None of us worries very much. It was disgorged just before World War II, thereby confuting Christian's theories on drinking mature champagne relatively soon after disgorging. Wines have a habit of mocking you.

Family lunch with the Roland-Billecarts at Mareuil-sur-Aÿ is always a pleasure, and not only for the delicious Billecart-Salmon Blanc de Blancs. Beautiful, ornamental gardens separate the office from the house. The dining room was once the cellar, and the Roland-Billecarts have restored the painted wall niches with great flair. Madame wheels in the food herself, Monsieur wears tweeds, and we talk of their recent visit to Scotland where they dropped in on the highlands and islands by helicopter – the only way to visit one's more isolated customers.

The interiors of Champagne houses are always easy on the eye, but they are not "decorator style" – Champagne women arrange their homes as they want them. They have lovely furniture and lighting, but they are also comfortable, as befits a hard, northern climate which means that a certain amount of time must be spent indoors. There is a good deal of wood panelling, dark at the Krugs, stripped paler at the Bizots and Rouzauds – Jean-Claude Rouzaud says wryly that people began to unvarnish their panelling following the emergence from the chrysalis of the beautiful "boiseries" at Les Crayères, the de Polignac former family home and now the famous Boyer restaurant. One problem common to nearly all Champagne houses is damp. Great care has to be taken not to put textile coverings on the walls without suitable insulation, otherwise telltale marks appear all too rapidly, especially after a winter as wet as 1987/1988.

Perhaps the most beautiful table setting in the whole of Champagne is at Roederer, dining with the Rouzauds. There is gold plate everywhere, gold and white china, and a fabulous arrangement of pink flowers in the centre. It reminds me of the reply given by a grand old man of Champagne when he was asked about the best moment to drink rosé champagne: "Ah, but my dear, you have supper when the sun is setting, the tablecloth and porcelain are pink, there are pink roses on the table, and you eat fresh salmon, lobster and strawberries. That is when to drink rosé champagne!" I have never yet managed to fulfil all the criteria at once, but I will keep on trying.

Summer holidays for the Champenois may mean Corsica, Biarritz or sailing off La Rochelle. But they must be back well before the vintage, which usually starts at the end of September. Nowadays, the Champenois are virtually besieged by visitors at this time, somewhat to their surprise, because the weather is not always as benevolent here as in more southern climes. But there is a good reason: the vintage in Champagne has retained its traditional nature more than any other. The rows of vines buzz with the chatter of pickers, rather than the rev of the motor, and the feast at the end of the harvest is always a highpoint. Elsewhere, this tradition has largely disappeared – a picking machine cannot sit down to table.

Then begins the busiest period of the year for selling champagne. The houses must have planned for the shipments to have left for foreign markets in good time, and this means careful planning of a disgorging programme so that the champagnes can be rested before leaving the cellars. The Champenois themselves are frequently required to make promotional visits at this time, the approach to Christmas, presenting awards, encouraging their sales teams, giving tastings, hosting receptions. The most important tastings, of course, are those when the new vintage is launched, but this can happen at any time of the year. Houses launch their vintage wines onto the market in very arbitrary manner. There is no set pattern; it is when they consider the champagne ready or, more prosaically, when they run out of the previous vintage.

Meanwhile, Reims and Epernay are preparing for "les fêtes". In the centre of Reims, the oyster stalls are out on the pavements, hugely tempting when one considers that the "vin de pays" is the perfect accompaniment. What I like is that you can eat them at any time of day. Arriving in Reims one Saturday afternoon in November, having missed lunch, we were able to share a dozen oysters and a half-bottle of champagne, just to tide us over until dinner. It was so much nicer than tea! The shop windows start to look tempting – Reims is a chocolate-lovers' dream, with a confiserie seemingly on every corner. Unfortunately, chocolates do *not* go with champagne. The centre of Reims also possesses a pâtisserie, Waïda, which makes the best "pains au chocolat" I have ever tasted. As Christmas nears, there is likely to be increased cultural activity, with concerts in the Grand Théâtre and art exhibitions in the town hall.

Christmas itself is a very family occasion. Gérard Boyer at Les Crayères closes down, as he says the Champenois do not want to go to restaurants over Christmas – they prefer to celebrate it at home, surrounded by children and perhaps grandchildren, although some escape to their chalets in Val d'Isère or Mégève. He also dislikes paying the exorbitant prices suddenly asked for truffles, foie gras and lobsters at this time of the year: "I do not want to have to pass on this kind of extortion to my customers."

Foie gras, predictably, features on quite a few Christmas menus in Champenois homes, and turkey is popular. The real speciality is boudin blanc aux truffes – white pudding with truffles – which goes splendidly with champagne, preferably a magnum. Many Champenois pride themselves on obtaining an English Christmas pudding, showing strong links with their oldest, and still their largest, export market. The Krug family drink an old Vintage (it was the 1962 in 1987) with theirs; Count Ghislain de Vogüé of Moët opts for Dom Pérignon. For what it is worth, I usually choose Roederer Rich, as the extra fullness copes so well with all that fruit. But I quite understand that a Champagne house cannot drink the product of a rival at Christmas!

Gérard Boyer, at home at Les Crayères in Reims, one of France's finest three-star restaurants. Happily for the guest who is staying here, after the meal of a lifetime it is a short journey up this staircase to the sumptuous bedrooms, with their view across the park and towards the Basilica of St-Rémi. Part of the panelled dining room resembles a very sybaritic library, part an elegant salon-conservatory. And the food is made for champagne: beautiful visually and full of tantalizing flavours.

CHAPTER TEN

SERVING CHAMPAGNE

There is something theatrical about serving champagne. Putting out special glasses, chilling the bottle, opening it, pouring gently and watching the bubbles rise: this is a ritual to rival the Japanese tea ceremony. There is a set series of moves, rather like a quadrille, which makes the anticipation all the keener. It always gives me a strange sense of history: how many fascinating people, on how many glittering occasions, have done precisely the same thing. They were probably just as mesmerized by the sparkle and froth as we are today. It is easy to muse as one sips that, long after we have left this world, new champagne lovers will still be raising their flûtes to toast one another.

Glasses

The history of the champagne flûte, which we consider relatively recent, is in fact far older than that of the much-maligned coupe. Certainly it was present in the Gallo-Roman era – appropriately enough, since the Roman crayères (the chalk quarries now used as cellars by many champagne houses) are such a feature of Reims life.

Some of the most glorious flûtes were, and still are, made at the glassworks on Venice's island of Murano: many have gold or bronze decoration and, although coloured glasses are frowned on by purists, the golden tracery perfectly highlights the topaz glints of champagne. In 17th-century Spain, classic flûtes were also in use, with the wine descending to the very foot of the glass. Velazquez's *Man with a Glass of Wine* is the portrait of a bon viveur who wishes to toast the onlooker, with the flûte held confidently at the base – obviously a practised drinker. There are, however, no bubbles in evidence! English flûtes of the Georgian period are especially elegant, beautifully balanced and a pleasure to hold and drink from. In 1983, Les Cristalleries de St-Louis in Lemburg, Moselle, made some grand Empire-style flûtes, copies of a set of glasses dating from 1898. They are hand-blown crystal and decorated with a frieze of engraved gold at rim and base, glasses "par excellence pour la grande soirée".

• • • • • • • • • •

"Champagne sparkles much more vigorously in a glass that is pointed than in one that is round or flat at the bottom. The old-fashioned tapering glass, called a 'flûte', is the one generally preferred in Champagne."
Champagne: Its History, Properties, and Manufactures, *Charles Tovey, 1870*

The coupe was first made by Venetian glassmakers working in England during the 17th century, but its heyday was in Victorian England and in 19th-century America. The Antique Porcelain Company of New York houses the most famous coupe of all – the alabaster-white Sèvres model, reputed to be a close copy of the breast of Marie Antoinette. One can admire the perfection of her figure while decrying the suitability of this shape as a glass for champagne. The wide surface area merely makes the bubbles disappear and the champagne warms with remarkable speed. The bouquet also is barely detectable. It needs the narrow opening of the flûte, or a classic tulip shape, to retain and hold the wonderful scent of champagne, one of its greatest joys.

The coupe is still with us, turning up in the most unexpected places. In one of the best dim-sum restaurants in Singapore we found they had champagne, which is a heaven-sent accompaniment to all the varied tastes of these little morsels. With great ceremony, and not a little fear, the bottle was opened and the wine poured into the widest of "wedding" coupes. We did not have the heart to deliver a lecture on ideal glass shapes. In any case, we were too busy drinking up quickly before the champagne became tepid.

To my surprise, the coupe also appears to be alive, if not exactly well, in modish French circles. Françoise Dorin, one of France's most successful contemporary novelists, begins *Les Lits à une Place* with a description of a rather strained silver wedding anniversary dinner. The wife lifts the "coupe de champagne" to her lips. . . and this is the smart moneyed set of 1980! However, we have to take it on trust that it actually was a coupe. Reims cafés still paint on their windows "champagne à la coupe!", but if you venture in and order one you are actually served a flûte. And when we found a cache of old Roederer Extra Quality at a family oyster restaurant in southwest France recently, we were offered coupes. But as we showed some alarm they were smilingly replaced, so obviously the two shapes can coexist.

Normally, one considers the official ISO/INAO tasting glasses as suitable for all types of wine, but I have found that champagne does not "mousse" very well in them, probably because the bowl is a little too wide at the base of the glass. There exists, however, a special version with a star on the inside where the bowl meets the stem, and this contact with something not quite smooth causes the bubbles to rise in a more satisfactory way. And two glasses that are sheer perfection, both from the aesthetic and the practical point of view, are the "Sommelier" flûte and the tulip called "Clicquot", shown on pages 196 and 197.

Although coloured glasses are never advisable for any type of wine, the beautiful Lalique glasses, clear in colour but with a beguiling pink flower linking the stem to the bowl of the flûte, are a glamorous novelty when drinking rosé champagne. There is a hint of decadence and daring in having something less than classic but still eminently classy. And what could be more apposite, since René Lalique was born in Aÿ.

Wherever you are, and whatever the conditions, it is really not worth drinking champagne out of mugs, paper cups or plastic beakers. You cannot see

• • • • • • • • • •

Flûtes are held
joyously aloft in a
scene of Regency
revelry in 18th-century
France, carved into the
soft chalk walls of
Pommery's
magnificent cellars in
Reims. This was well
before the coupe
became fashionable for
drinking champagne.
• • • • • • • • • • •

the mousse, you cannot smell anything, and the material comes between you and the champagne. I have it on impeccable authority that Bokassa, former self-styled "Emperor" of what is now the Central African Republic, drank Dom Pérignon out of mugs, and look what happened to him!

Tasting Champagne

Tasting, as opposed to drinking, champagne is normally left to professionals, whether it is the champagne houses themselves, wine merchants or restaurants deciding what to buy, or wine writers and commentators deciding what to recommend. Occasionally, the consumer likes to taste conscientiously, rather than to sip with pleasure, but not necessarily with concentration. This is usually to compare one champagne with another, perhaps to decide which wine to buy for a party or a wedding. Sometimes we want to take stock of what is in our cellar, or see if it is worth buying a case from the local store's special offer.

If you wish to assess a champagne, not only for its intrinsic quality but, more important, to see whether it is really the one for you, try it in the glass you would normally use. Suddenly switching glass shapes can play tricks on the taste or, at least, on the impressions you have of a champagne. It is essential that the glass is perfectly clean, whatever you are tasting, but it is doubly important where champagne is concerned, because the slightest lack of cleanliness will result in champagne losing its bubble and going flat. The worst thing of all is traces of detergent; any product of this sort is not actually necessary for washing glasses – cold or tepid water will do the job much better.

Naturally, champagne should be quite clear and brilliant and not in any way hazy. Nowadays, I doubt whether anyone would take the same attitude as Oscar Philippe, who owned the Cavour restaurant in London's Leicester Square during

The flûte has long been the traditional glass of Champagne, but it is fascinating to see the similarity with an English ale glass of the 1700s (far left). The reason is simple: the tapering shape did not so much facilitate the release of bubbles, but it enabled the wine (or ale) of the time, which was often cloudy, to clarify, the solid matter gathering in the narrowest part of the stem. The two champagne flûtes next to the ale glass are from the first half of the 1800s. Today's Baccarat flûte (fourth from left) is very fine indeed, as light as cobwebs, and the bubbles burst on the surface of the champagne like little shooting stars. For young champagnes, especially non-vintage and blanc de blancs, the slender, hand-blown flûte in the "Sommelier" range by the Austrian glassmaker Riedel (far right) is the height of elegance, elongated of stem and just the right weight to hold. It would be a crime to put anything other than a champagne of great finesse in such a glass!

This page, from left to right: The superb, long-stemmed tulip called "Clicquot" and made by the French glassmaker Portieux is perfect for vintage champagnes, for champagnes with a high proportion of black grapes, old champagnes or the grandest of prestige cuvées. There is sufficient width for the bouquet and flavour to open out in the glass, and the narrow V at the base enhances the mousse so that the bubbles resemble tiny silvery grains of sand spiralling upwards. The classic tulip next to it is the ideal all-purpose champagne glass which, happily, is also very good for all types of wine, both white and red. Victorian coupes were sometimes made with a hollow stem to stimulate the flow of bubbles, but the bouquet was quickly lost from the shallow bowl. The official "international" (ISO) tasting glass is suitable for most wines, but when it is used for champagne the mousse is disappointing. Far right: the glass used in Champagne for blending the cuvée.

the Belle Epoque. André Simon recounts how the 1895s threw a "blue smoke" sediment, so the champagne shippers offered to replace any cloudy bottles with clear ones. Only Oscar Philippe never exchanged any of his '95s. He listed them as "clear" and "thick", and sold them all with no trouble at all.

Colour is interesting: it can indicate the grape variety composition and the youth or age of the champagne. A young blanc de blancs will be very pale indeed, whereas a black-grape dominated wine will be more golden. Champagnes with a high proportion of reserve wine will also tend to have more colour. As champagnes age they gain in colour, but not necessarily in chronological order. Some years are more "tinted" with colour than others, even when young – especially in the past, when pressing was less tightly controlled. As a rule, the Chardonnay grape gives a greeny, hay-like colour, whereas the two black Pinots "go for gold".

Looking at the bubbles is one of the great pleasures of drinking champagne. There is something almost hypnotic about watching them spiralling upwards. Unfortunately, two glasses washed in exactly the same way can produce different results, which is a mystery we have yet to solve. There are two ways you can observe the effervescence: by watching the bubbles that should come up the middle of the glass, and those that attach themselves to the inside of the glass. Those that busy themselves by rising up the middle to the surface should be fine, continuous and long lasting. Those that stick to the side of the glass will probably be larger, but should also be persistent and abundant. A stream of tiny, strong bubbles is undoubtedly a sign of quality, apart from being the most fascinating sight in the wine-drinking world. Obviously, a very old champagne, particularly if it has been disgorged many years before, will have far fewer bubbles. The attraction, in this case, is in the concentration of bouquet and flavour.

The effervescence, or carbonic gas, of champagne underlines and amplifies the aromas – it throws them into relief. You can actually divide the aromas into three stages. The primary aromas come directly from the grape and are thus fruity, but they are less evident in champagne than in still wines. The secondary aromas derive from the alcoholic fermentation and are of a volatile nature: higher alcohols and esters. Although they are not strong in champagne, they do clearly contribute to the overall olfactory judgment of a young wine. The tertiary aromas stem from the "prise de mousse", and are not very well understood, but undoubtedly they contribute to the complexity of champagne and their presence signifies a wine with some bottle-age.

In the very nature of the ageing of champagne, two phenomena are at work: oxidation and reduction due to the presence of carbonic gas. The yeasts, as they gradually break down (autolysis), give off substances which add to the tasting and effervescent qualities of the champagne. But the process is so subtle that it is extremely difficult to evaluate, even for professional oenological researchers.

The bouquet of a champagne can be discreet, "classic" or powerful, a measure of the intensity or otherwise of the aromas. Then there is the judgment of the quality of those aromas. Do they have finesse and subtlety? Are they classically "champagne" in character? Can one detect a "terroir" or a grape variety? Or is the bouquet rather neutral, lacking aromatic richness?

There are groups of different aromas, too: those that are fruity, floral or vegetal. Ferns, ambergris, hazelnuts, apple, wild rose and honey might sound esoteric, but they are all terms used quite easily among the Champenois themselves. Biscuity, toasty and fresh-bread smells are among the most attractive of all the aromas of champagne – they are more pronounced in black-grape dominated wines. Some mature champagnes have an irresistible perfume of freshly roasted coffee – torrefaction in its nicest sense. Champagnes with a high proportion of Pinot Noir can smell of red burgundy (if you forget the colour), with that vague vegetal/farmyard nose, whereas pure Chardonnay champagnes can smell very like a Chablis – hardly surprising when you consider that, logically, this region should be attached to Champagne rather than Burgundy. Rosé champagnes often have a nose of red fruits, with strawberry dominating although, in extreme youth, raspberry can take the upper hand.

There is also the effect of the effervescence on the palate. Champagne should fizz gently in the mouth, with no excessive foam such as one would experience with a cheap sparkling wine. It should tingle and sparkle, throwing up all the flavours and taste sensations. It should be fresh and fruity, but not excessively so – too much freshness and you probably have green acidity, too much fruitiness and you will have a fruit cocktail, which is *not* what champagne is all about.

Sweetness and acidity are notoriously difficult to assess. One man's "acid" is another's "just fine", and one taster's "dry" is another's "far too sweet". But the taste of a champagne should "ring true". My particular dislike is a champagne

Far left: In the 19th century, the Russian Royal Court took to champagne like the proverbial ducks to something altogether less exciting. This Imperial flûte bears the cipher of Alexander I and a celebratory comment that "Paris is taken May 19, 1814". Centre: An American crackle-glass champagne jug, circa 1875–1888, gives a double effect of sparkling mousse. Right: By the 1880s, the Russian Court had succumbed to the prevailing fashion for the coupe.

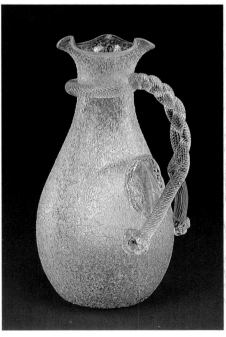

that was originally rather green (unripe) and acid and that has been overlaid with too sweet a dosage to try to mask the rawness. The whole never marries and the result is incompatible. I can tell after one sip: the green acidity descends to the pit of the stomach and stays there, and no amount of heavyweight camouflage can alter the fact.

Some people are disorientated by a high amount of mature reserve wine in a champagne – they erroneously judge the extra roundness and richness as a high dosage. But the difference is easy to see. The champagne with the generous amount of reserve wines is "complete", with the weight an integral part of the whole, whereas a high dosage will always be a separate component standing away from the wine itself, like paint applied to a badly prepared surface.

Old champagnes are a very subjective taste, more favoured by the British than the French and most Americans. The Swiss, too, positively wince at a mature wine. I have to confess that I like champagne at all stages of its life, providing it is good, from the youthful and sprightly, to the six-to-ten year old adult beauty in full bloom, to those grand old majestic champagnes of 20 years or more. The youthful froth gives way to complex precision, finally ending in rich, tawny maturity. If you do not like the taste of old champagne, by no means feel you should. Stay with the current vintages and the fresh sans année wines, and leave the old masters to the devotees, for those special occasions when one can savour them with all the time in the world at one's disposal. But variety is what many champagne lovers find intriguing, ringing the changes between the houses, the vintages and the blends. For each one there is an occasion and a mood.

Length on the palate after spitting or swallowing (but only professionals in a long lineup of wines will have to practise the former) is a sure sign of quality. Champagne shares this yardstick with all wines. If the aftertaste lingers until the next sip, it is almost certainly a good champagne.

Serving Champagne

In all the broadcasts I have done, by far the greatest number of questions from listeners involve champagne and when to drink it. Apparently, people tend to keep it too long, often in suspect conditions, as if afraid to open the bottle. This is a great mistake, as nothing could be simpler. Clearly one wants to chill champagne beforehand and most of us use the refrigerator for this, but don't put the bottle in the door because the constant opening and shutting is not ideal for fine wine. If taken by surprise, without time to prepare the champagne, plunge the bottle into a bucket filled with ice and water for a quarter of an hour. Even a few minutes in the deep freeze can be contemplated as an emergency measure, but don't forget it: abandoned bottles have been known to explode.

Champagne should be served at around 8°C (46°F) for the optimum effect of the carbonic gas and the maximum bouquet and flavour. This seems to suit young, non-vintage wines as well as all-Chardonnay blanc de blancs, but recent tastings have showed me that a temperature of 11–12°C (53°F) is actually better for weighty vintage champagnes or old wines, and it really improves those without any dosage. But remember that if you have many people in the room, or an array of candles, the champagne will warm up quickly. For a large party, champagne bottles can be buried in ice in a wine cooler – or, failing that, in the bath.

Champagne is remarkably resilient, and one of the few wines that can survive a journey in an ice box in the back of the car and emerge in top form at the picnic. But the cork can come out with some exuberance after a bumpy ride. Normally the cork should be eased out with a sigh, not with a bang. "Popping the cork" is a phrase to be forgotten rather than followed. Wine waiters were (and still are, in some flashy places) wont to open champagne with too much of a flourish, to attract the attention of diners and shame other hosts into ordering a bottle. Happily, these habits are changing, helped by better training. Ruinart have contributed greatly to this by their sponsorship of the Meilleur Jeune Sommelier (best young wine waiter) de France competition. Since 1977, wine waiters of less than 26 years of age have competed for this honour, and Ruinart also founded l'Association des Sommeliers. Their influence now spreads outside France, with competitions for the Meilleur Sommelier in Switzerland and Spain. Krug are responsible for the Krug Award which is given annually to the candidate with the highest marks in the Master Sommeliers examination.

To obtain the best results when opening champagne, remove the foil and the wire muzzle but keep a finger or thumb on the cork because it could then come out of its own accord. Normally, however, it has to be eased out, and this is best done by slowly turning the bottle rather than the cork itself. Always hold the bottle at an angle away from you, which helps the cork emerge more gently than if the bottle were vertical. Various gadgets have been developed that assist in removing recalcitrant corks and require no strength whatsoever.

When pouring champagne, pour a little for everyone and then go back to the beginning to "top up". This avoids frothing over. As an alternative, you might just occasionally like to serve a non-vintage champagne in a carafe. Some purists frown on this practice but it has a place in history, having been quite common in 19th-century France. When that delightful recollection of domestic life at the Château de Nohant, *A La Table de George Sand*, was launched in 1987 in Paris, the guests drank tisane de champagne "en carafe", a perfect evocation of the period. Traditionally, tisane de champagne is lighter than most (the connotation must be that it is for invalids), and I would think the carafe method best suits a blanc de blancs. There is a bustling brasserie specializing in fruits de mer near the Ecole Militaire in the 7ème arrondissement in Paris, and if you drop in there late at night for a dozen oysters they will still bring you the "house" champagne in a carafe. It is quite delicious, utterly effervescent, and the most dogmatic purist would be converted.

Storing and Buying Champagne

Always store champagne on its side in a cool, dark place, preferably at about 15°C (60°F). The colder the storage temperature, the slower the maturation of the

• • • • • • • • • • • •

Brillat-Savarin, or one of his disciples, is reputed to have said: "Champagne with its amber hue, its éclat, its sparkle and its perfume arouses the senses and produces a cheerfulness which flashes through the company like a spark of electricity. At the magic word champagne the guests, dull and torpid with good feeding, awake at once. This lively, ethereal and charming beverage sets in motion the spirits of all; the phlegmatic, the grave and the philosophic are surprised to find themselves amiable; in the wink of an eye (or the pop of a cork) the whole banquet has changed its physiognomy." Quite!

• • • • • • • • • • • •

wine. Thus, champagne that has never been moved from the colder cellars in the Champagne region will taste much younger than champagne that has been kept at 18° or 20°C (65–70°F). But as with all wines, wide temperature fluctuation is the most dangerous thing of all. Magnums mature better than bottles, and halves the least well of all. Never store champagne in the refrigerator, as it will tire the wine. Bottles that have been broached but not finished can be closed with a pressure stopper cork and kept in the refrigerator for a day or two, but it would be a pity to do this with a great old champagne.

Champagne comes in a range of bottle sizes. It is most unlikely that the largest will have had their second fermentation in the same bottle (wine being decanted from smaller sizes) so these giants should be drunk soon after purchase.

Quarter	18.75cl.	Rehoboam (or triple magnum)	6 bottles
Half	37.5cl.	Methuselah	8 bottles
Bottle	75cl.	Salmanazar	12 bottles
Magnum	2 bottles	Balthazar	16 bottles
Jeroboam (or double magnum)	4 bottles	Nebuchadnezzar	20 bottles

The only size bottle sadly missing from this list is the Imperial Pint (midway between a half and a bottle), beloved of Sir Winston Churchill and no less appreciated by me. It is a perfect size for those who find a half bottle a little too mean and a bottle a little too much of a good thing. Unfortunately, the European Common Market, in its wisdom, has outlawed the Imperial Pint. The last one I drank was a delicious Bollinger Special Cuvée, shared with my husband when my first book was published. This time, I think it will have to be a magnum!

Many people have wondered about the Old Testament nature of the names for the large champagne bottles. No one knows for sure why this is so, but there is a theory that the bottle manufacturers were once predominantly Jewish, and this led to the biblical vocabulary. But, we are flying kites. . .

I would certainly recommend laying down non-vintage and vintage champagne. If you keep non-vintage for a year or two after buying it, most of your guests will guess that it is vintage because the extra bottle-age gives it added complexity. Vintage champagne almost always needs a few more years in bottle after coming onto the market to show its full beauty – it is virtually a rule that any given vintage is at its best when it is no longer available in the shops. So the onus of storage rests with you.

But, of course, many of us buy a bottle of champagne on impulse, as a surprise for a dinner or as a gift. And that is fine, too, because top champagnes are sold when they are ready to drink. Naturally, there is some disparity between national tastes, with the French preferring their champagne on the youthful side, but some houses keep back the stock destined for Britain a little longer than that for the domestic market, so by the time it is in the shops it is ready for the British palate. When champagne is shipped to America and to all far-flung corners of the world, the journey can equal a few more months of bottle-age. The essential point to remember everywhere is to buy from a shop with a good turnover in champagne. Hot temperatures and ultraviolet lights in many stores are a catastrophe for champagne when it is exposed to them for any length of time. The champagne houses and the CIVC are beginning to work with stores in France on improving conditions of storage, offering incentives and prizes for the best-organized wine sections. This will undoubtedly encourage awareness of the problem and it is to be hoped that all the importing countries can follow suit.

Buying old champagne at auction can be rewarding. Only Dom Pérignon and Cristal go on steadily increasing in value, and many other excellent vintage and prestige cuvée champagnes are undervalued. This is because they are usually underrated and, if you like the taste of aged champagne, there are some bargains to be had. But develop a relationship with the auction house and, if you cannot taste the wine yourself, ask for the history of the champagne. This should give you some idea of how it has been stored. If it has been moved around from pillar to post it could be decidedly faded, but if, for example, it has been kept in a Scottish nobleman's freezing-cold cellar, you are in luck!

• • • • • • • • • • •
A perfect setting for enjoying champagne: the conservatory of Les Crayères, Gérard Boyer's restaurant in Reims.

CHAPTER ELEVEN

CHAMPAGNE AND FOOD

Some gastronomic deity must have decreed that this chapter should be written in the spring, during the short season for gulls' eggs. The combination of these little delicacies, freshly hard-boiled and served with celery salt and some brown bread and butter, with the most seductive champagne currently in your cellar, is inspired. It is curious that only the British seem to have stumbled upon the joys of gulls' eggs. Quails' eggs are not to be sneezed at, but they are not the same. The extra bonus is that in Britain there are so many seagulls that conservation is not a problem, although in some countries they are, quite rightly, protected. With them choose a creamy blanc de blancs, or a very fruity champagne such as Pol Roger or Perrier-Jouët, or a vintage that particularly favours the Chardonnay, such as 1982. It is a pity that the spring is too early for picnics, so plan these for a supper à deux.

Champagne "goes" with almost everything, but the trick is in finding what it goes with best. My research has been far-reaching, and extremely diligent – not a bottle has been left unopened on your behalf. The only combination I would not recommend is champagne with chocolate: contrary to popular belief, chocolate can be matched with some wines, but subjecting champagne to the ordeal is a crime. And grapefruit is out – but then its extreme citric character ruins any wine. I have not tried champagne with food I personally dislike, such as tripe, but that should not stop anyone else from experimenting.

Caviar and champagne is almost a cliché, but perhaps a misunderstood cliché for it all depends on which caviar. The dark grey Sevruga has a more definite, usually slightly saltier taste than Beluga, and I think vodka goes best with it. But the large-grained and lighter Beluga simply demands champagne – something like Louise Pommery or Grand Siècle to match the extreme finesse of the taste. The rare, nutty-flavoured Osetra or Oscietra caviar is perfection with an aged vintage champagne, 15 years old or more: the hazelnut taste seems to link the food with the wine. Try mature Salon or a Bollinger Année Rare. Of course, no "accompaniments" such as chopped onion will come anywhere near

• • • • • • • • • • •

"The advantages of giving Champagne, whatever limit, at the beginning of dinner, are these, that it has the greatest relish, that its exhilerating [sic] quality serves to start the guests, after which they seldom flag, and that it disposes people to take less of other wines afterwards." While I am not convinced of the latter point made by the 19th-century gastronome Thomas Walker, close observation of your own dinner guests will probably confirm the rest of Mr Walker's maxim to be accurate.

• • • • • • • • • •

this feast — only blinis, those plump little Russian pancakes, or plain toast are allowed. I did once revel, though, in a roulade of caviar, an exquisite "swiss roll" made with a soufflé mixture and filled with sour cream and caviar, matched with Dom Pérignon 1961 disgorged 20 years later in honour of the wedding of the Prince and Princess of Wales. Rules are made to be bent.

Caviar fits beautifully into a celebration with a Russian flavour. You can start with caviar and Roederer Cristal, the champagne of the Tsars. Then a plate of smoked eel and sturgeon with Roederer vintage can follow, and finally that utterly irresistible cream cheese and candied fruit concoction, paska, with Roederer Rich. Bliss indeed. In the background, the Russian Easter music of Bortniansky should be playing, or the deep velvety sound of Chaliapin. It is all enough to transport one back into another age.

Champagne and oysters: what could be more perfect after the theatre, or in the crisp early hours of Christmas morning after Midnight Service, or for Sunday lunch in Paris. Are oysters too salty, altogether too maritime, to flatter champagne? I don't think so, but you need a vibrant, fresh champagne, not a venerable old bottle. The non-dosage wines are superb, something like Piper-Heidsieck's Brut Sauvage or Laurent-Perrier's Ultra Brut. And if you are in New Orleans, revive the racy champagne-drinking days of the turn of the century and enjoy Oysters Rockefeller with some bubbly over brunch. Champagne seems to have extra pizzazz in the morning. The creamy, smoky flavour of kedgeree is a perfect match — but move on to coffee when you reach the toast and marmalade. Many chefs and restaurant owners find a glass of champagne marvellous mid-morning: it sets them up for the arrival of their public and makes their welcome just that little bit warmer.

Gérard Boyer at Les Crayères in Reims epitomizes the champagne chef. He and his father arrived from Paris at the beginning of the 1960s, and the Champenois took the talented duo to their hearts. Now Gérard Boyer is the most practised exponent of the art of marrying champagne with food, and he also uses it in much of his cooking. His champagne sauce made with a fish fumet and shallots is superb with any white fish. He recommends using old champagne in sorbets (and drinking champagne with smoked haddock). He also uses the verjus, or the acid juice from unripe grapes, most intriguingly for some sauces, but this is hardly a possibility for those of us who do not live next door to a vineyard. The juice of both Chardonnay and Pinot Noir can be used, but Gérard Boyer prefers the black grape, reducing it to a syrup and at the same time causing the acidity to disappear and enhancing the colour. Not every year produces the right kind of verjus, but 1987 was ideal because the grapes left on the vine after the harvest had both acidity and sugar.

Boyer composes the kind of meal with which you can choose just one champagne that will take you through every course: no fuss, no bother, just supreme enjoyment. You can, for example, start with his terrine de lapereau (young rabbit), and then go on to les huîtres au curry — oysters with a mere hint of the exotic East. The highly original (and equally effective) bar, or sea bass, à la

Caviar is one of the
great luxury foods of
the world, so naturally
it goes with the world's
most glamorous wine:
champagne. A
spoonful of caviar and
a sip of champagne –
somehow the briny
taste of the caviar
marries perfectly with
the biscuity flavour of
a grand, aged vintage
champagne. For
ultimate hedonism
there should be no
extraneous
accompaniments, but
blinis with sour cream
can be an exception.
• • • • • • • • • • •

vanille and marinated with olive oil comes next, followed by a consommé flavoured with fresh ginger – another influence from the chef's visits to China and Hong Kong. Then, the main course, a panaché de poissons: Saint Pierre (John Dory), red mullet and salmon, with truffles.

This was the dish that started me on the road to adventure, because I discovered just how ethereal the meeting of the black truffle and champagne could be. Colette preferred her beloved red wines of Burgundy with "le diamant noir" ("If you have no great Burgundy of impeccable ancestry to hand, then drink some wine from Mercurey, full-bodied and velvety at the same time" – *Prisons et Paradis*), and the Bordelais reach for the nearest bottle of claret. But a fresh black truffle and a bottle of great champagne is a marriage made to last. Another Boyer masterpiece is his asparagus and truffles, with which we drank Besserat de Bellefon's Brut Intégral 1979, the smoky dryness of the wine really opening up to the strong flavours in the dish.

Research continued at La Briqueterie restaurant at Vinay near Epernay, where a whole truffle en brioche was partnered with Cuvée William Deutz 1979, probably a little too light for the dish: it would have been better as an apéritif. We got it right, though, at L'Abbaye at Talloires, a former Benedictine monastery on Lac d'Annecy now given over to more worldly pleasures. Here I had the best truffles of my life, thickly sliced over a salad. The truffles came, unusually, from the area of Bugey, in the hinterland to the east of Lyon, and their scent was unforgettable. This we matched with Pol Roger 1975, and the maturity of this classic champagne was the perfect foil to the wild aromas of the black truffle.

*In a book written in
1755 on recipes used
at the Court of
France, Les Soupers
de la Cour,
champagne was used
in 67 of 352 meat
dishes, 76 of 266 fish
dishes and in 25 out
of 84 sauces.
Evidently, cost was
no problem at Court.*

over Barbary duck with vintage Moët rosé, followed by venison with bilberries, the first time I had tried champagne with game.

This was another road of discovery, which led to saddle of hare at the Auberge du Grand Cerf at Montchenot (between Reims and Epernay) with vintage Charles Heidsieck, and cold grouse and partridge with just about every champagne, provided it is not too light and too young.

Lest anyone think that champagne can only be served with luxury food, I will divulge that this book was conceived with my publisher in London over a lunch of bangers and mash and a bottle of champagne. The sausages were of the plain English variety too, although there is a marvellous recipe for champagne sausages which bears comparison with the hautest of haute cuisine. Nor do you have to serve poached salmon when you open a bottle of bubbly, although this *is* very nice: a modest fish pie made of more humble piscine cousins is a perfect backdrop to a really good champagne. Turkey with champagne is always a successful combination, and plain roast lamb, pink rather than overdone, is superb with a rosé. Blanquette de veau, a refined version of veal stew, with a blanc de blancs works very well, as do straightforward escalopes of veal or paupiettes filled with a duxelles of mushrooms.

It is a great mistake to feel that you have to stay within the repertoire of classic French cooking when serving a champagne. This most noble of wines is extremely eclectic, adapting to the food of countries that are often unlikely to see a bottle of the real thing. However, we are luckier, because with both the import of exotic restaurants and the raw ingredients for making the dishes ourselves, we can indulge in some very entertaining experiments.

Some of the most challenging are undoubtedly with the food of China. Certain regional Chinese cooking, such as that of Hunan and Sichuan, is less suitable than others because of the fiery nature of some of the dishes. But Shanghai and the East, the lands of fish and rice, lend themselves to this form of gastronomic experiment, and many dishes from Canton and the hot south can be enjoyed with champagne.

You could not make a better start than with dim sum, the Cantonese snacks, utterly appetizing in their diversity and contrasting flavours. A bottle of good non-vintage champagne is the ideal accompaniment to prawn dumplings, spring rolls, paper-wrapped prawns, pork dumplings, and chicken and glutinous rice wrapped like a fat bundle in lotus leaves. Hop from one mouthful to another, with a sip of champagne in between. The crab-meat dishes from the Yangtze delta are also ideal with champagne, although I would take a weightier vintage to match the richness. Roederer rosé goes equally well with steamed sea bass, Cantonese style with bamboo shoots, Chinese mushrooms and ginger root, or as served with basil at the Rouzaud home in Reims.

Rosé champagne also goes splendidly with North African couscous, the steamed semolina dish with chicken or mutton and vegetables. I like a soft non-vintage, perhaps a champagne with a fair amount of Pinot Meunier, with another steamed dish, Hainanese chicken rice, a favourite of that semi-tropical island off

**Salmon is one of the
great "naturals" with
champagne, white or
rosé. The king of fish
is nicest when
poached, with a
champagne sauce. This
is the time to bring out
quite a weighty
vintage, a champagne
with individuality and
character, or a rosé
with a Pinot Noir
flavour, to match the
solid texture of the
fish.**

the south coast of China and, by extension, among the Hainanese community in Singapore. Mildly spiced Kashmiri kormas are also delicious with champagne, the fresh green coriander a perfect foil to the intensity of bouquet and taste of a Pinot Noir-dominated wine.

The cooking of Champagne itself has never been particularly rich or grand; it is not a gastronomic region in the way that Burgundy or the southwest of France so ably demonstrate. A hard climate and northerly situation made Champagne better known for its potatoes and cabbages than for more luxurious food, and hearty soups and peasant salads were the staple diet. Freshwater fish and sausages such as boudins and andouillettes are also native to the region, and the "chasseurs" – the huntsmen – bring game to the table. For visitors to Reims, many of these country dishes can be tried at the restaurant Le Vigneron, which has the added advantage of a superb list of champagnes and a formidable collection of old posters and vineyard implements. The sweet-toothed can buy the famous pink biscuits of Reims from the pâtisserie-confiserie Fossier.

At Moët & Chandon's elegant Epernay establishment, the Trianon, guests are wooed by the cooking of Joseph Thuet, who was born at La Fère in the Aisne and has explored all avenues where cooking with champagne is concerned. Even the aspic at the Trianon is made with non-vintage Moët! A dish that is within the orbit of a competent cook is M. Thuet's monkfish and crayfish in champagne – you can substitute any firm-fleshed white fish if you do not have the "lotte", and

Pink lamb is superb with rosé champagne, one of the heavier styles rather than a lighter apéritif example: it works happily with a vintage rosé of ten or more years old, the maturity of the taste marrying well with the meaty flavour. It is more difficult to keep the rosiness in the lamb when it is baked in pastry, but it is worth getting the timing just right.

large shrimps can replace the "écrevisses". Nothing, however, can replace the cup of champagne you will need to give the dish that extra panache. It was at the Trianon that I once had a delicious soufflé glacé au café served with Dom Pérignon 1969, an inspired match, as aged Dom Pérignon often has a toasty, mocha bouquet which is captivating. And a sabayon made with champagne is a lovely variation on the heavier Italian zabaglione.

The Italians are great champagne lovers, especially the prosperous and sophisticated Milanese. At Giannino, one of the smartest restaurants of Milan, two of the most popular dishes are branzino, or sea bass, cooked with champagne, and zabaglione allo champagne con pesche, with champagne replacing the habitual Marsala in the whipped egg yolks and sugar concoction, which is then served with peaches.

The theatrical side of champagne makes it a natural for parties and celebrations, when a theme can be woven into the evening and imagination can run riot. A whole dinner can be planned around a colour: a pink evening, for example, with rosé champagne, pink tablecloth, salmon, lobster and strawberries, pink candles on the table and glasses with pink stems. A gold evening could match the orange-gold of the Clicquot labels, with a centrepiece of gold chrysanthemums or marigolds, and a cold orange soufflé to finish the feast. A stark black and white party could feature Lanson Black Label; a Cordon Rouge fling could have festoons of red ribbon; a rose evening would have Mumm's rosé

• • • • • • • • • • •

An array of Cantonese dim sum, utterly appetizing in the diversity of colour, taste and texture. Dim sum are usually only gently spiced, so you can have an aristocratic champagne as an accompaniment: Krug is splendid, with its big, imposing flavour.

• • • • • • • • • • •

"No other wine produces an equal effect in increasing the success of a party, and a judicious Champagne-giver is sure to win the goodwill and respect even of those who can command it at pleasure." (Thomas Walker, 1835.)

with Foujita's flower on the label matched by bowls of huge overblown roses. A Belle Epoque party, with Perrier-Jouët's enamelled bottle much in evidence, would recreate the atmosphere of Maxim's at the turn of the century.

Few things give greater pleasure in this world than offering someone "un petit repas au champagne". Whether it is in a restaurant, or an informal repast at home, a meal designed around a bottle of champagne will remain in the memory. Chef Jacky Michel at the Hôtel d'Angleterre in Châlons-sur-Marne hits exactly the right note with his warm rabbit salad, and oysters and scallops ensconced on a cabbage leaf. At home, braise a ham in champagne to feed a large family, or make scrambled eggs with smoked salmon for a champagne supper à deux.

I celebrated writing the last lines of this book with a little comparison of Iranian (darker and tangier) and Russian (milder, oilier and fishier) Oscietra caviar, accompanied by a gloriously opulent bottle of Bollinger RD 1975. Now *that* is a marriage made in heaven.

Champagne Drinks

As a general rule, my view is that champagne is far too good a drink to tamper with. With the vast diversity of tastes that the different houses provide, there is choice enough for the rest of one's champagne-drinking life. But just occasionally, in frivolous mood, it is fun to ring the changes. There is no point in using a vintage champagne or a cuvée de prestige for any of these drinks – it would be like using Romanée-Conti for coq au vin. A non-vintage champagne is fine.

Champagne punch is a novelty: try the Cardiff wine merchant S.D. Churchill's Lawn Punch, popular at the end of the last century.

Champagne Lawn Punch: Bring one cup of sugar and five cups of water to the boil, with the grated rind of an orange and a lemon. Skim, boil for five minutes, strain and, when cool, add some chopped ice, the juice of two lemons and three-quarters of a bottle of champagne (the remaining champagne is presumably to sustain the punch maker). If strawberries are in season, add about a dozen.

My favourite champagne cup comes from the 19th century, courtesy of Charles Tovey. It is really a sort of large-scale champagne cocktail.

Champagne Cup: Take one bottle of champagne, two bottles of soda water, a liqueur glass of brandy or Curaçao, two tablespoonfuls of powdered sugar, a pound of chopped ice (you don't need the ice if you have the means to keep your cup very cool) and a sprig of green borage, and put all the ingredients into a silver cup.

The best champagne cocktails in the world are now made at the Connaught and Ritz hotels in London. This is what they advise:

The Connaught Champagne Cocktail: The method is simply one of "building up" – put a cube of sugar in a glass, add to that the tiniest drop of Angostura bitters, then a teaspoon of Grand Marnier, next a teaspoon of brandy, top up with champagne and finish with a good-sized twist of orange peel, making sure that the oil from the peel goes over the drink (this is very important for the "Connaught taste"). Garnish with a cherry.

The Ritz Champagne Cocktail: Put a cube of sugar in a flûte, with a dash of Angostura bitters, add two dashes of brandy, which should just cover the sugar cube (too much spoils the taste of the champagne), top up with iced champagne and add a slice of orange and a cherry. This is a classic champagne cocktail, which stays the closest to the drink as it was originally made.

The most original, and perhaps the most delicious, variation of the champagne cocktail that I know of is the brilliant invention of the barman at London's Capital Hotel. You will be instantly seduced.

The Capital Hotel's Framboise Fizz Royal: Take a measure of eau de vie de framboise, a little fresh lemon juice, a little gomme (sugar) syrup and the fresh white of an egg, shake in a cocktail shaker, pour into a champagne glass and then top up very slowly with champagne so that it doesn't froth over. Decorate with a few fresh raspberries.

I have nothing whatsoever against Buck's Fizz (the French call this drink Mimosa), provided the orange juice is freshly squeezed. Fresh tangerine juice is tangy and intriguing, and a beautiful colour – try it half and half, or one-quarter tangerine juice to three-quarters champagne, depending on mood and time of day. A Champagne Bellini, with fresh peach juice, is wonderful mid-morning. Black Velvet is a very British drink: half champagne and half stout (Guinness), it is black, frothy and smooth, not for purists but definitely different.

• • • • • • • • • •

Soufflés are perfect with champagne, be they savoury (cheese, with a predominantly black-grape champagne) or sweet, when red fruits are in season. Here, the options are manifold: a grande cuvée de prestige (formal occasions in France invariably take this route), a rosé or a Rich. Ring the changes and see what you prefer. Try iced mocha and apricot soufflés too.

• • • • • • • • • •

GLOSSARY

Agrafe The metal clasp that secures the cork during the second fermentation. Now only occasionally used for cuvées de prestige, as the practical crown cap has largely replaced it as a temporary closure.

Assemblage Blending of the still wines.

Atmosphere The pressure of the effervescence in the bottle related to atmospheric pressure. (See page 51.)

Blanc de blancs White wine made from white grapes; in Champagne, exclusively Chardonnay.

Blanc de noirs White wine made from black grapes; in Champagne, Pinot Noir and Pinot Meunier.

Brut Very dry: champagne with a maximum of 15 grams per litre of residual sugar. (See page 53.)

Buyer's Own Brand (BOB) Wines produced under their own label for specific customers such as hotel groups, wine merchants and supermarket chains.

Cave Cellar, nearly always underground in Champagne.

Chaptalization Addition of sugar to the must to increase the potential alcohol level (see page 48).

Chef de caves Cellarmaster.

Coteaux Champenois Still wines from the Champagne vineyards.

Courtier Wine broker.

Crayères Chalk pits quarried in Gallo-Roman times to provide building material for Reims, converted by champagne houses into labyrinthian cellars.

Crémant Literally, "creaming"; a gentle fizz, at between 3.5 and 4 atmospheres rather than 5–6 atmospheres. Disappearing as a description.

Cru A growth, or village, e.g. Aÿ, Verzenay.

Cuve Vat in which wine is kept, or fermented, or both.

Cuvée A blend of wines which makes up a specific champagne. A producer refers to his wine as his "cuvée"; also the first juice from the presses (see page 47).

Cuvée de prestige A house's top "luxury" champagne, e.g. Roederer Cristal, Moët's Dom Pérignon.

Débourbage Removing impurities from the juice before the first fermentation. (See page 48.)

Dégorgé tardivement Disgorged later, so the wine has remained longer than usual on its yeasts.

Dégorgement Removing (disgorging) the sediment produced by the second fermentation in bottle.

Demi-sec Sweet: champagne with 33–50 grams per litre of residual sugar. (See page 53.)

Deuxième taille The last 205 litres of the main run of juice from the presses (see page 47).

Dosage Sugar added to (most) champagnes with the liqueur d'expédition to attain the required degree of sweetness or "roundness" (see pages 52–3).

Doux Very sweet: champagne with more than 50 grams per litre of residual sugar. (See page 53.)

Echelle Quality rating of the Champagne vineyards, from 100% for the grands crus, through 90–99% for the premiers crus, down to 80% for the lesser communes. The price of the grapes each year is determined by that decided for the 100%-rated vineyards.

Extra sec Dry: champagne with 12–20 grams per litre of residual sugar. (See page 53.)

Glace, à la The process of removing the sediment created by the second fermentation by freezing the neck of the bottle (see page 52).

Grand cru "Great growth": one of the 17 villages with a 100% échelle. (See page 59.)

Grande marque "Great name" or house; also a member of the Syndicat de Grandes Marques de Champagne (but see page 83).

Gyropalette Frame in which the process of remuage, or riddling, is done mechanically.

Habillage "Dressing" the bottle with label and foil; in Champagne, a particularly important part of the "image" of the house and its wines.

In-vitro Literally, in glass; the culture of vines under laboratory conditions (see page 47).

Liqueur d'expédition The mixture of wine and, usually, cane sugar used to top up the bottle after dégorgement (see page 52).

Liqueur de tirage The mixture of wine, sugar and selected yeast culture added to the wine to induce the prise de mousse, or second fermentation in bottle. (See pages 50–1.)

Malolactic fermentation The process by which harsh or "green" malic acid is converted into milder lactic acid. (See page 48.)

Marc In Champagne, both the capacity (4,000kg) of the traditional wine press and the pulp of skins, pips and stalks that remains when the juice has been run off.

Marque Brand, make.

Méthode champenoise Now usually refers to the method of secondary fermentation in bottle to produce the bubbles. But it is really the entire champagne process and the combination of the soil, climate and grape varieties of the region allied to the skill of the blending.

Millésime The vintage year, i.e. what "millésime" is your champagne?

Millésimé The wine of one year, i.e. a vintage champagne.

Mousse Sparkle or effervescence.

Mousseux Sparkling: in champagne, fully sparkling as distinct from "crémant" or semi-sparkling.

Must Freshly pressed juice, before fermentation.

Négociant Traditionally, a merchant or shipper; in Champagne, often also the champagne maker.

Négociant-manipulant (NM) A house or grower both making and selling champagne.

Négociant-non-manipulant Someone who sells champagne under his own name but does not make it.

Non-vintage (NV) The (undated) blend of current and reserve wines prepared each year to be consistent with the house "style".

Poignetage Shaking the bottles when they are moved during their time sur lattes, to keep the sediment suspended and make remuage easier.

Premier cru "First growth": villages with a 90–99% échelle (vineyard rating).

Première taille The 410 litres of juice that follows the vin de cuvée off the press (see page 47).

Prise de mousse The second fermentation in bottle that produces the bubble.

Punt The hollow in the base of the bottle (see page 178).

Pupitre Hinged board with holes into which the bottles are inserted for the remuage.

Rebêche The last juice extracted from the grape pulp after the main run; it can be made into cheap still wine but never used in champagne.

Récemment dégorgé (RD) Literally, recently disgorged, but the wine will have been maturing, sur pointes, in the maker's cellars, to be disgorged when required for shipment. The initials RD are a Bollinger trademark.

Récoltant-manipulant (RM) A grower who makes and sells his own champagne.

Remuage The process of shaking and turning the bottles until the sediment from the second fermentation is resting on the closure, ready for dégorgement. (See pages 51–2.)

Remueur The cellar worker who carries out the remuage.

Reserve wine Still wine reserved for use in future blends to make non-vintage champagne.

Residual sugar The sugar in the wine after the addition of the dosage (see page 52).

Riddling English word for remuage.

Saignée Some rosé champagne is made by the "saignée" method, literally, "bleeding", or draining off the juice from the skins when the right pink colour has been obtained. (See page 47.)

Sans année Non-vintage, i.e. wine without a date.

Sec Slightly sweet: champagne with 17–35 grams per litre of residual sugar. (See page 53.)

Second fermentation The prise de mousse, or the creation of the bubble in the bottle.

Skin contact The process of leaving the juice in contact with the grape skins for a brief time to absorb colour, used in the making of some rosé champagnes. (See page 47.)

Sur lattes The system of stacking bottles horizontally on thin strips of wood while the prise de mousse takes place. (See page 51.)

Sur lie The process of keeping a wine on its lees, or sediment, to obtain a more complex taste.

Sur pointes The system of storing bottles upside down, on their "points", or corks, after remuage, while they await dégorgement.

Temporary cork or closure The cork and clasp or crown cap used to seal the bottle for the prise de mousse (temporary because it comes off with the dégorgement).

Transvasage Transfer of wine under pressure (to preserve the effervescence), usually from standard bottles or magnums, the most practical sizes for remuage and dégorgement, to quarter or larger format bottles.

Vendange The harvest.

Vendangeur The harvester, or grape picker.

Vendangoir The accommodation provided for the pickers during the harvest.

Veuve Widow (as in Veuve Clicquot).

Vieilles vignes Ungrafted vines.

Vignoble Vineyard.

Vin clair "Clear wine": the wine when it has been cleaned of impurities after the first fermentation and is ready for blending.

Vin de cuvée The first 2,050 litres of juice from a pressing (see page 47).

Vin de taille The 615 litres of juice after the vin de cuvée.

Vintage In general, the harvest; in Champagne, also the wine of a single year, when the harvest has been of sufficient quality: then a date will always be shown on the label and the champagne is "vintage".

Volée, à la The old traditional method of disgorging by hand (see page 52).

SOURCES

I have occasionally quoted from some of the works of reference consulted during the writing of this book, when the phrase has seemed particularly apposite. Each quotation credits its author, but as a quick reference the main sources for these "bons mots" have been:

S.D. Churchill, *All Sorts and Conditions of Drinks*, circa 1893

N.E. Legrand, *Le Vin de Champagne*, 1896

Professor George Saintsbury, *Notes on a Cellar-Book*, MacMillan and Co., London, 1921

Thomas George Shaw, *Wine, the Vine, and the Cellar*, 1863

André Simon, *The History of Champagne*, © George Rainbird Ltd., 1962, the quote on page 176 reprinted by permission of The Rainbird Publishing Group Limited, London

André Simon, *The History of the Wine Trade in England*, London, 1905

Charles Tovey, *Champagne: Its History, Properties and Manufactures*, 1870

Henry Vizetelly, *A History of Champagne*, 1882

Thomas Walker, *The Original*, 1835

ADDRESSES

The following are the champagne houses profiled in Chapter VII. For information about visiting the houses, see page 80. If you are a good customer of one particular champagne house, ask your wine merchant to give you an introduction.

Ayala
2 boulevard du Nord
51160 Aÿ   Tel: 26.55.15.44

Besserat de Bellefon
Allée du Vignoble
51100 Reims   Tel: 26.36.09.18

Billecart-Salmon
40 rue Carnot
Mareuil-sur-Aÿ
51160 Aÿ   Tel: 26.50.60.22

Bollinger
Rue Jules-Lobet
51160 Aÿ   Tel: 26.55.21.31

Deutz
16 rue Jeanson
51160 Aÿ   Tel: 26.55.15.11

Gosset
69 rue Jules-Blondeau
51160 Aÿ   Tel: 26.55.14.18

Alfred Gratien
Gratien, Meyer, Seydoux & Co.
30 rue Maurice Cervaux
51200 Epernay   Tel: 26.54.38.20

Charles Heidsieck
3 place des Droits de l'Homme
51100 Reims   Tel: 26.85.03.27

Heidsieck & Co. Monopole
83 rue Coquebert
51100 Reims   Tel: 26.07.39.34

Henriot
3 place des Droits de l'Homme
51100 Reims   Tel: 26.85.03.27

Jacquesson & Fils
68 rue du Colonel Fabien
Dizy
51200 Epernay   Tel: 26.53.00.66

Krug
5 rue Coquebert
51100 Reims   Tel: 26.88.24.24

Lanson
12 boulevard Lundy
51100 Reims   Tel: 26.40.36.26

Laurent-Perrier & Co.
Domaine de Tours-sur-Marne
51150 Tours-sur-Marne   Tel: 26.58.91.22

Abel Lepitre/George Goulet
Grands Vins Chatellier
2/4 avenue du Général Giraud
51100 Reims   Tel: 26.85.05.77

Mercier
75 avenue de Champagne
51200 Epernay   Tel: 26.54.71.11

Moët & Chandon
20 avenue de Champagne
51200 Epernay   Tel: 26.54.71.11

G.H. Mumm & Co.
29 rue du Champ de Mars
51100 Reims   Tel: 26.40.22.73

Bruno Paillard
Rue Jacques Maritain
51100 Reims   Tel: 26.36.20.22

Joseph Perrier
69 avenue de Paris
51000 Châlons-sur-Marne   Tel: 26.68.29.51

Perrier-Jouët
26 avenue de Champagne
51200 Epernay   Tel: 26.55.20.53

Philipponnat
13 rue du Pont
Mareuil-sur-Aÿ
51160 Aÿ   Tel: 26.50.60.43

Piper-Heidsieck
51 boulevard Henri-Vasnier
51100 Reims   Tel: 26.85.01.94

Pol Roger & Co.
1 rue Henri Lelarge
51200 Epernay   Tel: 26.55.41.95

Pommery & Greno
5 place du Général Gouraud
51100 Reims   Tel: 26.05.05.01

Roederer
21 boulevard Lundy
51100 Reims   Tel: 26.40.42.11

Ruinart
4 rue des Crayères
51100 Reims   Tel: 26.85.40.29

Salon
Le Mesnil-sur-Oger
51190 Avize   Tel: 26.50.53.69

Taittinger
9 place Saint-Niçaise
51100 Reims   Tel: 26.85.45.35

Veuve Clicquot Ponsardin
12 rue du Temple
51100 Reims   Tel: 26.40.25.42

The CIVC (Comité Interprofessionnel du Vin de Champagne) is the official body that regulates the champagne industry and is a useful source of additional information.

CIVC
5 rue Henri-Martin
51200 Epernay   Tel: 26.54.47.20

INDEX

PICTURE CREDITS

Commissioned photographs by Nic Barlow appear on the following pages: 12, 13, 17, 18, 19, 25, 27TL/TR, 29BL, 46, 49TL, 51, 59, 60/1, 67, 69, 70, 72/3, 75L, 79, 91, 99, 101, 105, 110, 113T, 117, 119R, 129, 140, 141, 143, 151L, 152, 165, 168, 169, 174, 175, 179, 186, 187, 191, 195.

Other photographs: 6: MB/Photo: Simon Wheeler; 14: Sonia Halliday and Laura Lushington; 16: Lauros-Giraudon; 21: Moët & Chandon (London) Ltd; 24L/R: Mary Evans Picture Library; 27B: Veuve Clicquot; 28 TL: Leonetto Cappiello © DACS, 1988; 28TR: Joseph Perrier; 29R: Kharbine – Tapabor; 32: David Cannon/Allsport; 33: Norman Lomax/Impact Photos; 34: Homer Sykes; 37: Nils Jorgensen/Rex Features; 40TL: Moët & Chandon, London; 40TC: Kharbine – Tapabor; 40–41: Lelli & Masotti/Teatro alla Scala; 41TC: The Kobal Collection; 41C: The Raymond Mander & Joe Mitchenson Theatre Collection; 41R: J. R. Prints; 43: Sotheby's; 48: Kharbine – Tapabor; 49TR: Bruno Paillard; 50: Kharbine – Tapabor; 53: Kharbine – Tapabor; 82: Moët & Chandon (London) Ltd; 85: Billecart-Salmon/ Photo: Patrick Guerin; 88T: Bollinger; 88B: A la Carte Magazine; 93: Deutz Delas Diffusion; 103: Heidsieck & Co. Monopole; 107: Jacquesson et Fils; 113 BL/BR: Krug; 119L: Laurent Perrier; 121: John Johnson Collection/The Bodleian Library, Oxford; 124: Roger – Viollet; 126: Collection Champagne Mercier/Photo: Patrick Guerin; 130: © DACS, 1988/Jean-Loup Charmet; 132L: Kharbine – Tapabor; 132R: Jean-Loup Charmet; 137L/R, 139: Perrier-Jouët; 146: Alexis Duclos/Gamma/Frank Spooner Pictures; 148T/CL/ CR/B: Pol Roger; 156: Ronald Elmer; 158T/CL/ CR/B: Louis Roederer; 164: Taittinger; 170: Veuve Clicquot/Photo: Michel Jolyot; 185L/R: A la Carte Magazine; 196/7: MB/Photo: Sally Cushing; 199L/ C/R: The Corning Museum of Glass; 203: Revue Maison & Jardin/Photo: Jacques Bachmann; 207/ 208L: The Anthony Blake Photo Library; 208R: A la Carte Magazine; 209L: The Robert Opie Collection; 209R: Harlingue-Viollet; 210/211/212: A la Carte Magazine; 213/215 and back cover: The Anthony Blake Photo Library.